UNCOMPROMISING ACTIVIST

The Johns Hopkins University Studies in Historical
and Political Science

132nd series (2017)

Seth A. Johnston, *How NATO Adapts: Strategy and Organization in the Atlantic Alliance since 1950*

Katherine Reynolds Chaddock, *Uncompromising Activist: Richard Greener, First Black Graduate of Harvard College*

Uncompromising Activist

Richard Greener, First Black Graduate of Harvard College

KATHERINE REYNOLDS CHADDOCK

JOHNS HOPKINS UNIVERSITY PRESS   BALTIMORE

© 2017 Johns Hopkins University Press
All rights reserved. Published 2017
Printed in the United States of America on acid-free paper
9 8 7 6 5 4 3 2 1

Johns Hopkins University Press
2715 North Charles Street
Baltimore, Maryland 21218-4363
www.press.jhu.edu

Library of Congress Cataloging-in-Publication Data

Names: Chaddock, Katherine Reynolds 1945– author.
Title: Uncompromising activist : Richard Greener, first black graduate
   of Harvard College / Katherine Reynolds Chaddock.
Description: Baltimore : Johns Hopkins University Press, 2017. | Series:
   The Johns Hopkins University studies in historical and political
   science. 132nd series (2017) ; 2 | Includes bibliographical references
   and index.
Identifiers: LCCN 2016052558| ISBN 9781421423296 (hardcover : ac-
   id-free paper) | ISBN1421423294 (hardcover : acid-free paper) | ISBN
   9781421423302 (electronic) | ISBN 1421423308 (electronic)
Subjects: LCSH: Greener, Richard Theodore, 1844-1922. | African
   Americans—Biography. | African American political activists—
   Biography. | African American scholars—Biography. | African
   American diplomats—Biography. | Harvard College (1780–)—Students
   —Biography. | University of South Carolina—Faculty—Biography.
   | Howard University. School of Law---Faculty—Biography. | Passing
   (Identity)—United States—Case studies. | United States—Race rela-
   tions—Case studies. | BISAC: HISTORY / United States / General. |
   SOCIAL SCIENCE / Black Studies (Global).
Classification: LCC E185.97.G796 R48 2017 | DDC 327.730092 [B] —dc23
   LC record available at https://lccn.loc.gov/2016052558

A catalog record for this book is available from the British Library.

*Special discounts are available for bulk purchases of this book. For more
information, please contact Special Sales at 410-516-6936 or specialsales@
press.jhu.edu.*

Johns Hopkins University Press uses environmentally friendly book
materials, including recycled text paper that is composed of at least 30
percent post-consumer waste, whenever possible.

For Adrienne and Brett Reynolds,
my most valued and essential sources of support

CONTENTS

UNCOMPROMISING ACTIVIST

A Search for Identity

THE ABANDONED ROW HOUSE in the Englewood area of Chicago's South Side had suffered years of human and animal squatters. Termites had bored into the wood, and vandals had made off with anything of even minimal value. But just before the structure's scheduled demolition in 2009, Rufus McDonald of the contracted clean-out crew spotted something still untouched. A heavy old steamer trunk in the attic had somehow escaped scavengers. Although his fellow crew members advised pitching the bulky trunk, McDonald opened it. He put some of its contents—documents, papers, and a few books—into a paper bag. Later, he took them to a rare book dealer, who quickly identified two crumpled items: an 1870 Harvard College diploma and an 1876 University of South Carolina Law School diploma. Surprised and pleased to recognize the still-readable name of the graduate, the dealer immediately asked McDonald, "Do you know who Richard Theodore Greener was?"[1]

. . .

Richard T. Greener, widely acclaimed as one of the most eloquent and effective voices for the cause of racial equality during the late nineteenth and early twentieth centuries, was also well known as the first black graduate of Harvard College (class of 1870). Later, he became the first black professor at a southern public university, a law school dean, an inspiring writer and orator, a black diplomat to a country of white citizenry, and more. Yet, curiously, his name is now scarcely mentioned among the historic figures who have battled for extending the rights of US citizenship across color lines.

Beginning as the tale of a scrappy black kid learning street smarts, Greener's life story could be viewed almost as a classic American narrative of bootstrapping determination and well-earned achievement. However, his extraordinary journey was punctuated with plenty of wrong turns, missed opportunities, professional frustrations, personal tragedies, and bitter disappointments. Most crucial, there was always the race issue. A handsome, light-skinned "black" man with mixed ancestry, Greener faced accusations from fellow blacks that ranged from getting too cozy with white folks to attempting to pass as white. On the other hand, he experienced race discrimination in employment, housing, transportation, and services. His opportunities sometimes expanded due to his pale complexion; they also contracted due to his African American ancestry. His straddle of the black and white divide became as much a part of his life story as did his numerous accomplishments and setbacks.

Born in Philadelphia (1844) and raised in Boston and Cambridge, Massachusetts, the young, energetic Greener quickly developed an ability to be everywhere and know everyone. He was still in his teens when he rowed on the Charles River with his friend Oliver Wendell Holmes Sr., read Latin with George Herbert Palmer, attended lectures by Ralph Waldo Emerson and Henry Ward Beecher, helped guard Wendell Phillips from an angry mob at a rally of abolitionists, and sat spellbound at numerous antislavery meetings graced by Frederick Douglass and Senator Charles Sumner. When his father departed for the California gold mines and never returned, eleven-year-old Richard left school for a succession of jobs that would help support him and his mother. His avid networking among employers and acquaintances eventually landed him a benefactor and some generous friends who helped him get to Oberlin Collegiate Institute, Phillips Academy at Andover, and Harvard College.

His employment after graduation was again a rapid succession of jobs. In 1873, after a brief teaching stint at one black high school and a short time as principal at another, he gained an appointment as a professor, and soon also as librarian, at the University of South Carolina, which had been newly integrated during the Reconstruction era. There, he enjoyed little noticeable color discrimination and much meaningful work with students and colleagues. During that time, he married a lady from an elite black family in Washington, DC, earned a law degree, undertook political and academic oratory throughout the state, and welcomed the birth of his first child. At the close of his fourth year of academic work, Reconstruction ended, and the university returned to its original segregated condition. Although Greener would never again reside in South Carolina, he would long refer to it as "my adopted State."[2]

A move to the nation's capital yielded a patronage appointment at the Treasury Department for several years, a two-year-long deanship at Howard University Law School, and a partnership in a law practice. He delivered public lectures and published essays for the black cause, campaigned for liberal presidential candidates, and had more children. Later, he worked in New York City as secretary and chief fund-raiser at the Ulysses S. Grant Monument Association. Finally, in 1898, Greener went to Russia after being appointed by President William McKinley as the first US diplomatic representative to the Siberian city of Vladivostok.

For all his education, way with words, recognition, and networks of friends and colleagues, Greener perpetually faced professional and financial crises. Personal dramas and changes in political sentiments led to stretches of underemployment or unemployment. He launched into seemingly attractive, but unsuccessful, business investments. His public speaking and political campaigning took time away from building his law practice and enjoying his family. And something always happened to shorten his various professional stints. Integration ended at the University of South Carolina, and Greener was out. Howard University Law School suffered low enrollment during his time as its dean, and Greener was out. The Grant Monument Association board experienced infighting and resignations, and Greener was out. After McKinley's assassination, the new president Theodore Roosevelt had his own ideas and obligations for diplomatic patronage assignments. Once again, Greener was out.

It is possible that Greener could have better weathered changing winds in professional and political assignments if he had been someone else. But he was a black man who could be outspoken about his opinions, assertive for his race and himself, and blatantly self-confident about his abilities and worth. The hard work that got Greener through Phillips Andover and Harvard supports sociologist Ralph Turner's contention that American education favors "contest mobility," in which "common sense, craft, enterprise, and daring" are keys to status and reward. However, when Greener confronted the world of working professionals, "sponsored mobility" was also in play, limiting social and economic advancement to citizens who could display "the appropriate qualities" for promotion to elite status by existing elites.[3] His success at Harvard was laudable and noteworthy, but that alone was not enough to carry him to the professional heights his classmates could expect to achieve.

While working for the Grant Monument Association and living in New York, Greener's marriage faltered. His wife and five children stayed there when he went to Vladivostok. All were light complexioned, and they soon changed their names and slipped across the color line to become white citizens who claimed a bit of Spanish heritage. Greener never saw them again. In Vladivostok, where he had substantial additional diplomatic responsibilities during the Boxer Rebellion and the Russo-Japanese War, he lived with a smart, worldly Japanese woman with whom he fathered three children. He hoped for another foreign assignment, possibly even in that part of the world, after his recall from Russia. But that never happened, and he never again saw his Japanese family.

· · ·

Greener's ideas about race issues of the time—especially discrimination, civil rights, and segregation—were collected from his own experience and infused with his commitment to blunt candor. One of his earliest firsthand experiences in the struggle for equal opportunity occurred when he was the twenty-eight-year-old principal of the Preparatory High School for Colored Youth in Washington, DC. He eagerly and publicly promoted the idea of integrated schools, which were not at all what the board of trustees of the colored schools of Washington had in mind. At the University of South Carolina, he pushed state legislators for funds for a preparatory program and scholarships as a way to begin leveling the playing field for black students. Often quoting the accomplishments of black soldiers, inventors, writers, and others in lectures and in print, he saw no reason why blacks should be set apart or treated as lesser beings in any area of endeavor. Any hint of deficit among black citizens was not innate, he argued, but a temporary result of the circumstances of slavery, poverty, and indefensible treatment by whites. He believed that what had been characterized as "a negro problem" was, in fact, "a white problem." Misguided and mistaken, whites treated the negro "as a member of a child-like race" who could not think, speak, or act independently. Greener had scores of examples of high-achieving blacks to prove his points, but his own keen intellect made him perhaps the best evidence of his convictions. Harvard professor Henry Louis Gates Jr. has described him as "a leading intellectual of the time."[4] Yet Greener was determined not only to convince readers and audiences but also to encourage action. He pushed elected officials for the passage of the Civil Rights Act of 1875 and for federal action to enforce the Fourteenth and Fifteenth Amendments, but every sign of victory seemed laced with backsliding in practice.

In retrospect, Greener could not have experienced a worse time to be an eloquent and determined advocate for racial uplift. During his adult life, in the late nineteenth and early twentieth centuries, the progress he hoped to facilitate in that area became more and more difficult to attain. Abolitionists had scored their triumph with the Emancipation Proclamation and the outcome of the Civil War. At the close of Reconstruction, however, rights and opportunities for newly freed blacks, most of whom were in the South, began a great and long-term regression. Although there were many individual achievements and successes, especially in the northern and western states, the struggle waged by Greener and other busy activists accomplished little in the way of widespread legal, economic, and social advancement for black Americans during that period. Education became legally separate and not at all equal, segregation heightened views of white superiority, voting became a gauntlet of poll taxes and tests, employment was no place for equal opportunity, and lynchings and burnings went unchecked. Adding to the frustration of these realities, they existed at a time of enlightened legislation by Progressive Era politicians who believed in fair labor practices, trust busting, urban renewal, and professional public service. These politicians were indifferent, however, to establishing equal opportunity across the races.

It is hardly surprising that at the turn of the century, Greener was satisfied to build a new career in a distant country. In far eastern Russia, a part of the world experiencing growing US interest in commercial opportunities and foreign policy, he could be part of something moving forward. When he returned to the United States in 1906, he no longer hoped to see significant change during his lifetime. As he declared to W. E. B. Du Bois, "The White American is not yet freed from his prejudices, cruelties, meanness, hypocrisy!"[5] Nevertheless, in the last fifteen years before his death in 1922, while living with relatives in a predominantly white area of Chicago, he continued writing and speaking for the cause of racial equality. Although he had once needed and courted the largesse of Booker T. Washington, whose influence with well-placed whites was often key for black job seekers, he had become disillusioned with Washington's schemes and power maneuvers. However, he attended the 1909 National Negro Conference that supported Du Bois's adamant activist stance and became a precursor to the National Association for the Advancement of Colored People. But Greener's days at the forefront of equal rights work were by then dampened by his age and his doubt.

As noted by historian Michael Mounter, Greener had a "troubled but distinguished career."[6] He also had a troubled but rich life. Those realities are the conundrums at the heart of this biography. How is it that someone so accomplished and widely recognized never seemed to reach the very top of his field as a long-renowned standout? How much was the idea of skin color, with all its ambiguities and vagaries, to blame? Why was there so much disappointment, and even heartbreak, in Richard Greener's life? How much can be explained by timing, national mood, good and bad fortune, or racial inequality? And how much came from within the individual at the center of the story? And, of course: What is the story behind the documents found in a trunk at least six miles from Greener's Chicago residence?

Greener's story is also about the post–Civil War era, a time of hopeful and heroic efforts toward full opportunity amid the reality of continuing racial divide and enforced inequality. As an exemplary pioneer and vigorous advocate for the rights of black Americans, Greener met with many successes and many disappointments that illuminate the ongoing struggle to define the meaning of full citizenship in a democracy.

CHAPTER ONE

Boyhood Interrupted

FREDERICK DOUGLASS, often celebrated in northern states for his consummate oratorical skill and reasoned abolition arguments, was not at all well received at an 1847 invited speech in Pennsylvania. A barrage of rotten eggs and rocks accompanied jeers and catcalls from the excited audience. Some shouted, "Throw out the nigger!" A local newspaper explained, "Douglass is a darkey and a tool for the enemies of our country."[1]

For several decades before the Civil War, when abolitionists and slavery advocates publicly teemed with anger, the northern state of Pennsylvania was viewed as "uneven antislavery ground." Brotherly love was in especially short supply in Philadelphia. Five major race riots occurred there between 1832 and 1849, when one in every thirteen city residents was classified as Negro—almost twenty thousand total, giving Philadelphia the largest black population of any northern US city.[2] The numbers had swelled as benevolent organizations and Underground Railroad operations in nearby Maryland and Delaware assisted in northward movement for black families—from fugitives at risk of capture to freeborn at risk of kidnapping. Combined with an increasing influx of immigrants, including thousands who fled Ireland during the Potato Famine, the growing black laboring class quickly became the subject of resentment among Philadelphia's underemployed whites.

Even generally compassionate Quakers were sometimes skeptical on race questions. One prominent Philadelphia Quaker noted of local black citizens, "The popular feeling is against them . . . the interests of our citizens are against them. . . . Their prospects, either as free or bond men, are dreary and comfortless." Free black men in Pennsylvania lost the right to vote when an 1836 court decision curiously interpreted the state constitution as indicating that they could not be truly free. In the ensuing years, they were subject to mob terrorism on the streets, home burnings, slum dwelling, and what W. E. B. Du Bois called "a tide of prejudice and economic proscription" that worsened as "the foreign element gained all the new employments which the growing industries of the state opened."[3]

Given the bleak circumstances, the departure of Richard Greener's parents from Baltimore for Philadelphia remains a mystery. His father, Richard Wesley Greener, was born in Baltimore in about 1809 and had numerous friends and relatives there. His paternal grandfather, Jacob Greener, taught in a Baltimore school for colored children. A free black born to former Virginia slaves, Richard Wesley found work in dyeing, cleaning, boot blacking, and various other labor-intensive activities. He also was an agent for William Lloyd Garrison's abolitionist newspaper, the *Liberator,* founded in Boston in 1831.[4] A slave state on its way to becoming a Civil War border state, Maryland was a hotbed of debate about the treatment, employment, and education of black citizens. In about 1840, Richard Wesley Greener married Mary Ann Le Brune, and the couple soon moved to Philadelphia. Le Brune was the light-skinned daughter of Alphonse Josef Le Brune, a Spaniard from Puerto Rico, and Mary Connelly Le Brune, "a negress."[5] Their son, Richard Theodore Greener, born in Philadelphia in 1844, was immediately notable for his fair complexion. One of his friends would later describe him as "very little tinged [with] the hated color."[6]

Attracted to the large and active Philadelphia Naval Shipyard, opened in 1801 as the first naval shipyard in the country, Richard Wesley Greener managed to establish himself as a seafarer. At about the time of his son's birth, he began work as a steward on various ships, including the USS *Princeton* during its service along coastal Mexico in the Mexican-American War. He was then employed by the firm Glidden and Williams, owners of a fleet of nimble three-masted clipper ships popular for their speed in getting passengers from the eastern seaboard to California and Europe.[7] As first steward on the clipper *George Raynes* during a voyage from Portsmouth, New Hampshire, to New Orleans and on to Liverpool, England, Greener was able to take his young son along. Although Richard Greener later stated that he was ten years old at the time, other reports indicate he was several years younger.[8]

While his father was away at sea, young Richard began his schooling—first at a Baptist church school for black children and then at the Lombard Street School, more often called the Bird school after its principal James Bird. Opened in 1822 as the first public school in the area for blacks, it managed an academic reputation far better than expected, given its approximately fifty students for every teacher.[9] It was not long before the family moved again, this time to Boston. The elder Greener was soon attracted by exciting California gold-rush tales—possibly from clipper-ship passengers on their way to San Francisco or perhaps from reports published in the *North Star,* Douglass's antislavery newspaper. In 1853, Greener headed west. His son later recalled that "he succeeded well for a while" in gold digging but then met with illness. Mary Greener and young Richard never saw him again, and the last evidence of Richard Wesley was a US Census indicating he lived in Yuba County, California, in 1860.[10]

• • •

Richard T. Greener was nine years old when the family moved to Massachusetts, known as a place where "Negroes had won virtual political and legal equality." However, at about 1.3 percent, Boston's black citizens represented a far smaller portion of the city's population than did Philadelphia blacks at the time. Most black residential neighborhoods reflected racial segregation, including the lower slopes of Beacon Hill, which were collectively referred to as "Nigger Hill" by locals. In the 1850s, immigration was just beginning to spawn signs of diversity, as "an increasing number of white faces and Irish brogues blended with the other sights and sounds of black neighborhoods." Skin color mattered. Those Boston citizens officially categorized as mulattoes were "generally more skilled, held more property, and were a bit less residentially separated from the white society than the darker members of their race."[11]

While public schools were integrated in towns like Lowell, Salem, and New Bedford, Boston still maintained educational segregation. Challenged by black activists and local parents, the city's Grammar School Board had formed a special committee to look into the matter and determined "a promiscuous intermingling in the public schools disadvantageous," due to community sentiment and white citizens' natural tendencies toward discrimination. School integration would only put "poor and ill-educated colored children . . . into disadvantageous competition and association with the more advanced and wealthy white children."[12] Boston public schools resisted integration until 1855, when state legislation was passed to force the inclusion of all races.

Greener later reported that when his parents found no adequate schools for him in Boston, they settled in nearby Cambridge, where he attended the integrated Broadway Grammar School for two years. The liberal education available there included Latin, literature, English, and mathematics.

Although Greener absorbed it all and began to develop a preference for arts and literature, he left school at eleven years old to "help support my mother."[13]

Even for a plucky and energetic pre-teen, however, it was not easy to find odd jobs in Boston. Black Bostonians typically were found in manual labor or service work, employed as mariners, house servants, waiters, barbers, bootblacks, porters, cooks, seamstresses, and hod carriers. By midcentury, the influx of immigrants created an employment squeeze even among those jobs. One Bostonian of the time claimed that "it is ten times as difficult for a colored mechanic to get work here as in Charleston [South Carolina]." Douglass lamented in 1855, "Every hour sees us elbowed out of some employment to make room perhaps for some newly arrived immigrant." Even well-educated black professionals faced disappointing employment realities. The nation's first black lawyer, Macon B. Allen, a member of the bar of Suffolk County, Massachusetts, found his legal services in scarce demand, "owing to the peculiar custom of the New England people, and especially Boston people, to sustain those chiefly who are of family and fortune, or who have been long established."[14]

Young Greener found work first at a shoe store and later as an office boy at the Pavilion Hotel, a large group of apartments. There, he was befriended by Thomas Russell, a well- regarded Massachusetts native and superior court judge who made his large library available to Greener whenever he had time to peruse it. Then about thirty-three years old, Judge Russell had graduated from Harvard College in 1845 and remained in Cambridge to study at Harvard Law School. He eventually became an outside examiner of Harvard student work and a Harvard overseer. Greener's self-education further expanded when he befriended Maria S. Cook, who began instructing him in French.[15]

Greener easily made friends of all ages, and he soon became well acquainted with Oliver Wendell Holmes Sr. An adept mentor to those he called "my young folks," Holmes doubtless instilled in his young friends respect for his contention, "I always believed in life rather than in books." Although the wealthy Andover- and Harvard-educated Holmes had a huge personal library, he was determined to live an active life beyond his scholarly roles as a poet, lecturer, author, doctor, medical reformer, and Harvard Medical School professor. He kept what he called a "fleet" of three boats on the Charles River, including a racing skeleton, a flat-bottomed skiff, and a dory. These allowed him to travel "around the Back Bay, down the stream, up the Charles to Cambridge and Watertown, up the Mystic, [and] round the wharves."[16]

On boating excursions with Holmes, Greener was generally accompanied by his friend Charles Blaney, a youngster of about his own age whose father was a tender on a drawbridge across the Charles River between Boston and Cambridge. For a young boy with street sense and working responsibilities, the conversation with his fellow boaters was as stimulating as the adventure was exhilarating. Greener later maintained that from Holmes he "got most of my real philosophy of life, and learned to read ever after [from] him." Happily for the impressionable Greener, Boston and Cambridge provided close proximity to the big names in commerce, culture, education, and politics. More than a half century after his boyhood, he still enjoyed the "blissful memory" of seeing Senator Charles Sumner, Henry Wadsworth Longfellow, and James Russell Lowell walking arm in arm along a Boston street.[17]

• • •

Boston also provided Greener with his earliest opportunities to observe firsthand the political battles and national debates about the abolition of slavery, hunting down fugitive slaves, the idea of "colonization" to encourage black emigration to other countries, and the continued union of the states. Boston citizens had begun to organize for racial justice in the 1830s, perhaps prompted by the growing popularity of the *Liberator,* which was part journal, part newspaper, and very much a uniting voice for black action. William Lloyd Garrison, its white abolitionist publisher, had managed to attract an audience up and down the East Coast for essays about injustices, news about black issues, and articles by black writers who might never have otherwise broken into print.[18]

During the 1850s, racial justice controversies among Bostonians were heightened by the Fugitive Slave Act (labeled the "Bloodhound Law" by abolitionists for the dogs that sniffed out escaped southern slaves), the Dred Scott decision of 1857, and the John Brown raid of 1859. Divisions grew sharper between citizens calling for abolition of slavery and those calling for means to stop the spread of slavery. Abolitionists favored an immediate end to all slavery throughout the country, even at the risk of a union dissolved. Many more New England citizens, however, disapproved of slavery but thought that as long as it was not extended to new territories and states it might gradually disappear. Typically, these "nonextentionists" found the abolitionists fanatical in their zeal for action, reckless in their disregard for the principle of private property, and careless toward the ideal of maintaining one united country.[19]

Greener would later pinpoint that time in Boston as "the storm and stress of 1855–62."[20] As a spirited teenager, though, he delighted in the excitement. The city was a beacon for eloquent abolitionist orators such as Douglass and Garrison. Young Greener managed to find time and the means to join the audiences crowding Boston's halls and churches to hear the fiery rhetoric of the skilled and emotional speakers who defined the abolition movement. Such occasions typically drew factions on various sides of slavery questions and were often subject to disruption by boisterous citizens.

Lifelong Boston resident Wendell Phillips was preeminent among orators of his time; he was "the silver tongued, matchless one," according to Greener. A vocal abolitionist, he was one of many who advocated the solution of allowing the slave states to leave the union. He also joined the struggle for women's rights and universal suffrage. Seventeen-year-old Greener was present at an 1860 gathering that included Phillips and later would be remembered for turning particularly violent. Planned as a meeting to commemorate the anniversary of the execution of abolitionist John Brown, the event hosted a star-studded roster of antislavery orators. Among those joining Phillips were escaped slave turned Boston pastor John Sella Martin and Douglass, who had recently returned from Canada where he had fled after being sought for arrest as a Brown co-conspirator.[21]

The hall chosen for the occasion, the Tremont Temple, was packed with vocal antislavery citizens and surrounded by anti-abolition mobs that gathered outside. These included many worried about national commercial consequences if the southern plantation economy were to end and some concerned about a change in the idea of what constituted legal property. A loud shouting match broke out, soon punctuated by pushing and punching on and around the speakers' platform. Douglass, who was thrown down a staircase during the melee, later observed that the anti-abolition forces present were "a gentleman's mob. Its rank and file, not less than its leaders, claim position with the upper classes of Boston society."[22] Several participants were injured before the group holding the meeting decided to relocate to the Joy Street Baptist Church, where John Sella Martin was pastor. Greener moved with the speakers and helped to guard Phillips, while a loud mob gathered outside the church. Although many antislavery supporters were attacked when they left the church, local police managed to keep violence to a minimum. Douglass later boasted, "The actors in the disgraceful and scandalous riot failed to convert Boston into an echo of Charleston, and to make Massachusetts an appendage of the blood-stained cotton fields of the Carolinas."[23] Greener was impressed by both the eloquence of the speakers and the anger of the opposing crowd, and no doubt such events strengthened his resolve to support the cause of racial justice. Moreover, by listening to eloquent speakers such as Douglass, Phillips, Sumner, Henry Ward Beecher, and Ralph Waldo Emerson, he learned a great deal about oratorical excellence.

· · ·

The teenaged Greener was pleased when he began working for a well-regarded Boston wood-engraving operation, D. T. Smith & Co. With his interest in art and longing to someday study art abroad, he was happy to begin to learn the technique and business of what might become a profession for him. Not quite a year after hiring Greener, however, his employer became angry and struck him. Greener later recalled, "I couldn't consent to work for him anymore."[24]

In about 1861, he went to work as a porter and night watchman at the silver, watch, and jewelry firm of Palmer and Batchelders. Established in 1817, the firm earned a reputation for crafting fine silverware and jewelry. Augustus E. Batchelder, then aged thirty-six, had become a partner in 1846, adding a younger generation to the two Palmers and two Batchelders who already shared ownership in the business. One of them became Augustus's father-in-law when Lucy Ann Palmer married Augustus in 1853. Lucy Ann's younger brother, George Herbert Palmer, would eventually claim fame as a Harvard philosopher.[25]

Greener, who was "obliged to remain in the store at night," found he had time to read enough to become familiar with business and banking and to continue his study of French. Batchelder encouraged Greener's education in all areas, and George Herbert Palmer helped him learn some Latin. While Greener hoped for a promotion and his employers found him deserving, they were "afraid to attempt it." Their concern may have been due to his race or his lack of formal education, or both. In any case, Greener was encouraged to continue studying, with the hope that he would eventually have the opportunity to get back into a school and perhaps even prepare for college. His optimism about getting and using an education began to grow when, after Union victories at Shiloh and Antietam, he considered the possibility that the Civil War might result in the United States "placing the colored people in a less humiliating position."[26]

Among the noted New England abolitionists of the time was controversial colonization advocate and zealous John Brown supporter Frank B. Sanborn. Arrested in Concord, Massachusetts, for complicity in Brown's slave uprising at Harper's Ferry, Sanborn was released by a forceful mob of his neighbors and friends. Sanborn's participation in planning the uprising as one of Brown's "secret six" group of advisors and fund raisers might seem unexpected for a Harvard-educated, twenty-eight-year-old headmaster of a private school. But Sanborn was no ordinary stiff-collared headmaster. A New Englander by birth (New Hampshire) and inclination, he demonstrated a spirit of independent thought and his coeducational Concord School was a model of progressive teaching, experiential learning, and student freedom.[27] When Greener began to suspect that he might have a chance at a formal college education, he contacted Sanborn about preparing for it at Concord School. Sanborn was immediately encouraging and even met with Greener in Boston to talk about the school. The possibility of attending Sanborn's school was appealing to Greener, but his employer and educational benefactor, Batchelder, would have other ideas.

CHAPTER TWO

Being Prepared

A UGUSTUS BATCHELDER KNEW a few things about Oberlin College in Ohio: It admitted male and female students, black and white; it had both a college preparatory program and a college; and, along with its surrounding community, it had earned a reputation as a hotbed of abolitionist sentiment and evangelical missionary zeal. In sharing this information with young Greener, Batchelder was quick to add "how cheap it was"—the annual tuition was $10 to $14—and he offered to help support Greener through the two-year preparatory course. Greener determined that the opportunity was "a decided gain" over other educational options, and, with tutoring in Latin from Harvard student George Herbert Palmer, he hoped to arrive at Oberlin with every chance of success.[1]

Founded in 1833 on swampy, forested, flat land thirty-two miles southwest of Cleveland, Oberlin Collegiate Institute was named for John Frederick Oberlin, a pious German Lutheran. Part of a Utopian community dedicated to spiritual salvation and spreading the word to the untamed American West, Oberlin began admitting African American students in 1835. That decision was not made without controversy. The students had polled their ranks about the possibility and found that a majority did not favor integration (26 for, 32 against). John J. Shipherd, one of Oberlin's founders and a proponent of racial integration, found it necessary to promise that the school would "not fill up with filthy stupid negroes." The school's New England financial agent was certain that "as soon as your darkies begin to come in in any considerable numbers . . . the whites will begin to leave." After several attempts, the board of trustees passed its radical commitment to black higher education by one vote. As Oberlin historian Geoffrey Blodgett remarked, that benevolent action happened when the college "was still very hungry for students and money, had no president and few notable teachers, and seemed on the brink of collapse."[2] Fortunately, the idea was favored by the country's abolitionists and revivalists, whose ranks and support for Oberlin were steadily growing.

Initially, Oberlin Collegiate Institute charged no tuition; instead, students worked to help farm the property and maintain the buildings. In 1850 its name changed to Oberlin College, and its emphasis shifted from manual labor and theology to a liberal arts curriculum. However, it did retain its preparatory course for students not quite ready for college work. Most early students did not graduate from a full course of study in the college or preparatory department but simply got the learning they needed and moved on. Of approximately one hundred black students who came to Oberlin in the first thirty years after its integration, thirty-two earned degrees from Oberlin. They generally comprised from 2 to 5 percent of the student body in any given year.[3]

• • •

In 1862, Greener walked onto an Oberlin campus graced with stately classical buildings of buff Ohio sandstone. The local community, with 20 percent black residents, was known for its support of the black students, and campus life was known for its mix of race and gender among students who lived and learned together. The collegiate area had a literary program (generally for female students) and a Bachelor of Arts program. Fanny Jackson, later Fanny Jackson Coppin, a student in the mostly male collegiate course while Greener was there, explained the differences as nondiscriminatory, but sometimes daunting, in her memoir.

> The faculty did not forbid a woman to take the gentleman's course, but they did not advise it. There was plenty of Latin and Greek in it, and as much mathematics as one could shoulder. . . . Then, one day, the faculty sent for me—ominous request—and I was not slow in obeying it. It was a custom in Oberlin that forty students from the junior and senior classes were employed to teach the preparatory classes. As it was now time for the juniors to begin their work, the Faculty informed me that it was their purpose to give me a class, but I was to distinctly understand that if the pupils rebelled against my teaching, they did not intend to force it. Fortunately for my training at the normal school, and my own dear love of teaching, tho there was a little surprise on the faces of some when they came into the class, and saw the teacher, there were no signs of rebellion.[4]

That Fanny Jackson was a black woman teaching white students, both male and female, testifies to an unusual atmosphere of tolerance and community. It would seem that Oberlin was just the right place for Greener, ambitious to be educated and anxious to succeed. Yet the college, starting in the mid-nineteenth century with a new president, "moved steadily toward a more conservative stance on race and gender." As historian Ronald Butchart observed, "Throughout the last half of the nineteenth century, African Americans who had attended or graduated from the college fought a difficult rearguard action to hold Oberlin to its initial promise." Greener joined the preparatory course three months late, and in spite of his tutoring in Latin, he struggled to keep up. However, showing the verbal adeptness that had attracted his Boston patrons, he quickly was recognized for his abilities in oral presentations. Public speaking, including lecture and debate, would from then on be his most recognized talent.[5]

Greener's preparatory teachers were mostly advanced students in the college program, and he would later claim, "My preparation at Oberlin was far below the eastern standard. . . . Nothing of interest occurred there, except that I had considerable practice in speaking and debating."[6] In 1881, however, reviewing a textbook on Greek grammar by Professor W. S. Scarborough, an African American, he recalled his impressive introduction to the language at Oberlin.

> There rises before me as I write the vision of Tappan Hall and N. W. Colonial, at Oberlin where first the sounds of that melodious language awakened the thoughts as yet untamed. Here is the copy of Crosby's Greek lessons, even then well thumbed, with which we began the arduous accent of Parnassus. Here, too, is the card with numerals representing so many sections of Greek Grammar committed so deeply to the memory's care that even now they spring into place by the law of association.[7]

His introduction to Greek seems to have been something "of interest" to Greener after all. Indeed, for a black student to learn Greek at that time was an achievement with meaning beyond personal educational goals. Fanny Jackson Coppin, who also managed to conquer Latin and Greek at Oberlin, recalled the prevailing sentiment "in defense of slavery," noting, "It is said that John C. Calhoun made the remark, that if there could be found a Negro that could conjugate a Greek verb, he would give up all his preconceived ideas of the inferiority of the Negro."[8]

Even amid their demanding studies, Oberlin students during Greener's time were greatly interested in the raging Civil War and the possibility of emancipation. In July 1863, following the first draft in US history, violent protests erupted in New York City. Over one hundred people were killed,

stores were looted, and blacks were subjected to lynching and injury. Oberlin students did not need to be drafted, however. Thirty-five percent of
the student body, some 850 students, left voluntarily to join the war. Later,
Greener recalled, "I belonged to the Ohio National Guard while at Oberlin
and was attached to a company of students. Never saw any active service.
Would have joined the first-Ohio colored regiment as Sergeant Major, but
my mother would not give her consent, and I was then under age." When
he entered Oberlin, he was in fact eighteen, the age required for enlistment,
but it was unlikely that military service seemed attractive to him. Black men
at that time could enlist in the Union military only as menial workers, not
as soldiers. It was not until the following year, with the establishment of
the Bureau of Colored Troops, that joining fighting forces became possible
for black men. There is evidence, from a teacher's record, however, that
Greener and other Oberlin classmates "made a commitment to educate
freed slaves in the segregated South." After the war, more Oberlin graduates
went south to teach freed slaves than graduates of any other school, and
many stayed in the South.[9]

Greener studied hard and advanced to the senior preparatory class for
the 1863–64 school year. He took part in debates, played chess, and made
a few friends. During the winter break, he taught school at Samantha in
Highland County, Ohio. As summer graduation neared, however, he ran
into what he termed "colorphobia" among several of the twenty-three members of his Preparatory Department class. An article in the *Commonwealth,*
a Boston newspaper, flashed the headline "Prejudice at Oberlin College!"
and reported that Greener had been squeezed out of his deserved position
of student-elected valedictorian by students who campaigned against him
because of his color. While there may have been occasional racist sentiment
on the part of some students, the article got the facts wrong. The Preparatory Department did not honor a valedictorian or salutatorian, but it did
allow a dozen student-elected speakers to participate in an exhibition held
at commencement time. Oberlin representatives reported that Greener may
have suspected racism because he was not elected to that group. Later, he insisted, "I was chosen one of the twelve speakers at the exhibition." However,
since he did not manage "as high an appointment as I thought I deserved,"
he decided to leave Oberlin rather than continue to its college level.[10]

Fanny Jackson defended Oberlin to the *National Anti-Slavery Standard,*
pointing out that all students there received fair and kind treatment without

regard to race. If there were a rare exception to that, she noted, it would only be at the hands of a student from the South, of which there were very few.[11] It is difficult to discern what actually happened. It is possible that Greener, with his streetwise urban upbringing, was highly alert to any hint of racial prejudice and prepared to speak out when he felt he'd been treated unjustly. Others at Oberlin may not have noticed or experienced racial tensions, or perhaps they chose not to react to slights that did occur. It is telling that it was a newspaper in Boston, where antislavery and racial justice were hotly defended, that reported the story. Student political intrigue also might have played a part in the drama. Greener soon gave up his protest and returned to Boston.

• • •

Batchelder and Greener agreed that he needed at least another preparatory year before attempting to enter college. Greener first tried to gain admission to Phillips Academy, Exeter, in southern New Hampshire, but officials there felt he was not ready for the senior class. Instead, with Batchelder's continuing support, he went twenty miles up the road to Phillips Academy, Andover. He entered the senior class, probably qualifying for free tuition and reduced cost for room and board as an "indigent student."[12]

Founded by Andover mill owner Samuel Phillips Jr. in 1778, in the midst of the Revolution, Phillips Academy aimed to inculcate Christian values in its students. Phillips, who supplied George Washington with gunpowder, came from generations of Puritans and was eager to ensure the preservation of the traditions and values of the past, especially orthodox Calvinism. Thus, the preamble to the school's constitution noted its founding as a "humble dedication to our heavenly benefactor" and outlined a course of instruction that included English, Latin, writing, arithmetic, sciences, and "the great and real business of living."[13]

By the time Greener arrived in the fall of 1864, Phillips Andover was a thriving boys' school of over three hundred students, insulated and isolated from the Civil War, and under the firm influence of Samuel Harvey Taylor. Taylor, who had been principal for nearly thirty years, was himself an institution—conservative in outlook, dictatorial in manner, and dedicated to the classics as the essential subjects for study. Appropriately, Andover historian Frederick S. Allis Jr. titled his chapter on the Taylor years, "The Dictatorship of Samuel Harvey Taylor."[14] Students lived in terror of the man they called Uncle Sam, and Greener, in his address at his fiftieth reunion in 1915, remembered his first run-in.

> When I entered the precincts of the Academy and was taken in hand by good Dr. Taylor (who had received only good notices about me in advance) I was somewhat surprised on the first morning of my entrance, when I was sitting feeling very meek in the backseat, to have my name shouted out before the entire 300—"Greener!" I was astounded, shocked. Again it was repeated—"Greener, you may leave the room." I rose cautiously, put my books together and with the utmost ease and comfort, straightened myself to a military gait and walked down the hall, bowed to Uncle Sam, as I termed him, went to the door, closed it carefully, and when I knew it was well closed I shook my fist at him through the door. When the class came out to proceed to the recitation room, No. 9 (which you may know), he was the last man to go up, but I followed him. I said, "Dr. Taylor, you sent me out of the room." "Yes, sir." Another step he took up. I said, "I was not conscious of having done anything and I don't know why you sent me out." Another step up. He looked at me fiercely and said, "You were whispering, sir." Another step up. I said, "I was not whispering, sir. I have not been here long enough for you to know whether I am truthful or not, but I say I was not whispering." When he reached the top he said: "Well, sir, if you were not whispering your whole manner indicated levity." I came out, naturally chagrined, went to the second house in the English Commons, and flung the books on the bed, and felt like fighting the bed. One of the boys seeing me said, "What is the matter, Greener?" and I related the circumstance. He said, "Why don't you know what is the matter?" "No," I said, "I was not whispering." "Why," he said, "Dr. Taylor has given you the first degree for boys that he knows have got mischief in them. He generally looks after them in advance."[15]

Perhaps the preemptive penalty worked, for Greener quickly became a model student. He was the only black student during his time there, although several others had attended earlier without graduating. Following Uncle Sam's advice about the best way to prepare for college, he chose the curriculum in the Classical Department. He next chose to reject religious faith, explaining, "I joined the 1st Independent Baptist Church in Boston in 1861 under the mistaken impression that I was converted. Being convinced of my error, I procured an honorable dismissal, I think while at Andover."[16]

Greener undoubtedly found the senior, or third-year, curriculum rigorous and demanding, given its strict emphasis on reading and translating Latin and Greek. He decided he would not even attempt to climb to the top of his class but would be more than happy to just keep up. His three terms—autumn, winter, and summer, three-and-a-half months each—included: (1) Virgil (continued from previous year), *Anabasis* (continued from previous year), exercises in comparing the Latin with the Greek, Liddell's *History of Rome,* and Doderlien's Latin synonyms; (2) works of Sallust, Homer's Iliad, translations into Latin and Greek verse, ancient geography, and Smith's *History of Greece*; and (3) Virgil (completed), translations from Latin into Greek and Greek into Latin, studies reviewed.[17]

Recitations, daunting daily tests of learning, required a great deal of study time. But completely absent was any attention to science and mathematics. Several years after Greener's days at Andover, students protested, insisting that without more math and science they were unprepared for Harvard. Intense immersion in the classics likely contributed to Greener's later writing style, with its lengthy, convoluted sentences and heavy use of allusions. Greener later remembered Dr. Taylor's teaching with gratitude: "I have never had a book upon literary composition, that did me as much good as his criticisms on the Latin and Greek authors. It was owing to this, perhaps, more than anything else throughout my career, that I have been able to make whatever little literary efforts I have made."[18]

Although the only student of African American ancestry at the school during that time, Greener joined with his fellow students to fully enjoy all aspects of the Andover experience. He quickly entered into activities on the beautiful campus of red-brick Georgian buildings, sweeping lawns, and great trees. An enthusiastic participant in informal student baseball and football skirmishes, sledding, and skating, he was known as "fun loving and well-liked." As expected, he excelled in public speaking and debate, thriving in the Philomathean Society, the oldest secondary-school debate club in the country. He later recalled his prominence "on two out of its three exhibitions while there, first with a declamation, and in the summer term with an oration."[19] During his last term, summer 1865, he was chief editor of the *Mirror,* the Philomathean literary journal.

Horace Deming, from Palmyra, New York, also a member of the Philomathean, became a close friend. During their final term, he wrote home about his plans for spending the fourth of July with Greener in Boston.

In the morning at 8 o'clock there is a boat race on the Charles river, then a concert in the common with 8 bands with cannons for base [*sic*] drums, a pro-

Richard T. Greener at Phillips Academy, Andover, 1865, at age twenty-one. Courtesy of Archives and Special Collections, Phillips Academy, Andover, Massachusetts.

cession in which will be General [Robert] Anderson (of Fort Sumpter [*sic*]) and Commodore [David] Farragut, an oration, a balloon ascension at 5 in the P.M., and fireworks in the evening, besides an anti-slavery picnic in the woods near Framingham, where Wendell Phillips and Fred Douglass will be and other prominent speakers. Quite a programme for fun, isn't there?[20]

There seemed little evidence on the campus of the great events shaking the nation. Taylor would not change his educational plans for a war. As one student remembered, "The fact is that during the year [1862–63] that I was at Andover the war had very little effect on student life. We were absorbed in study (no [formal] athletics in those days) and Andover Hill was so remote from scenes of conflict that the roar of battles was like the sound of breakers on a far distant shore. . . . The battle of Gettysburg, July 1, 2, and 3, 1863, made very little impression at the time." Nevertheless, when word of the surrender at Appomattox reached the campus, Greener led his classmates on a grand parade through Andover and was chosen as the orator for the occasion. He would later refer to his Andover class as "The Great Appomattox Class of 1865."[21]

The final issue of the *Mirror* under Greener's editorship carried this homage to the president who had been assassinated during his year in the senior class. Although unsigned, it was surely penned by Greener.

> Would that that great and noble man could have been spared; but since it could not be thus—since the salvation of the country demanded his life—let us thank God that our nation is preserved, and that such a man as Abraham Lincoln has been spared to us so long, and that he has had the power and the wisdom to carry us safely through the foulest rebellion that ever existed. . . .
>
> . . . On him rested the responsibility of saving our national honor, of saving everything that was dear to us; to him we owe more than we can ever pay. Washington obtained for us our national independence; Lincoln preserved our country and gave freedom to the slave.
>
> . . . Whatever storms of war or treason may beat against her sides, they shall never move her from her broad and strong foundation of liberty and freedom, strengthened by the life-blood of three hundred thousand patriots, and by the life of our lamented chief, Abraham Lincoln.[22]

Apparently, Principal Taylor's relentless classicism had left its mark. As his days at Andover came to a close, Greener wrote a flowery entry in Horace Deming's autograph book.

> If the sharing of each other's plans, the stimulating of one another, the happy days that we spend together, the picnicking on "Byron's hill," and the triumphs of Philo and "1st Greek," should come across your mind while at home, think of me whose friendship for you is not founded merely on class relations. My heart, though buoyant at the thought of leaving Phillips, feels sad to think that we must part. Hoping nevertheless that we may meet again, and that I may have the opportunity of fulfilling my promise, I remain Dear Horace, ever your True Friend & Classmate, Richard T. Greener.[23]

Greener's graduation photograph shows a handsome, self-assured young man, well-dressed and clean shaven, with neatly barbered curly hair. At the end of a year of acceptance and accomplishment, he was at last prepared to take on his next challenge: a college education. In pursuing it, he would take with him the touchstone motto of his Andover class: "I shall find a way or make one."[24]

CHAPTER THREE

Experiment at Harvard

ICHARD GREENER'S ENTRANCE into Harvard in 1865 was not only
a groundbreaking event but also a nostalgic homecoming for the
twenty-one-year-old, who fondly recalled the adventures of his Cambridge adolescence. He recalled entering Harvard Square and skipping
among "her green and elms and red brick educational factories." He had
frequently managed to watch the festive celebrations of the college com-
mencements, after which he would sneak into the anteroom of Harvard
Hall to listen to chatter between students and alumni.[1] While the Harvard
residence halls in which he lived as a student were less familiar, it was perhaps a comfort that he knew their surroundings so well.

With Greener's admission, Harvard College took its second memora-
ble stride toward racial integration. Beverly G. Williams was a seventeen-
year-old scholarly prodigy at Hopkins Classical School in Cambridge when
he was admitted in 1847 as the college's first black student—amid loud protests from many students and faculty, as well as some local citizens. Sadly,
he died of consumption shortly before the start of the academic year. Thus
Greener would become the first of his race to attempt to conquer the full
undergraduate curriculum and earn a Bachelor of Arts degree from the
venerable institution on the Charles River—a place where just a few decades earlier the only blacks in evidence were those brought as servants to
wealthy undergraduates or employed by the college as janitors or waiters.
The likelihood of his success was notably dim upon his admission, which
was "heavily conditioned" by a skeptical faculty taking a wait-and-see approach.[2]

• • •

Greener's mentor and chief financial backer, Augustus Batchelder, was itch-
ing to see the educational experiment of a black student succeeding at Andover carried on to Harvard. He found a receptive audience in Harvard president Thomas Hill, who soon expressed the college's interest in "seeing the

experiment fairly tried." Elected to the post in 1862, the multitalented Hill was a mathematician, naturalist, and Unitarian minister who had served as president of Antioch College during the three years preceding his move to Boston. Although never a forceful leader and recalled as having "the air and appearance of a kindly, eccentric country minister," Hill had clear objectives for moving Harvard beyond its usual embrace of history and tradition. One of these, raising the median age of incoming freshmen above seventeen, was a particularly good fit for Greener, then in his twenty-first year. Hill also hoped to improve and expand graduate education at Harvard and to add variety and choice to undergraduate studies through electives. Importantly, he was committed to racial equality through academic merit, and he was willing to go to bat for Greener, declaring, "I love the young man and admire his spirit."[3]

The Harvard College that greeted Greener in 1865 would change a great deal by the time he graduated. The Civil War had touched the campus only slightly, since there was no real enthusiasm in New England for students leaving college for the battlefield. Most of the few southern students left shortly after the war broke out in 1861, but students from other regions were much less likely to join the conflict. Even Robert Lincoln, the president's son, stayed at Harvard until he graduated in 1864, after which he opted for what one historian labeled "a safe staff appointment." Total undergraduate enrollment hovered close to four hundred. The classical curriculum, emphasizing studies in Greek and Latin, mathematics, history, philosophy, and elocution, continued to be prescribed, as did daily chapel services. The Harvard boat club raced throughout the area, while crew races against Yale and between Harvard undergraduate classes grew increasingly popular. A college cricket club played against club teams in the Boston area. Baseball arrived during the Civil War, and the first intercollegiate game, in 1863, resulted in genuine excitement: Harvard 27, Brown 17. Still more dramatic was the first varsity baseball game in 1865: Harvard 35, Williams 30.[4]

Shortly after Greener's arrival, change became the watchword—generally meaning change toward bigger, more modern, more progressive. As noted in the *Nation*, a popular monthly, that process would soon create a curriculum that "opened to the undergraduates wider opportunities for the gratification of individual preferences and tastes than is furnished at any other of our older colleges." The long-required ancient Greek and Latin language and literature were made voluntary after the sophomore year. Then, following lengthy debate about the idea of student choice and what it might mean for sparking interest and creating paths to wider varieties of professional pursuits, studies beyond the first two years allowed growing numbers of elective courses. While advanced Latin and Greek studies were among those electives, so were Italian, Spanish, German, chemistry, poetry, natural history, and other subjects. A new scientific spirit on campus also marked the years immediately following the Civil War, with ongoing arguments for and against Darwinism highlighting newer academic disciplines and pitting star faculty like naturalist Louis Agassiz (against) in ongoing debate with star faculty like botanist Asa Gray (for).[5]

Perhaps even more significant to many students, the ban on Greek fraternities, imposed by the faculty in 1857, was lifted in 1865. Not surprisingly, some groups did not have to make much of a comeback, since they had been kept alive by "leading a surreptitious life." Clubs, such as the Hasty Pudding, the Porcellian, and the Institute of 1770, continued their long history of literary and social activities, and they were joined by even more clubs after 1865. If clubs and fraternities provided too little diversion, students could take advantage of improved transportation to go elsewhere. As President Hill fretted, "The passage of horse-cars to and from Boston, nearly, if not quite, a hundred times a day, has rendered it practically impossible for the Government of the College to prevent our young men from being exposed to the temptations of the city."[6]

• • •

Greener's arrival on campus was relatively understated, and undoubtedly many of his fellow freshmen were initially uncertain whether he was considered a different race from the rest of them. However, several New England and Midwestern newspapers picked up the story: "The first colored student admitted to Harvard College is Mr. Richard Greener, some twenty-two years of age, who yesterday passed a rigid and satisfactory examination." Although there is no recorded evidence that he was treated differently by his peers in the class of 126 freshmen, Greener was slow to join the mainstream of college activities and interactions. He was assigned a single room in College House dormitory, where it was well recognized that "the poor and struggling lived." While he surmised that his "fit for college was inadequate" and that he would have to work more diligently than many classmates, he later recalled, "I felt confident I could keep up with my class."[7]

Greener's strong suit continued to be oral communication—debate, declamation, and oratory. Only weeks after his arrival on campus, he was able
to compete for the freshman Lee Prize for excellence in reading aloud. The
one-two finish, recorded by university librarian John Langdon Sibley in his
diary, was both even-handed and ironic: "Prizes for reading assigned to
Freshmen: first prize to [Robert] McLeod, a rebel officer who lost his arm
in the rebel service and the second to Greener, who is of African descent."
Greener's prize was a welcome ten dollars worth of books.[8]

It soon became apparent that elocution, one of the required freshman
courses, was Greener's only area of certain success. The other compulsory
studies for that year were Greek and Latin language and literature, French
grammar and literature, and mathematics. Greener was not naturally inclined to mathematics and would have barely performed adequately on that
part of the admissions examinations. The freshman year emphasis was geometry and algebra, and he struggled mightily, while just barely keeping up
in his other coursework.[9]

While Greener may have been hampered by his limited early academic
exposure, it is also likely that he experienced loneliness and some stress as
the sole student representative of his race. False impressions of him circulated
among the other students, who speculated about him. Upon graduating, he
recalled that among those were rumors "that I had escaped from slavery with
innumerable difficulties; that I came direct from the cotton field to college;
that I was a scout in the Union army; the son of a Rebel general, etc." Even
classmates who knew him well did not seem to realize that "instead of drifting
from the South, I was a Boston boy." President Hill concluded by the end of
Greener's first semester that he "came here under the great disadvantages of
an inadequate preparation, of having almost no friends, and of being the
first student known to have entered this College with African blood in his
being. He has been on the whole well treated by the undergraduates and has
made a very pleasant impression on the students and the faculty."[10]

The situation soon deteriorated. In the second term of his freshman
year, the faculty voted that Greener should be "dropped for conditions not
made up and for failure of Mathematical Examinations."[11] Hill and Batchelder, however, were unwilling to let their Harvard College test case fail
so quickly. Hill wrote immediately to Batchelder to assess his willingness
to attempt to save the situation, asking if he might foot the bill for private
tutoring, a repeated freshman year, or both.

[Greener's] mathematical preparation was so utterly insufficient that he cannot possibly keep up with his class in that department. No one left in the class has received less than about double the credit given him by the mathematical tutor. Meanwhile as in other studies his preparation was only moderately good, the faculty deems it impossible for him to catch up with his class in mathematics without the ruin of his other studies or of his health. They therefore strongly recommend him to withdraw from College and come back in September to join the next freshman class.

He is of course averse to doing this. . . . One reason of his desire to go on with his present class is undoubtedly his great unwillingness to be a burden for another year upon the gentlemen who so generously bear his expenses. I write to ask you whether this burden cannot be removed—whether gentlemen cannot be found who will say to him, "Be of good courage, take the task more deliberately, accept the urgent advice of the faculty, and be assured that we will very cheerfully bear the additional expense."[12]

Batchelder replied immediately, agreeing to help. He added that "Mr. Greener's friends will certainly thank you" and reminded Hill that "we believe him to have the necessary latent ability to be an honor to the race." Perhaps somewhat chagrined that it was he who encouraged Greener to go to Oberlin, Batchelder noted the "unfortunate" preparation by which Greener "lost the year or more he spent at Oberlin." But, he had no doubt that Hill's recommendation for Greener to take on private work, followed by a repeated freshman year, could be managed.[13]

A month later, it began to appear that Greener might not be required to repeat his first year after all. President Hill wrote to Batchelder that "the faculty had so much sympathy with Greener on account of his race that they consented to give him a longer trial, to May 1, on condition of his taking on a private tutor in mathematics." Apparently, however, the tutor was only able to take Greener so far. At the close of the academic year, the struggling student failed his year-end mathematical examination, and the faculty voted unanimously that he be dropped from his class. President Hill reported the bad news to Batchelder, adding, "I am rather disappointed that his bright, amicable character proved insufficient to carry him. . . . I wish with all my heart that we could graduate him, if not in 1869 at least in 1870." With Batchelder's unwavering help, Hill got his wish. Greener was reluctant to drop back a class, and he blamed much of the problem on "some members of the faculty and certain tutors."[14] But his determination to one day earn a Harvard diploma and the encouragement of supporters like Batchelder allowed him to swallow his pride and return for another year as a freshman—again alone in a room in College House.

• • •

During his second freshman year, 1866–67, Greener started to find his footing socially and academically. By a stroke of good luck, a second black student enrolled in the freshman class—a Phillips Exeter Academy graduate whom Greener saw "nearly every day until he left in the junior year." Additional changes and modernization at Harvard contributed to a vibrant spirit throughout the community. The start time for compulsory early morning chapel was pushed up to 7:30. Plans for making all courses in Greek and Latin voluntary after freshman year became a reality by 1867. Sophomores joined upperclassmen in being allowed some elective courses. Such steps foreshadowed a time when neither required prayers nor required courses would be in favor at the nation's oldest college.[15]

Student journalism, and thus communication relevant to student interests, got a boost with the founding of the *Harvard Advocate* in 1866. Published fortnightly during the academic year and initially called the *Collegian*, it was touted as the first Harvard newspaper. "For the first time the pompous shape of a magazine was abandoned," an early article reminisced: "Opportunity was given for the publication of such light and bright articles as should better express the thoughts and knowledge of the undergraduates than could imitations of more serious work." Although the faculty managed to suppress the publication of the *Collegian* after three issues, it soon bounced back as the *Harvard Advocate*. It went underground for much of its first two years, and the administration threatened expulsion of the editors. Yet, students continued and eventually won the struggle for the right to publish a paper "which should express undergraduate opinion, even when that opinion differed radically from the views held by the governing body of the college."[16]

Thus, students aired complaints about their college, reported on boating and baseball, reviewed books and plays, and contributed witty discussions of social life. For students like Greener, who could easily revert to the fringe of collegiate life, the *Harvard Advocate* was able to motivate engaged involvement. Additionally, Greener contributed short articles and reviews

to the publication during his junior and senior years. His article on a collection of engravings donated to Harvard caught the eye of Sen. Charles
Sumner, a beacon for civil rights in the US Congress, who asked about the
author and soon began a friendship with him.[17]

Harvard's Pi Eta Society was established by members of the class of 1866
as a senior society founded "to promote social fellowship among its members with literary and dramatic inclinations." Greener eventually became
a member and, although there is no indication he took part in the group's
well-known theatrical productions, he undoubtedly enjoyed his association
with some of Harvard's especially creative students. He would later note
that he also served as vice president of a secret society and was a member of
"a radical religious club."[18]

Particularly fortunate for Greener was Nathaniel Thayer's 1865 bequest
establishing a student-run club to provide meals to needy students "at actual cost; the students themselves having direction of the tables." Thayer
Club participants—initially about 150 undergraduates—could eat well while
avoiding costly charges for board in private homes or the Harvard com-
mons. With its own dining hall, kitchen, club officers, and monthly meetings, the group charged student diners two dollars a week. Greener was a
charter member.[19]

• • •

Finally, by his sophomore year, 1867–68, Greener was ready to hit his college
stride. He moved to Stoughton Hall, a busy four-story dormitory prominent in Harvard's main quadrangle. For the first time, he acquired a roommate: Horace Deming, his friend during Andover days and now a Harvard
freshman. Deming was outgoing and quick to get to know his fellow students, many of whom also became friendly with Greener. The two would
continue to room together through Greener's junior year. In his final year,
he roomed with a fellow senior, Oscar Fitzallan Seavey. Greener even enjoyed some social life off campus, including parties with male and female
acquaintances. His new confidence could at times be off-puttingly arrogant,
according to his friend Frances Anne Rollin. The daughter of free blacks in
Charleston, South Carolina, Rollin came to Boston to research a biography of Martin Delany, an outspoken abolitionist and one of the first three
black men admitted to Harvard Medical School. When she asked Greener
to comment on some early drafts of her biography, she was disappointed

to find him "cynical and apt to discourage instead of acting otherwise. He lives in a grand intellectual sphere and is accustomed to only perfection."[20]

Clearly, Greener had decided that acceptance across racial boundaries was crucial to having a favorable experience at Harvard. He had white friends, and that served him well when he wanted to submit an article to the *Harvard Advocate*, borrow a book, or join a group walking down to the Charles to watch a boat race. He was surrounded by whiteness, he was amiable, and he enjoyed fully participating in student life. Such ease and involvement with whites, however, could be viewed by fellow blacks as pandering or pretense, detracting from his own or others' activism for the black race. W. E. B. Du Bois would later take a very different approach as a Harvard student. He decided on adopting "voluntary race segregation" and claimed that doing so assured that he was "not obsequious" to white fellow students and faculty. He simply stuck to his studies and associated with a few black members of the surrounding community, "cutting myself off from my white fellows" and remaining "firm in my criticism of white folk and in my dream of a self-sufficient Negro culture even in America."[21]

As an upperclassman, Greener participated in informal athletic games and rowing on the Charles. He later recalled being "everywhere treated as a friend and companion" and "took part in all the scrapes." He also won first place in Harvard's Boyleston Prize for Elocution competition of 1868, receiving a $50 reward. He understood that he would not quite make the very top academic ranks: "The first representative of the negro race at Harvard wisely determined to curb a very strong desire to carry off a *summa cum laude* in college, in order that he might preserve his health, and, by a prolonged and useful life, reflect, in some small degree, honor on the ancient University which gave him her blessing." Nevertheless, Greener would go on to win another Boyleston Prize, a second place in 1870, and first place among seniors vying for the Bowdoin Prize in dissertation writing on an assigned subject. His heavily researched essay, "The Tenure of Land in Ireland," argued for reform and even at one point "compared the relationship between Irish tenants and their English landlords to the relationship between slaves and masters in the antebellum South."[22]

The Richard Greener who twice had been a worried freshman sprinted toward his finish line as a worldly senior. To that end, he began to expand the reach of his efforts well beyond the brick and ivy campus. At the start of his senior year, in August 1869, he launched a fledgling public-speaking career with an appearance at the Institute for Colored Youth in Philadelphia. It was an auspicious start. The *Philadelphia Evening Bulletin* puffed his upcoming appearance by noting, "He is a young colored man of excellent character and of fine ability, and his elocution is pronounced by Boston critics to be of no inferior character." Greener combined reading from popular works with his own original oratory in a style reviewed as "pure, very careful, elegant and strikingly natural." He undoubtedly enjoyed reading the paper's praise of his "full mellow voice, [speaking] without apparent effort, which evidently pleased the audience."[23]

That same summer, Greener was thrilled to make a pilgrimage to Rochester, New York, to visit the "grand man" he so revered, Frederick Douglass. According to his later recollections, both the hero and the hero worshipper were in their elements. For Greener, it was an "idyllic visit" to the comfortable Douglass home, complete with a model hostess in Douglass's wife Anna, "a grand character." He and Douglass "talked philosophy, history, discussed the leaders in politics and thought of the time, in all of which he showed himself well informed, critical and a systematic reader." Douglass played his violin and recounted his European travels. Of these, he particularly remembered meeting Alexandre Dumas, père, in France, and he confided to Greener that his own long, unruly hair was worn in imitation of the great author.[24]

Class Day, a senior celebration prior to commencement exercises, was a day and evening spectacle among the Harvard campus buildings and pathways; those lucky enough to have tickets were invited to all events. The activities of June 1870 began in the morning with the seniors marching together to the campus church to hear odes and benedictions. Then there was a breakfast at the home of Greek professor William Watson Goodwin, an affair that included the faculty and the newly inaugurated Harvard president, Charles Eliot. When the class filed back to the church, they heard Roger Wolcott deliver the senior oration, entitled "Enthusiasm." Surprisingly, the speech itself was subdued and cautionary. Wolcott reminded, "Full well indeed do we know that danger lurks on the path before us . . . eagerly we would press on to encounter and overthrow it." Later, all participants made the rounds of "swell spreads" of punch and food sponsored by various groups and clubs throughout campus. There was dancing on the green in the afternoon, a reception at President Eliot's residence, the planting of the class ivy, more orations in the evening, a band concert, and a glee club appearance. The governor and lieutenant governor of Massachusetts attended, as did two

Twenty-six-year-old Greener at Harvard College, 1870.
Courtesy of Harvard University Archives.

past Harvard presidents, US Secretary of the Interior Jacob Cox, and Gen. William Tecumseh Sherman.[25]

It had already become apparent that many of Greener's classmates would head to law school, most likely at Harvard. Others would gravitate to medical school or go directly into banking, teaching, or a family business. One vital purpose of a Harvard degree was to launch future networking with classmates and other Harvard graduates. The class of 1870 was well positioned in that direction as its polished and connected graduates glided out of Harvard Yard toward their various places among the heady possibilities of the Gilded Age. Orator Roger Wolcott, for example, inspired enough voter enthusiasm to be elected lieutenant governor and then governor of Massachusetts. Classmate William Fisher Wharton served as US assistant secretary of state. Two Adams family members from Massachusetts, Brooks and George, went on to Harvard Law School and successful legal careers. Newton Dexter became the editor of Denver's *Rocky Mountain News*. Arthur Cutler started slowly as a private tutor of hopeful Harvard applicants, including young Teddy Roosevelt; he went on to establish the Cutler School in New York City. Willis Farrington became a well-known tennis star. His sports prominence among class of 1870 alums was second only to that of golfer Laurence Curtis, who traveled extensively in Europe, returned to popularize the game in the United States, and, in 1894, founded the US Golf Association.[26]

For Greener, a young black man with what was considered a white man's education, professional options were far more circumscribed. By the time he graduated, he had determined that a law degree would be an excellent foundation for his proclaimed "chief desire"—to lead a "literary life" of speaking and writing. However, he knew that course would have to wait until he achieved a far more solid financial footing. In an autobiographical sketch written at the time, he mentioned his fondness for art and particular interest in "metaphysics, general literature, and the Greek and Latin classics when divested of grammatical pedantry."[27] Unfortunately, then as now, such pursuits were far from where the money was.

Understanding that his interests might not match his immediate needs, Greener stated that his long-term goal was "to get all the knowledge I can, make all the reputation I can, and 'do good.' "[28] While his demonstrated success at Harvard was a singular and significant occurrence, his demonstrated reality—that even a Harvard education could not open doors equally across the races—may have made an even more important point.

An Accidental Academic

U PON GRADUATION FROM HARVARD in 1870, Greener well understood the reality of his immediate circumstances. After the years at Oberlin, Andover, and Harvard, he had substantial debts, including at least one institutional loan from Harvard.[1] He would not think of asking for any further educational funding from Augustus Batchelder. Law school was out of reach, as was foregoing precious wage-earning time for a legal apprenticeship. Without targeted professional preparation, political connections that could help him get a government job, or a family business to join, twenty-six-year-old Greener found his options sorely limited. Teaching or journalism—limited for him to black schools or black newspapers—were the only likely career paths remaining.

• • •

The coeducational Institute for Colored Youth (ICY), which included high-school-level work and a preparatory program offering both a classical curriculum and a normal-school course, was located in Philadelphia's black community on Shippen Street (later Bainbridge Street). The institute's roots reached back to an 1832 bequest from the estate of a wealthy and benevolent Quaker, Richard Humphreys, who wanted to provide educational opportunities to "descendants of the African race" who might take up teaching, agriculture, and/or mechanical arts.[2] Early in the nineteenth century, normal schooling for blacks was nearly nonexistent in the South and exceptional in the North. At the start of the Reconstruction era, when the US census reported 80 percent of African Americans over fourteen years of age as illiterate, the Quaker managers of ICY had moved its location twice and reduced its orientation toward preparing students for trade and farming. They had accentuated the institute's teacher-training mission, acquired a building that could house up to four hundred students, and installed a rigorous curriculum. Studies included English, classics of philosophy, Latin, Greek, geometry, trigonometry, life sciences, social sciences, chemistry, and religious instruction. Final oral examinations were required for graduation and open to the public.[3] What has since been characterized as a "negroes-teaching-negroes experiment" had blossomed into an exemplary academic success that attracted scores of visitors every year who wanted to transplant its methods or simply marvel at the students' accomplishments.[4] Eventually, the institute would become Cheney University.

In 1870, the ICY had as its principal the diminutive and determined Fanny Jackson. An expert teacher of "vast knowledge, refined manner, religious beliefs, and plain dress," according to her biographer, she also would prove to be an "aggressive and outspoken leader." She had arrived straight from Oberlin three years earlier to teach and take responsibility for the ICY Girls Department. When the principal, Ebenezer D. Bassett, was appointed US minister to Haiti, Jackson was ready to head the school. Her promotion over her colleague Octavius Catto, the highly regarded head of the Boys Department, may have surprised some, but it made only good sense to the ICY managers. Catto's biographers later noted several differences that led to Jackson's promotion over her male colleague: "She had a college degree. She did not pester the managers periodically for raises. Her name was in the newspapers now and again, but for accomplishments in the classroom." And, as one of the Quaker managers explained to a disappointed Catto, "Thou had not kept thyself somewhat fresh in all those branches which are allotted to the station of Principal."[5]

Greener had crossed paths with Jackson at Oberlin when she was a student in its Collegiate Department, gaining experience by teaching preparatory students. Greener's complaints that "some colorphobia shown by several classmates" stood in the way of his election as a top Oberlin graduate and Jackson's response in defense of Oberlin had created differences between the two, but those were six years in the past by the time Greener graduated from Harvard. In August 1870, he was hired as an assistant to the principal and soon took on some of Catto and Jackson's responsibilities while they were traveling that fall. By late 1870, he took charge of the ICY English Department, with an annual salary of $1,400.[6]

Undoubtedly, Greener found Philadelphia an intriguing and even exciting crossroads of northern and southern sentiments in the aftermath of the Civil War. Positioned between Delaware and New Jersey, the city of nearly 700,000 residents—not quite 4 percent of them considered "negro"—was slower than many others to integrate public places such as railways, streetcars, theaters, museums. The continuing racial discrimination motivated a rising generation of black activists, organizers, protestors, and politicians. The Fifteenth Amendment to the US Constitution, giving citizens the right to vote regardless of "race, color, or previous condition of servitude," had been ratified just months before Greener arrived, and racist objectors had not yet fully perfected the use of discriminatory tests and taxes that would later effectively nullify it. Philadelphia's African American population was bustling with anticipation about the next election and busily meeting, lecturing, and organizing to get out the vote.[7]

Among Philadelphia's vocal and well-known black citizens was Greener's cousin, Isaiah Wears, a popular barber, president of the Social, Civil and Statistical Association of the Colored People of Pennsylvania, and a highly regarded speaker and black suffrage advocate. He had been selected by the National Convention of Colored Men to address the US House of Representatives Judiciary Committee during the Fifteenth Amendment debate and had famously upended the idea of "giving" all races the right to vote. Instead, he claimed that the right was already "ours because it is yours. . . . It is one of the pursuits of happiness." Other Philadelphians prominent in pushing for increased black voices and votes included Amherst-educated abolitionist Robert Purvis; renowned Underground Railroad conductor William Still; principal of the Vaux School for black children, Jacob C. White Jr.; social and political activist William D. Forten; and, of course, Octavius Catto. Fanny Jackson, committed to equal rights across gender and race, generally took a less conspicuous approach to her advocacy. At Oberlin, with its mostly tolerant and largely white student body, she could report, "I had forgotten about my color." That changed when a streetcar conductor blocked her entrance onto his white-only car during a fierce rainstorm, her "first unpleasant experience in Philadelphia." Her subsequent activity in community speaking and organizing eventually led her to conclude she "had always had two schools—the Institute and the Philadelphia black community."[8]

Greener arrived at ICY just as Catto was making plans to leave. After discussions during the summer with influential black friends in Washington, DC, Catto had been asked to consider becoming the superintendent of District of Columbia colored schools. With a board of trustees and superintendent separate from those of the white public school system, Washington's black schools were overflowing with 2,700 students. They had grown so fast after the Civil War as to outstrip attempts at establishing coherent curricula and consistent policies. When the ICY managers seemed unlikely to waive their requirement for three months' notice of resignation, Catto instead decided to remain at ICY but to take a one-month leave of absence. Greener took on his responsibility for the Boys Department, while Catto spent his leave in Washington developing new curricula for the black schools, including courses, learning topics, and textbooks.[9]

• • •

The 1870 elections clearly indicated that the passage of the Fifteenth Amendment had done nothing to quell racial bigotry among many citizens. Political organizers urged black voters to vote early and vote Republican. At some Philadelphia polls, however, local police shoved aside blacks standing near the front of lines to make way for white citizens. At other polling places, groups of white voters simply swarmed past blacks. The general chaos accompanying attempts to deter black voting prompted US marshal E. M. Gregory to use his authority to appoint special deputies to preserve order. He promptly deputized marines from the Philadelphia Navy Yard. That act infuriated Mayor Daniel Fox, a Democrat, who claimed on election day that "this city is in a state of profound peace."[10] With Fox ending his first mayoral term the next year, the more racist members of his party readied themselves to limit black, mostly Republican, voting by any means possible.

Greener was just a few blocks from the ICY building when he saw a white man shoot at an unarmed black man on the morning of the 1871 election. When he reported it to the police, he was told that the white man was actually one of their own, a "special policeman" for the day. The day did not go well. Several black men were shot at on their way to the polls before voting began. Complaints mounted about policemen clubbing black voters and shoving them out of lines at the polls, and citizens appealed to local judges to issue arrest warrants for violent police officers. Rioting broke out, and ICY closed several hours early that day in order to get students safely home as soon as possible. Catto walked toward his home by a route he selected purposely to avoid the worst of violence.[11]

He had almost made it home when a white man passed him on the street, then wheeled around to yell at him. The man shot Catto three times before running away. One shot pierced Catto's heart, and he died instantly. Greener was one of the first on the scene after his colleague fell in the street. Other

ICY colleagues soon joined him, and they all gathered at a nearby police station where Catto's body had been carried. Three black citizens were killed in the city that day, and many more injured. At the polls, voters had overwhelmingly leaned Republican and elected William Stokley, who would serve as Philadelphia's mayor for three terms.[12]

The local press was incensed at thirty-two-year-old Catto's murder and quickly reported it as an act of racial bigotry carried out by Frank Kelly, a local political mobster for Democratic Party strategists.[13] Five years later, after being captured in Chicago, Kelly would stand trial and face more than a dozen witnesses who saw him shoot Catto—most from nearby front porches and a stopped streetcar. A jury of twelve white men found him not guilty.

Catto's funeral was much like an affair of state. All city offices and many schools closed for the occasion. W. E. B. Du Bois would later describe it as "perhaps the most imposing ever given to an American negro."[14] Catto had helped to form a short-lived colored infantry company during the Civil War. Now, he lay in full military dress in an ornate open casket at the military armory on Broad Street. An estimated five thousand mourners filed past, including prominent black men and women from Washington, DC, to New England. A huge parade of bands, civic organizations, honor guards, carriages, military companies, city employees, and ICY students followed the horse-drawn hearse on its three-mile route to the burial site at Lebanon Cemetery. Wears gave the keynote address at a large meeting of black citizens memorializing Catto and others who had died on election day.

> To us these scenes are nothing new. Their horrible and community-disgracing record dates back a whole generation. . . . The party that stands guilty of the crimes of today is the same class of merciless persecutors that have followed and dogged us as no other people in this country have been followed, and this, too, under the blazing sunlight of a Christian civilization. Whenever and wherever we have made any effort to lift ourselves, mobs were sent to burn our dwellings, our schoolhouses, our churches, and our orphan asylums, hanging us to lampposts and clubbing us to death on the highways. . . . There are men claiming position in the higher walks of life who have nothing but their color to recommend them, hence they fight for it in this way; they labor to keep alive public sentiment, the logical consequence of which is the murder of our people.[15]

W. E. B. Du Bois later interpreted Catto's murder, with its community-wide "outburst of indignation and sorrow" among citizens of every race and class, as finally exposing the "barbarism and lawlessness in the second city of the land" and thereby initiating opportunities to move toward racial justice in Philadelphia. For the first time, a black Philadelphian might find "a disposition to grant him, within limits, a man's chance to make his way in the world."[16]

Richard Greener was quickly appointed to step into Catto's place as temporary principal for the Boys Department of the ICY. As it did for many black citizens, the tragedy of Catto's murder further motivated Greener's interest in voicing the case for racial justice. His speaking reached larger audiences in the immediate aftermath of Catto's death, as he addressed several meetings of blacks who protested the killing and organized to demand an end to racism. Also becoming vocally supportive of gender equality, he was enthusiastic about a speech on "the conservation of our own talent" by Fanny Jackson, and he remarked that her oratorical ability demonstrated "that intellect [was] independent of sex."[17] His writing gained traction as he became a regular correspondent to the *New National Era,* founded by Frederick Douglass in 1870 as the first national newspaper for black citizens and published in Washington, DC. By 1873, Greener would join Lewis Douglass and John A. Cook on the editing team of the paper.

Shortly before Catto's death, Greener's first lengthy published essay had appeared in the *New National Era.* Titled "Individuality," it centered on the idea that "most of us are so wedded to creeds, and dogmas, and methods . . . that there is scarcely less diversity in the average thought—political, ethical, or educational—than there is difference in the garments of the State's prison convicts." He admonished his largely black readership to avoid "allegiance to the common creed merely because it is common," and he maintained that any individual and any race could only progress if people refused to remain too comfortable with the status quo or too meek to act on their own convictions. Citing noted thinkers from Shakespeare and Milton to Martin Luther and Wendell Phillips, his advice reflected his own inner struggles about a vision for his professional future.[18]

It was clear to Greener that his endeavors in speaking and writing were more suited to his personal preferences than were his teaching activities. He wrote to Sen. Charles Sumner that although he considered his position at ICY quite good, it was not at all the career he longed for. "Mr. [Frederick] Douglass is the only colored lecturer and consequently the field is open," he pointed out. "Some partial success in speaking and writing at Cambridge leads me to think I might do passably well."[19] Additionally, he still hoped to study law and was making a small start by apprenticing on occasion in the Philadelphia law office of Edward Hopper.

Undoubtedly eager to increase his sphere of possible influence, Greener took a prominent part in meetings among black men concerning the passage of the Civil Rights Bill then working its way through committees in the US Congress. Proposed in 1870 by Senator Sumner, the bill would give all citizens, regardless of color, equal access in accommodations, transportation, places of worship, public schools, cemeteries, theaters, museums, cemeteries, and the like. Sumner had wisely introduced it as an amendment to a bill giving general amnesty to former Confederate fighters. By January 1872, the bill had not yet reached the floor of either the Senate or the House of Representatives. To help keep it moving, Greener traveled to Washington as one of four leaders of a delegation of prominent black citizens that would meet with congressional representatives and with President Ulysses S. Grant to push for the legislation. Delegates from Arkansas, Philadelphia, Richmond, and Washington, DC, joined together to call on the president, with Greener heading the Philadelphia contingent and bringing a petition bearing two thousand signatures in favor of the bill.[20]

Greener well understood that among elected officials the idea of civil rights was as much a political issue as a racial-justice issue. At the White House, he noted to President Grant that he represented 14,000 black male voters of Philadelphia who desired Grant's support in "securing that which the name citizen would imply we are already enjoying, but is, as far as the colored people are concerned, to an extent a farce." He further reminded the president that the current situation not only affected freed slaves in the South but also "stamped with inferiority and degradation 300,000 colored voters who have not been slaves. It is a lamentable and sad fact that the only country wherein caste is recognized is in free America."[21]

Although President Grant agreed that black citizens were being denied rights and privileges, he felt that simply getting adequate enforcement of the Fourteenth and Fifteenth Amendments might solve the problem. He told the group that "not having read the bill attentively, he was unable to speak as to the specific provisions contained therein." However, he did think there was enough in it to "commend itself to the thoughtful consideration of those who are called upon to legislate."[22]

Later the same month, Sumner addressed the Senate in support of his Civil

Rights Bill, using examples of racial discrimination provided by Greener, whom he called "no unworthy representative of his race." In a somewhat watered-down version, the bill became the Civil Rights Act of 1875, passing into law without barring discrimination in schools, churches, or cemeteries. In the words of one of many blacks who had worked for passage, it was simply "a patched up apology for a Civil Rights Bill."[23] Eight years later, the Supreme Court declared it unconstitutional. Ironically, the lone dissenter in that decision, John M. Harlan, was also the only former slave owner among the nine justices.

• • •

Greener returned to Philadelphia with an expanded circle of political contacts and activist friends from the Washington delegation. He was now convinced that any start he could make on his desire to "get into public life" would be far more likely to happen in Washington than in Philadelphia. Writing to Sumner as a valued friend and advisor, as well as a key professional and political connection, Greener asked for his "opinion with reference to my own plans." He reminded Sumner that he desired legal training and practice, and he noted that he knew a number of people in Washington who might help him obtain a position that supported his desire to "have leisure to fit myself for public life in the best way." He hoped Sumner would "consider this matter and advise me."[24] Undoubtedly, he wanted not only advice but also Sumner's active efforts to open doors that would lead to a suitable position in Washington.

It is likely that Sumner also took up the issue with his influential friend William Wormley. One of the wealthiest black businessmen in the nation's capital, Wormley was also a member of the three-man Board of Trustees of Colored Schools of Washington and Georgetown. He thought of Greener for possible leadership of the city's first public high school for nonwhite students, the Preparatory High School for Colored Youth (later M Street High School and then Dunbar High School). Founded in 1870 in a church basement and soon moved to shared space in another black school, the school had a college-preparation curriculum that included English grammar and literature, mathematics, geometry, trigonometry, astronomy, mental and moral philosophy, and foreign languages.[25]

Wormley's colleague on the board, John Gray, was also favorable toward Greener. However, the Preparatory High School already had a competent principal: Mary Jane Patterson, who in 1862 had been the first black woman to receive a BA from Oberlin. Like Greener, she had taught at ICY in Philadelphia after graduation. She had been made principal of the Preparatory High School in the fall of 1872. Board president Henry Johnson worried that the $1,500 salary that Wormley proposed for Greener was higher than necessary, especially since Mary Patterson was doing a fine job with a $900 salary. Although nobody objected to a male principal commanding higher pay, Johnson was unable to get his two board colleagues to agree to his proposal of a $1,200 salary, which would have been $200 below Greener's annual pay in Philadelphia.[26]

Greener was offered the Preparatory High School principalship in September 1872. He had been at ICY long enough to make a positive impression, and some in the community hoped he would turn down the new opportunity. The *Philadelphia Christian Recorder* reported, "Prof. Greener has made so many friends during his stay in this city and is so popular with the Board of Managers of the Institute that it is doubtful if he will accept, or the Institute will be willing to lose him."[27] However, Greener wasted no time in giving notice to the ICY board. Johnson, still fretting about Greener's salary and the financial condition of the Preparatory High School, wrote to members of the ICY board suggesting they not let Greener go and noting that possible upcoming changes relating to the Colored School Board would likely make the job less favorable for him. Greener, nevertheless, took over as principal of the Preparatory School in January 1873. Mary Patterson stayed on as a teacher.

The District of Columbia had the largest community of black residents of any city in the country. It had swelled with black migration during and after the Civil War, and had quickly become, in the words of one historian, "the center of Negro 'society.'" This circumstance was at least partly due to the city's "large Negro professional class, including teachers in the segregated public school system, doctors, dentists, and lawyers, and large numbers of Negroes employed in the federal government." Notably, observed E. Franklin Frazier, Washington's elite "Negro society" was largely "composed of the upper-class mulattoes who, in fleeing from the persecution and discrimination in the South, brought to Washington the social distinctions and color snobbery that had been the basis of their ascendancy."[28] Greener had all the attributes to fit right into the top echelons of black society in his new locale.

However, some early misunderstandings created initial friction between the new principal and upper administrators. Greener was chagrined to find no appointment made for an assistant, which he believed he had been promised. Eventually, he was able to appoint his old friend Charlotte Forten, a well-known civil-rights activist from Philadelphia, who had taught former slaves on South Carolina's coastal islands. He also felt he had not been given adequate orientation to his new work by the superintendent of black schools, George F. T. Cook. And Johnson, who was school board president, felt Greener's suggestions for curriculum changes toward building a true preparatory school implied criticism of the board of trustees.[29]

Greener quickly became a participant in Washington's black community. With his college education and light complexion, he would have been easily embraced by the city's color-conscious elite blacks, an element labeled by one black journalist as "pin-headed dudes and dudines." He had been initiated into the black freemasons of Philadelphia, and he associated with the Washington Masonic bodies. Within a few months of moving to Washington, he joined groups advocating civil rights, supporting insurrectionists in Cuba rebelling against Spanish rule, and promoting integrated schools. As the principal speaker at an Emancipation anniversary celebration, he exhorted black citizens to fight for their rights, vote Republican, and form "a community of interest" by "devoting ourselves to deeds—to the serious work of consolidating our influence and wielding our just power." In his oratory and his writing, he campaigned for racial justice, desegregated education (generally referred to as "mixed schools"), and women's suffrage, announcing to a wide audience his commitment to and promise of leadership for his race. He also participated with other prominent blacks in denouncing the Colored School Board decision to not purchase a portrait of Senator Sumner.[30]

• • •

Perhaps the refusal to buy the Sumner portrait was the last straw. Greener had always been candid in his opinions, even when they were counter to those in power. It didn't help that the Colored School Board composition and selection process had changed shortly after he became a principal. The board size expanded from three to nine members, with Johnson retaining the position of board president. Unfortunately for Greener, "seven of the nine trustees of the new Colored School Board were loyal supporters of Johnson's policies." After Greener had been in his position for about three months, the board asked Superintendent Cook to conduct an examination of the condition of the school and its costs. The school didn't fare well. The report found furniture and equipment suffering lack of maintenance, and student discipline seemed lax. Yet the cost per pupil had nearly tripled in less than a year.[31]

During the spring of 1873, when Greener joined the editorial board of the *New National Era,* he was presented with even more opportunities to address racial issues in editorials and opinion pieces. He and his fellow editors were particularly incensed at the Colored School Board for combining two schools and appointing a white teacher as principal of the consolidated school. The paper's editorial objecting to such "injustice and apparent prejudice" undoubtedly did not endear Greener to the already skeptical Superintendent Cook.[32]

By the end of the school year, various factions involved with the schooling of blacks in Washington, DC, resorted to unrestrained battles of words and nerves. Final examinations of Greener's students, oral and open to the public, were attended by notables like mental-health advocate Dorothea Dix and women's-rights campaigner Mary Carpenter. They were impressed by student displays of learning in Latin, philosophy, mathematics, and other subjects. D. Augustus Straker, a prominent black Washington lawyer claimed, "These exercises reflect great credit on Mr. Greener." Yet, Superintendent Cook and trustee George Vashon, who were in charge of the examinations, reported to their colleagues that the students had fallen behind in nearly all subjects and proposed to the Colored School Board that Greener be removed from his position. The editors of the *New National Era,* including Greener, published an attack on board president Johnson that characterized his policies as "dogmatic, autocratic, and spiteful" and maintained his "unfitness" for the job.[33] Shortly thereafter, the board voted for Greener's removal.

Eventually, community members lined up for either Greener or the trustees of the Colored School Board, voicing their opinions throughout the summer in newspapers and meetings. The *Christian Recorder* added that the action has "awakened the bitter indignation of the people at several mass meetings representing the wealth, intelligence, and progressive spirit of the community." Editors at the *Washington Republican* concluded that Greener's support of mixed black and white schools was the key reason for his removal and pointed out, "He is in the fullest confidence of all the parents." A "committee of prominent black citizens" visited the governor of the District of Columbia, Henry D. Cooke, to enlist his authority to get Greener reinstated. Perhaps most telling, the students of the Preparatory High School met and drafted a resolution of protest against "the removal of our beloved and able teacher R. T. Greener." It included an expression of "our gratitude to Professor Richard T. Greener for his incessant labors with us, and for the good which we have derived from him during the last six months" and noted that his removal "is a loss which will ever be felt by this community."[34]

It soon became apparent, however, that the trustees would not back down from their decision to terminate Greener's appointment. Greener spent the summer writing for several newspapers, meeting with rising black leaders advocating for racial justice, and visiting with Sumner. He had begun to study law in the office of the US attorney for the District of Columbia. He also had begun to court a lovely and accomplished lady friend, Genevieve Ida Fleet. A twenty-four-year-old music teacher for a group of black schools that included Greener's Preparatory High School, she was from a prominent Washington family. Her father, James H. Fleet, who was listed as mulatto in the 1860 census, had been one of the few young black students admitted to Lancaster School in Georgetown, the first white male public school in the area to try limited experiments with educating female students and black students. After attending Columbian College (later George Washington University), he became an outspoken abolitionist and well-regarded music teacher. When Greener met her, Genevieve Fleet had been promoted to principal of an all-grades black school and lived with her mother and a brother in the upper Georgetown area.[35]

In early October, Greener received a letter from the secretary of the Board of Trustees of the University of South Carolina. Would he accept an appointment as a professor there? Apparently, James Alfred Bowley, a relatively new university board member, either knew or knew of Greener and had suggested him for the faculty. Bowley, who had escaped from slavery in Maryland as a child, had become an educator in Georgetown, South Carolina, and a representative to the state legislature during Reconstruction. Greener, uncertain about accepting, was being encouraged by Charles Sumner and others when he received a second letter from the university, informing him that the board had elected him professor of "moral and mental philosophy, sacred literature, and evidences of Christianity."[36] The

South was a mystery to Greener, and Reconstruction politics were chaotic, but a professorship at a newly integrated university was too inviting to refuse. There, he would have the academic cachet generally reserved for well-educated white men, as well as the opportunity to contribute to enhanced futures for black citizens.

CHAPTER FIVE

Professing in a Small and Angry Place

A RRIVING AT THE COLUMBIA, South Carolina, railway depot in the autumn of 1873, twenty-nine-year-old Richard Greener would have noted one new sight in particular: numerous black citizens, as well as white, populated the wide wooden platform. Mostly men, they sat on benches or leaned on posts, waiting for trains of three different railroads operating through the state capital at the time. They varied in skin color from very light to very dark. Typically, these travelers included the rough-hewn cotton farmers and day laborers who had been making their way out of rural areas since Emancipation. Others among South Carolina's black citizens, however, "lived in conformity to a standard far superior to that of many well-to-do white families of the North."[1] The genteel sorts were notable for well-clipped mustaches and clean-shaven chins, and sported any head gear available, from worn felt slouch hats to stiff stovepipes.[2]

Greener would have been well aware that South Carolina had four black citizens for every three white citizens.[3] When those blacks had been stashed away in plantation slave quarters or surviving free on the wrong side of the tracks, the South could still celebrate its "whiteness." Now, the recently emancipated seemed to show up everywhere, exercising new rights that ranged from mingling in public places to voting. Listening to their speech patterns and accents, Greener, with his urban mannerisms and educated diction, might have considered that he would fit in better with his new faculty colleagues at the University of South Carolina—all were white. In fact, during Reconstruction, "fitting in" across races was somewhat possible. In the face of federal occupation and black voting, the conservative whites of the defeated Confederacy seemed less in evidence around Columbia than in earlier times. One well-traveled black South Carolinian of the time remarked, "I think the whites of the South are really less afraid of contact with colored people than the whites of the North." However, many of those "whites of the South" were actually sympathetic "carpetbaggers" newly arrived from the North and local "scalawags," whose liberal leanings on race issues seemed particularly heinous to many of their white neighbors.[4]

In Reconstruction-era Columbia, racial mixing had its own rules. Blacks were served at integrated bars and ice cream parlors but excluded from the large hotels. In theaters and lecture halls, blacks were readily admitted, but, as one local white citizen found, "a wide berth is given them by the white audience if the hall be not crowded." Likewise, while a white passenger would not sit beside a black person (except a personal servant) on a train, "the negroes, however, are permitted to, and frequently do, ride in first-class railway and in street railway cars."[5]

The press in South Carolina accurately demonstrated the post–Civil War agitation among the white populace about the black citizens who were now state legislators, shopkeepers, share croppers, voters, teachers, tenant farmers, and so on. Black and white Republicans of the "Radical" wing of that party, which by 1870 held the majority in the state legislature, were scorched in print for supporting racial integration and black political leadership. Angry correspondents referred to "black imps" in elected offices and dubbed their mixed-race counterparts "bob tailed white men."[6] One South Carolina newspaper referred to "gibbering, louse eaten, devil worshipping barbarians from the jungles of Dahomey" and railed about "the hell-born policy which has trampled the fairest and noblest States of our great sisterhood beneath the unholy hoofs of African savages and shoulder-strapped brigands." Another daily proclaimed, "Richard T. Greener, who has recently been inducted into the chair of Moral and Mental Philosophy in the University of South Carolina, is a colored man, or in other words a negro. As a consequence thereof, metaphysics will now be made as clear as mud."[7]

Yet, when a black postmaster, Charles M. Wilder, was appointed in Columbia, the *Charleston Daily News* grudgingly admitted that he "has but little education and moderate ability. . . . But, he is the most decent Negro of the radical party that could have been appointed." The *Chesterfield Democrat* described black Republican state legislator Henry Shrewsbury as someone who "resisted indignantly all the corrupting influences at Columbia . . . is intelligent and understands the true interest of all classes to be endangered by the arts and schemes of unprincipled adventurers against whom he has taken a decided stand." Reporters and authors also were quick to depict skin tones as they differed among black or partly black citizens, using labels such as "quite black," "full black," or "light-skinned."[8]

• • •

From the horse-drawn buggy that carried him the several blocks from the train station to campus, Greener got his first glimpse of South Carolina's capital city. It was small, compact, and certainly not bustling. The streets were not paved or even graveled. The mostly wood, rather than brick or stone, buildings included five hotels and plenty of taverns. But the town of about eleven thousand had an appealing, almost languid, southern charm. Red and gold leaves fell steadily on the wooden sidewalks on sunny autumn days, flashing in the sun and softening the view of many structures not yet rebuilt since the wartime devastation.[9]

Had the train station been closer to the northern edge of town, Greener would have passed the large Victorian home occupied by Tommy Wilson and his family. Then a gangly seventeen-year-old, Tommy would later help chart the country's course of racial inequality. By that time he would be called by his middle name (and his mother's maiden name): Woodrow. Born in Virginia, he had moved to South Carolina when his father was appointed to a professorship at Columbia Presbyterian Seminary. During his presidency forty years later, and much to Greener's disappointment, Woodrow Wilson would abruptly end integration in federal agencies in Washington, DC, by signing off on the segregation of office facilities and hiring practices. He rationalized this as in no way a racial injustice but rather a "plan of concentration" that would separate black workers into "certain bureaus and sections" where they were "less likely to be discriminated against."[10] As expected, they were also less likely to be hired, retained, or promoted.

The South Carolina state capitol building, only partially completed during the Civil War years, still showed evidence of the devastating fires associated with the 1865 southern victory lap celebrated by Gen. William Tecumseh Sherman's troops. Just south of the state house, the main entrance to the University of South Carolina led into a campus of twelve large two- and three-story buildings. Facing one another across a wide expanse of grass and trees, the stately brick structures housed classrooms, faculty residences, the president's home, student lodging, a library, dining facilities, and a chapel—all behind a nearly seven-foot-tall brick wall, erected in 1835 to curtail student freedom.[11]

To the university's good fortune, and that of neighborhood squatters who moved quickly into campus structures from their war-ravaged homes, some campus buildings had been used as Civil War hospitals for sick and wounded soldiers, Confederate and Union. Therefore, out of a humane impulse during the triumphant Union march through the conquered South, General Sherman's forces had posted guards to discourage looting and burning on the Columbia campus. At the start of the Reconstruction era, federal troops were garrisoned just outside the university walls to keep order during the turmoil of change. The soldiers hoisted the Stars and Stripes on their training grounds across the street from the campus, and they managed to develop a tentative relationship with the community, which grew to tolerate them and occasionally interact with them. Many Columbians strolled by the encampment at dusk to listen to bugle music, and the garrison baseball club even challenged students in the college club to a game.[12]

The long, tree-studded campus midway that provided park-like space between the two lines of campus buildings was appealing, and the fine brick buildings, though on a smaller scale, might have reminded Greener of the college structures he had known in Cambridge and Philadelphia. The leaking roofs and broken windows then endemic to nearly all the University of South Carolina buildings would not have been immediately evident at first sight.

A residence had been promised to Greener. Ever skeptical about how things worked across racial boundaries, he might have expected to be isolated in a structure tucked away in a seldom-traveled corner of campus, such as a converted smokehouse or potting shed, thought suitable for a lone black professor. Instead, he was assigned to Lieber House, an imposing three-story Georgian building directly across from the university library and just inside the main campus entrance. There was some irony in installing the university's first black professor in a building named for the renowned political scientist Francis Lieber, who had been a faculty member from 1835 to 1856. Although Lieber, who continued his career at Columbia University in New York City, had been sympathetic to the North and abolition during the Civil War, he was pessimistic about racial integration. While it might mean freedom for the black race, he predicted that it would also "lead to the degeneration of the white race."[13] Just prior to Greener's arrival, Lieber House had been occupied by another Harvard alumnus, Robert W. Barnwell, class of 1821, who had served in the US Congress and as president of South Carolina College.

Greener's assigned residence also came with a housemate. Newly hired chemistry professor William Main Jr. struck Greener as mild mannered and intelligent. Like Greener, he was from Philadelphia. He had graduated from the University of Pennsylvania and then traveled extensively in the western territories as a mining engineer. When the two new and youngest faculty members met, they shook hands and uttered a few words of greeting. While Greener may have been a bit puzzled as to how the mixed-race residential arrangement would work out, Main seemed not at all reluctant to reside under the same roof with him. The large duplex building, constructed in 1835 as a residence for two faculty families, could easily accommodate both scholars in separate living quarters.[14]

• • •

Greener quickly recognized that he and Main were part of a new guard of faculty hired since the campus reopened after a nearly four-year wartime hiatus. In fact, by the time Greener arrived, there was no old guard. The largely black university board of trustees, ushered in as a result of widespread black voting for the state legislators who appointed the board members, foretold the likelihood of an integrated student body, substantial white recoil, and general confusion on campus. The idea of university desegregation had been stalled by attempts at compromise in the state legislature at the start of Reconstruction—including an 1868 bill that proposed turning the Citadel military college in Charleston into an all-black, nonmilitary school. Editorializing on that possibility, the *New York Times* concluded that the development of a separate black college would be preferable to integrated higher education: "Everybody, black and white, who is not a monomaniac, sees that to force the two races in the same colleges upon the people of the State [of South Carolina] would be to inaugurate a struggle, out of which the white would come out very much worst and in which the negro would be annihilated."[15]

The most prominent faculty members, impatient with the ambiguity of legislative control during political turmoil, had decamped early in the postwar years. They were soon followed by outraged colleagues who envisioned blacks on campus in the near future. Student numbers dwindled for the same reason, sinking to only sixty-eight in the 1872–73 academic year, with the inclusion of law and medical schools adding only a few more. Still, the new university trustees held fast to the vision of an integrated campus, announcing that "a spirit so hostile to the welfare of our state, as well as to the dictates of justice and the claims of common humanity, will no longer be represented in the university."[16] Many remaining students quickly withdrew after October 7, 1873, when South Carolina secretary of state Henry E. Hayne registered in the medical school as the university's first black student.

As he became acquainted with his colleagues, Greener realized he was in the midst of a very mixed academic bag. The small faculty, gathered from men who supported Republican politics and racially mixed education, ranged from opportunists and politicians to do-gooders and scholars. Greener was clearly in the final group. Three of his fellow professors were ministers from the Northeast who had helped to establish churches and missions in the postwar South. One had served as a president at a small Methodist seminary, one as a rector in an Episcopal church, and one as a chaplain at the South Carolina Lunatic Asylum.[17]

Shortly after his arrival, Greener hastened to visit the library, a stately columned structure designed from sketches by Washington Monument architect Robert Mills. When it opened in 1840, the building was the first freestanding college library in the United States. Amazingly, most of the impressive collection of nearly forty thousand volumes had survived the war years, although much of it was in deteriorating condition.[18]

A new librarian, Erastus Everson, had been elected by a slim margin of the voting trustees after four successive ballots involving eleven applicants. Following service in the Union army, Everson had become an archetypical northern carpetbagger with a knack for politics and self-promotion. He first worked on settling title claims concerning the disbursement of plantations throughout South Carolina. Soon, however, he hopscotched to journalism, reporting news and founding several Republican newspapers in Columbia, while investing in other small businesses on the side. A still-active freelance researcher and writer who served as a correspondent to the *New York Tribune* and the *Charleston (SC) News*, he was ill prepared for the more tedious effort of dealing with the library's books and catalogs. Yet, he had made friends in high Republican places, and he soon was able to manage the campus library as a part-time job by limiting its hours of operation to 9 a.m. to 1 p.m. each weekday. And, by naming a deputy librarian, he was able to absent himself from campus when necessary.[19]

Greener had a great deal of respect for professor of ancient languages and literature Fisk P. Brewer, a kindly scholar who had graduated from Yale and studied Greek in Athens before taking a professorship at University of

North Carolina and a tour as US consul to Greece. He was revered by his students. Nevertheless, former faculty member James Reynolds echoed the contempt of many local Confederates when he characterized all new professors from out of state as men "unknown or known only to be despised."[20]

Greener's arrival as the first African American faculty member—professor of moral and mental philosophy, sacred literature, and evidences of Christianity—lacked any real outward drama, and he had not expected any. He realized that his Andover and Harvard credentials, as well as his brief teaching experience, qualified him well above most of his new colleagues. The real campus drama had already happened with racial integration of the student body. And a second commotion quickly followed when the legislature announced that another new group would be coming to campus— women. The newly founded South Carolina Normal School, coeducational and integrated, would have two campus buildings as its home.

Although indignant about conservative white attitudes toward integrated education, Greener managed to keep his resentment in check during his early days as a professor. He was determined to enjoy the company of several fine colleagues and to busy himself with efforts aimed at the success of his teaching and of the students and university. He was, after all, exactly what the sitting governor of South Carolina noted upon his arrival: an individual "cultivated and refined, and an honored graduate of grand old Harvard." A correspondent for the *Christian Recorder* who attended a Latin class taught by Greener reported: "It was composed of white and colored boys. Their seats were arranged alternately. . . . They were neatly dressed, very gentlemanly in their manner and were equally good scholars. I saw not the slightest evidence that the contact was 'degrading' to either."[21]

Among black and white liberal friends and university colleagues in Columbia, Greener's race was generally not of note, and he was proud of his faculty position on a fine campus. During his first year as a professor, he made his first alumni gift to Harvard College: a set of seventeen photographs of the stately South Carolina campus buildings, taken by his colleague, Professor Main.[22] The gift sent the message that the unique graduate of four years earlier was doing well.

• • •

If Greener could have stuck to his resolve to focus solely on the teaching and administrative tasks at hand, he might have managed to smoothly travel the racially charged path between angry local conservatives and social-justice liberals. Instead, he soon jumped into the fray, on campus and in the state legislature, by advocating for more black applicants and students. Even without the deep pockets of the old cotton economy, the South Carolina legislature was generally willing to appropriate funds for scholarships and other needs. Actual spending, however, often was curtailed by other priorities. By 1874, substantial efforts were needed to attract more students to campus in the wake of many white student departures and to assure that African American students with poor academic preparation got up to speed for college.

A month after his arrival, Greener was the lead speaker at a meeting of faculty and state legislators on the needs of the university. He was in his oratorical element. Teetering between eloquence and brashness, he pushed for dozens of full scholarships to be awarded to several students from each of thirty-four counties. Even though a new agriculture and mechanical university for black students was being founded nearby with federal land-grant funds, Greener recognized that its resources would be separate but never equal to those of majority white institutions. He railed against "the idea of establishing simply colored schools at this day" and noted that "poor white boys" might also avail themselves of the scholarships he proposed.[23]

The local Democratic newspaper proclaimed the scholarship idea "a scheme to buy students," but a Republican counterpart noted that objections came "with ill grace from those who are responsible for the ignorance they hold up to the public scorn." Ultimately, the state legislature in its 1873–74 session passed an act providing 124 full university scholarships—each $200 annually—to be apportioned by county populations. Greener's colleagues, impressed with his forceful approach, soon unanimously voted for him to deliver the faculty oration at Public Day, the annual community-wide commencement celebration.[24]

The victory of the scholarship funds would be short-lived. Many underprepared black applicants could not pass the university's entrance examinations, even though Greener chaired the committee that developed exam questions and kept them within reach of very average students: "Express in words the value of DCXCIX." "Name the five principal countries of Europe." "Give the feminine of hero." But the campus needed warm bodies in order to continue, so Greener pushed the idea of a preparatory group of "sub-freshmen" boys who would be counted as students while they studied for another try at their entrance exams. Although he insisted to Sen. Charles Sumner that he was "not in love with school teaching," he extended his instructional hours to work with sub-freshmen in Greek and Latin. Encouraged by his own success following his repeated freshman year at Harvard, he insisted, "These young men, by their studious habits and gentlemanly behavior, have proved themselves worthy of the bounty of the State." Yet, even as student numbers started to climb, state officials railed against the "motley crowd" of preparatory students.[25]

All too aware of the prospects that awaited black youths from rural South Carolina with substandard secondary educations, Greener argued passionately that to keep them at the university was a far better option than "to dismiss them to the several Counties where absolutely no opportunity for higher education lay open to them." Although the first group of sub-freshman final examinations were graded with "much leniency," most grades were below 68 percent. Soon after, however, Greener reported that thirty of nearly forty sub-freshmen attained average grades of 70 percent or above, with ten of those reaching 85 percent and above.[26]

In advocating for continuing the sub-freshman concept, Greener experienced his first full-fledged clash with local authorities, especially with State Superintendent of Education Justus K. Jillson. A New Englander by birth, Jillson had moved south from Massachusetts in 1866 as a teacher for the Freedmen's Bureau and a white Radical Republican. He served two years in the state legislature before his appointment as education superintendent and his concurrent service as secretary to the university board of trustees. He strongly supported integrated schools. But he also was a stickler for standards and insisted that during his two visits to campus he found many scholarship boys who were "not entitled either by reason of poverty, merit or scholarly attainments to receive the bounty of $200 annually provided by the state." He concluded that the legislative act providing scholarships was "a miserable farce." The board of trustees voted to discontinue the sub-freshman class after fewer than two years—a move that likely relaxed faculty admission decisions concerning true freshmen. A printed circular about admission to the law and medical schools noted, "A good English preparation is required; but what is lacking in this respect may be made up after entrance." The subsequently cool relationship between Greener and Jillson is evident from their curt written communications, such as one sent after Greener inquired about the provision of writing supplies. Jillson replied, "I was in my office today from 10 a.m. to 4 p.m. Be so good as to send directions as to the kind of Writing Paper you want."[27]

• • •

A number of academically and financially able young black men had left South Carolina immediately after the Civil War to seek higher education at integrated or historically black colleges in the North. Now that these men could be educated in their home state, Greener and his colleagues viewed them as potential transfer students. Francis L. Cardozo, then the elected state treasurer and a future law student at the University of South Carolina, visited Washington, DC, to encourage students at Howard University to leave for South Carolina. As one of the most powerful politicians in the state, Cardozo could make a convincing case for good opportunities in the South. Greener traveled back to Washington in early 1874 and helped support the recruitment effort among Howard students he knew. Six Howard students transferred into the freshman, sophomore, and junior classes in Columbia in 1874. Cardozo loaned them funds for their travel expenses back to South Carolina.[28]

However, Greener's more important motivation for visiting Washington during the Christmas and New Year holidays was to visit the lady he had left behind, Genevieve Fleet. (He called her "Genie.")[29] While she offered an opportunity for a loving relationship and a family, she also held a social status among black Washingtonians that could only help Greener. They married in September 1874, with just enough time for Genevieve to move to the Columbia campus before the start of fall semester.

Along with enjoying matrimony, Greener had a very good academic year. The student body, largely due to an influx of black youngsters, had grown to a more respectable 166, many of them relatively unprepared black boys who benefited from Greener's preparatory lessons. The state normal school operating on campus added another thirty-nine students. Always a strong orator, Greener hit his stride after receiving statewide kudos for his graduation day speech in honor of his recently deceased friend, Charles Sumner. He now found himself frequently invited to speak throughout South Carolina and beyond, especially on racial equality in education and often at church gatherings. He also wrote for local papers about the ongoing need for civil rights, and one paper printed a poem of his under the pseudonym "Niger Nigrorum." And, pursuing a long-time goal, Greener registered as a student in the university law school in the fall of 1874.[30]

Greener's light skin likely enabled him to associate more easily with both black and white citizens during that fraught time. One friend noted his "olive complexion. . . . Caucasian features and curly hair," remarking that Greener was "a Spanish looking personage rather than one to be taken as belonging to the proscribed race." Genevieve also was pale-skinned and comfortable in white company. The political prominence of South Carolina blacks who were not very "black" at all was striking. Francis Cardozo, the light-skinned son of a Portuguese Jewish father and freed black mother, was educated at the University of Glasgow in Scotland and was the first nonwhite American elected to a statewide office when he became South Carolina secretary of state in 1868. The two nonwhite lieutenant governors of the state, Alonzo J. Ransier, elected in 1870 before being elected to the US Congress in 1872, and Richard H. Gleaves, elected in 1872, both had pale skin and were of mixed race. Such also was also the case with Samuel J. Lee, the first nonwhite state legislator to become speaker of the House; South Carolina secretary of state Henry Hayne; powerful legislator and state land commissioner Robert C. DeLarge; and legislator and lawyer Paris Simkins, among others.[31]

Reconstruction historian Thomas Holt demonstrated that 43 percent of South Carolina's state and federal elected officials from 1868 to 1876 were classified as mulattoes, while "only 7 percent of the state's general African American population was mulatto." Many objectors to Republican dominance in the state grudgingly claimed that mixed-race "blacks" were preferable to darker-skinned blacks and lily-white carpetbaggers, with one newspaper determining that "the quadroons and octoroons of the Senate are infinitely superior in personal appearance to their white Yankee and native compeers." Clearly, attitudes that were supposedly about race were very much about color.[32]

· · ·

By 1875, with the possibility of weakening Republican political control both nationally and in South Carolina, horror stories about black-dominated institutions aired frequently in the conservative newspapers and over back fences. White Democrats were eager to promote the "radical university" as a prostrate establishment populated strictly with unprepared black students and a few poor whites. Students soon joined in trying to convince the general public otherwise. T. McCants Stewart, a particularly smart and polished transfer student from Howard University, described the reality of the integrated campus in letters published in the *Washington (DC) New National Era*: "Both races are represented in the University classes. In the Professional and College departments more than one-half of the students are white. Within the past week twelve new students applied for admission. More than one-third of them were white." Later, he continued: "The two races study together, visit each other's rooms, play ball together, walk into the city together, without the blacks feeling honored or the whites disgraced. . . . Our library contains thirty thousand volumes and an excellent collection of paintings and sculpture. The college literary society alone has a library from twelve to fifteen thousand volumes."[33]

Another group of students published in the *Daily Union Herald* of Columbia, contending that "far from being broken up, the university has more students now than it has had for the last eight years. . . . It was prophesied that the admission of colored students would never be endured, that it would break up the university; but white and colored students are now pursuing their studies amicably together, and there is no war of races or other chimeras."[34]

Greener, however, found the political and economic climate growing less favorable for the fate of the university and for the fate of black citizens nationwide. He began to speak out on both counts. He joined two colleagues in sharing a list of campus grievances with South Carolina governor Daniel Chamberlain. They complained that "not one lecture room in the University proper is adequately provided with seats and blackboards" and that open fireplaces were used for heat due to the absence of stoves. Furthermore, "the want of advertising, catalogs, and general printing is crippling to a certain extent the efficiency, both of instruction and discipline." Mortimer Warren, principal of the State Normal School on campus, added, "We have had no books, maps, charts or aids of any kind. The State is pledged to assist us to all these and has done nothing for us." He and his pupils got by on several borrowed or donated dictionaries, encyclopedias, and devotional singing books. In addition to material resources, Greener stewed about student conduct. Their absence from regular prayer sessions was a problem, as was their presence at a new barroom opened just two blocks from campus. Finally, he drafted and pushed through a policy that "no student, except the preparatory students during their recess, shall be allowed to play upon the campus or on the grounds in the rear of the University buildings from 9 am to 4 pm."[35]

On the national scene, Greener continued as a vocal supporter of the Civil Rights Bill introduced in 1870 by Sumner. It had bogged down in the usual morass of committees, debates, recesses, and changes. The process sputtered on after Sumner's death in 1874, eventually producing a truncated version that forbade racial discrimination in public transportation and accommodations but stripped out earlier language related to integrating schools and churches. In a nearly full-page article in the *Daily Union Herald,* Greener maintained, "The uncertainty with regard to our civil rights renders us liable to insult daily, no matter how pious, virtuous, patriotic or intelligent we may be." He noted that "the fifteenth amendment gave back to us the rights which always belonged to us, and had been only withheld through fraud and force," but noncompliance too often meant that blacks were "told to seek our redress in local courts or trust to the variable of public opinion." Insisting that it was impossible for "state law to protect us in the exercise of civil rights where no judge or jury can be found to look beyond their prejudices and hatreds," he pleaded for "a real civil rights bill" that was both national and comprehensive. Of the compromise bill finally limping toward a vote in Congress, he concluded, "This emasculated bill does not give us what we ask, nor what we have had a right to demand."[36] Two months later, President Grant signed the emasculated bill into law. Eight years later, even with its watered-down provisions for civil rights, it was declared unconstitutional by the US Supreme Court.

• • •

Already one of the busiest faculty members, as well as a law student, Greener embraced even more overload. He was a frequent public speaker in South Carolina and beyond, he served on the Columbia Board of Health, and he was appointed to a commission to revise the state school system. He joined the Union League of America, a nationwide organization promoting equal opportunity across the races, and represented South Carolina on its national executive council. In 1875, he became the first black scholar elected to the American Philological Association, and he was determined to be an active member. More importantly, he became a father; his son Horace Kempton Greener was born in September 1875.[37] When librarian Erastus Everson disappeared that year, Greener volunteered for one more large academic undertaking.

Without a word to his university colleagues, Everson simply vanished from campus. There was some worry that he had met with the hostility of the Ku Klux Klan or other elements angry about his vocal support of integration through his newspaper work. It was also thought that, fearing for his safety, he might have left the state. Greener went to the library and began taking charge. The faculty soon formally appointed him librarian.[38]

The situation and organization at the library was equivocal at best. A library sub-committee of the board of trustees had recently reported the "management of the library under the auspices of E. W. Everson has been the most efficient and satisfactory." Yet, their report also noted "scores of books, pamphlets and records now in confusion." Greener, with his familiarity with the libraries at Harvard and Andover and with a clear agenda for making his own mark, noted that he found the library "in great confusion owing to the accumulation of books and the disorder in which they had been left." The building itself was in deplorable condition. After use as a hospital for wounded Confederate soldiers and as a meeting place for state legislators, it had fallen victim to crumbling ceiling and wall plaster, buckling and molding shelves, a leaking roof, and vandalism by angry patrons who defaced books and artworks in fury at the radical university.[39]

Greener found that many books were misclassified and inaccurately shelved due to Everson's "ignorance of Greek, Latin or French." A catalog Everson had started was a manuscript list, rather than a more modern card catalog reflecting "the latest methods now in vogue in the best libraries." Additionally, Columbia citizens had borrowed books and never returned them. Greener discovered that one prominent local physician had been keeping forty of the library's medical volumes, many of which had been borrowed more than a year earlier.[40]

With the help of two students, Greener worked throughout the summer of 1875 to accurately classify and reshelve thousands of volumes, getting them in order for cataloging by a fulltime librarian who would be his successor. A reporter for the *Charleston News and Courier* visited after Greener took charge and observed "a marked change from the dust, [and] chaos of books and confusion" he had seen on an earlier visit. Determined to improve the messiness of the interior, Greener installed new brackets and shelves, hung ten large portraits, and placed a collection of busts of prominent men on wall pedestals. Cicero, Demosthenes, James Madison, Thomas Jefferson, and John C. Calhoun were all represented. He also prepared a forty-page report on the collection for inclusion in a US Department of the Interior book on major libraries.[41]

No extra compensation had been arranged when Greener took on the librarianship. However, when the board of trustees seemed ready to appoint a new librarian, Greener was quick to inform them that it was "only reasonable" that he should be paid for his nearly six months of service to the library. He suggested that pay equivalent to what the librarian would have received during the summer-break months (August through October) would suffice, along with $200 for his student assistants. He also renewed a request he had made a year earlier, asking for $150 for repairs he had made at his own expense when moving into his residence on campus.[42] The trustees agreed.

With the appointment of a full-time librarian, his duties in the library ended, and Greener was ready to take a greater interest in off-campus political concerns. He quickly recognized that the future for continuing liberal Republican leadership in South Carolina was uncertain at best. Daniel H. Chamberlain, a Yale graduate and lawyer who had come from Massachusetts to South Carolina in 1866, had promised state government reform when elected a Republican governor in 1874. He quickly managed to remove some of the dubious, and likely corrupt, appointees of his Republican predecessor, and he vetoed legislation that appeared to be only personally beneficial to elected representatives. But he was a moderate, not Radical, Republican and above all a politician. Determined to create a larger white base than the radical wing supplied, he once noted that his leadership would help "keep the party from going over to negroism." Unwilling to completely alienate the growing numbers of black voters, however, he singled out popular and capable black politicians for praise. Of Cardozo's work as state treasurer, he announced, "I have never heard one word or seen one act of Mr. Cardozo's which did not confirm my confidence in his personal integrity and political honor."[43]

Some reforms of the Chamberlain administration, especially in taxation and state debt control, seemed to increase efficiency and fairness. Others, such as removing many black trial justices and proposing cuts to university appropriations, seemed only to increase his own political standing with white Democrats. After a year in office, Chamberlain had become, as characterized by historian Eric Foner, "the toast of upper-crust Democratic society, making the rounds of Charleston literary associations." One local observer at the time described the governor as "talented, ambitious, and unscrupulous," as he seemed to variously support black Republican or white Democratic preferences. Indeed, he managed to replace some unsuccessful black political appointees, but he likely did so as much to improve his own standing among white conservatives as to truly reform state government. Chamberlain's fusion politics fizzled when the resulting polarization among Republicans substantially improved the Democratic political outlook for the upcoming 1876 state and local elections—foretelling unsettled times ahead for the integrated university and the black citizens of South Carolina.[44]

CHAPTER SIX

The Brutal Retreat

THE PRINTED CIRCULAR, ready to be nailed on trees and wooden posts or read aloud at gatherings of South Carolina's black citizens, stated, "Colored Democrats, you shall be employed at fair wages; you shall have houses to live in. You, in voting the Democratic ticket, have looked at what is your good. . . . The Radical Negroes shall not be employed. If any man in the [Third South Carolina Congressional] District shall employ a Radical Negro, or rent him a storehouse or a dwelling house, he shall be asked to leave. . . . Businessmen, are you not ashamed to have a black Radical Negro waiting on you? If you cannot get a Democrat, do the work yourself."[1]

South Carolina Democrats understood throughout Reconstruction that their most immediate chance for ending Radical Republican government control was to apply economic pressure on black citizens and liberal whites to join the conservative ranks. Near general election times—every two years for governor and legislators—such pressure frequently resulted in physical skirmishes. And in the highly contested elections of 1870, barroom brawls escalated to ride-by shootings by paramilitary groups on horseback. As summarized by historian Rayford Logan, "So determined were most white Southerners to maintain their own way of life that they resorted to fraud, intimidation and murder in order to reestablish their own control of state governments."[2] When a legislative investigating committee questioned residents of Newberry County, fifty miles west of Columbia, about a deadly incident just prior to the 1870 elections, the answers were not exceptional.

"Do you know of any murders committed in this County before or at the election?"
"I cannot remember exactly how many now."
"Did you, or did you not, hear of any scouting party or bushwhackers?"
"Yes, as rumor."
"Do you believe that there was a free expression of the people at the general election?"

"I do not."

"State an instance of force resorted to [in order] to prevent persons exercising their political prerogative."

"There was the killing of Lee Nance, Johnson, and others, for their political opinions."[3]

• • •

Immediately following the Civil War, election campaigns for national congressional offices were subject to a bit less scheming and violence than those for state and local offices. This may have reflected cards stacked heavily against Democrats in the Confederate states. A conservative white politician—by definition a Democrat in Reconstruction South Carolina— might have a chance as a candidate for state legislator from a white and black local district, but he would have a steeper uphill battle running for US representative, with scant support from a wider group of black citizens, liberal white citizens, and carpetbaggers. Yet, when Democrats gained control of the US House of Representatives in 1874, conservatives in South Carolina and elsewhere became much more optimistic about the political future. And when new House members began to investigate and publicize various real and imagined irregularities among office holders in the Ulysses S. Grant administration, southern Democrats redoubled their determination to take control at all levels of elected office.[4]

Richard Greener joined many fellow Republicans in expressing skepticism about returning Governor Daniel H. Chamberlain to another term. Chamberlain had not only courted Democrats through appointments and promises but was openly critical of the operations of the University of South Carolina. He suggested that the integrated campus should be turned into a high school for training young people in practical subjects. However, when he proposed that the university's annual appropriation be cut by 33 percent, the Republican legislature slightly increased the budget item.[5] Greener, an alternate to the state Republican convention in September 1876, was still in the camp of radical Republicans, while Chamberlain politicked as a reform Republican who had indeed managed to curb some abuse and wastefulness in state expenditures during his first term as governor. At the September Republican nominating convention, it quickly became obvious that the reform group would carry the day. Chamberlain was easily nominated, and although fellow radicals had pushed Greener for the superintendent of education nomination, a reform candidate was also chosen for that place on the ballot.[6]

Chamberlain's Republican base was undoubtedly softened by his political inconsistencies related to garnering support and spreading spoils among some Democrats, as well as his proposals for budget cuts in education and social services. Therefore, when Democrats nominated for governor their Confederate hero, cavalry leader and brigadier general Wade Hampton, the conservative prospects looked at least somewhat favorable. Born into a wealthy Charleston family that owned multiple plantations, Hampton was a college-educated, upper-crust conservative whose detest for the policies of Reconstruction nearly matched his tolerance for armed vigilante activities to support Democratic causes. Such activities were growing and spreading throughout the state, organizing as local militant rifle clubs, which first affiliated with the Ku Klux Klan and then organized as the newly formed "Red Shirts." The mounted, rifle-toting Red Shirts were a daunting presence at Democratic and Republican meetings, protecting participants at the former and intimidating them at the latter.[7]

In a statewide race with black and white male voters, Hampton tried to distance himself a bit from the menacing Democratic outbursts. Instead, he supported "force without violence."[8] Still, masses of Democrats regularly disrupted Republican meetings and political rallies by gathering in the hundreds and galloping through crowds on horseback. They also boycotted Republican businesses and refused to make loans or rent land to Republicans. Hampton, eager for political converts, emphasized his support of black voting rights—as long as property ownership and literacy requirements were met—with promises of "free men, free schools and free ballots."[9]

The violent political conflicts of 1876 began in July, just as the country was mourning the death of Gen. George Custer at that last stand in Montana territory and celebrating the centennial of the Declaration of Independence in Philadelphia with the first official World's Fair. In the tiny town of Hamburg in western South Carolina, two white men on horseback disrupted a Fourth of July celebration by cantering through a local black militia company drilling in the streets. Several days of accusations about who was responsible for the clash ended when white gun-club members poured into Hamburg from other towns. During subsequent gunfire, two black people were killed. Five others were murdered after being captured by a Red Shirt group. The nationally publicized "Hamburg Massacre" was followed by numerous violent events during the South Carolina political-campaign season. One, in the town of Ellenton, not far from Hamburg, left one hundred black citizens and several whites dead. In Cainhoy, near Charleston, one black man and four whites died in the only such clash where white fatalities were greater in number than black fatalities.[10]

A native South Carolinian and thoughtful white essayist of the time, Belton O'Neall Townsend, explained the root of the problem: "The whites regard the negro as an inferior animal, admirably adapted to work and to wait, and look on him, 'in his proper place,' with a curious mixture of amusement, contempt, and affection. It is when he aspires to participate in politics or otherwise claim privileges that their hatred becomes intense."[11]

• • •

Although disappointed by the Chamberlain nomination, Greener quickly committed to pushing for Republican victories, especially in the state legislative races but also in the contests for governor and for US president. His first child, Horace, had died at nine months old in May, and the summer months had allowed Greener more time with his wife, who was again pregnant. Now, with the election two months away and the university's fall start postponed until after election day, he was ready to hit the campaign trail.

The Republican State Executive Committee asked Greener to speak in the northwestern quadrant of the state—northwest of Columbia toward the Georgia and North Carolina borders along the southern slopes of the Blue Ridge Mountains. Accepting their request would mean stumping for Republicans in hotly contested races in many small and fairly isolated towns dotting the rural campaign trail. And, as Greener well knew, it also meant the likelihood of encountering violence. Benjamin Tillman, a participant in the Hamburg Massacre who would eventually become a white-supremacist South Carolina governor and senator, proudly explained the goal of Democratic rifle clubs as "terrorizing the Negroes at the first opportunity . . . and then having the whites demonstrate their superiority by killing as many of them as was justifiable." He would later boast that the 1876 elections had signaled "the triumph of Democracy and white supremacy over mongrelism and anarchy."[12]

The first campaign rally in the area, at the town of Newberry in mid-October, presaged a long line of contentious occasions to come. There, Republicans had agreed to include Democrats in a discussion of issues, but it was not truly a debate: "When Republican speakers tried to address the crowd, they were bombarded with cries of 'that was a damn radical lie.' Greener was repeatedly called a 'God-damned nigger' by some Red Shirts."[13] Democrats—politicians and rowdy supporters—surrounded Greener on the platform and drowned out his speech. Finally, two Newberry boys who were also students at the university approached and exhorted their professor to leave before violence broke out.

At another Republican rally in Newberry later in October, organizers were somewhat better at limiting disruption. Greener was able to be heard when, according to a local Democratic newspaper, he "attacked the character of [Democratic presidential candidate Samuel J.] Tilden and proved to his own and some of his hearers' satisfactions that he [Tilden] is the grandest rascal on earth." He then "eulogized [Republican presidential candidate Rutherford B.] Hayes as the most immaculate and most sainted, the most gifted statesman imaginable." A rally in the tiny town of Pickens, however, did not go so smoothly. The Republicans had not widely announced the location of their political gathering, so when Greener stepped up onto a table in front of the post office, there was little initial excitement. The local paper reported that about 250 mounted Democrats in "their campaign regalia" then rode into town and soon "came riding up with hats in hand, making a welkin ring for Hampton. . . . A circle was formed around the improvised Republican stand, completely closing in all the Republicans." Although loud cheers for Hampton erupted, Greener somehow managed to finish his speech "but was frequently interrupted."[14]

Greener may have been relieved to occasionally appear before smaller audiences—such as the one in Walhalla, an Appalachian mountain town of not quite four square miles. It was reported as "a small affair," at which "attendance was quite limited on account of Robinson's Circus exhibiting at [nearby] Seneca City on that day, which proved a much greater attraction to the colored people." Nevertheless, jeers and shouts cut short Greener's speech, and the local postmaster saved his life when one of the disruptors started to aim a pistol at him. Yet, when he spoke nearby at a courthouse in the tiny town of Oconee, an estimated one hundred white Republican citizens joined the audience in support of their party's platform of expanding educational, economic, and political opportunities beyond the state's well-heeled elites.[15]

Traveling by a combination of railroad trains and carriages, Greener weaved his way through large and small towns in the mountain foothills of the state's northwestern section, generally accompanied by local office holders and hopefuls. He later recalled a campaign trip to Greenville most vividly, describing that "our party rode in three carriages all the way up the mountain to Pickens [County] Court House, escorted all the way by a double line of red-shirted horsemen, rifles across the pommel. . . . My speech took so well, I was invited to the red-shirt camp and, against the remonstrations of my associates, went." In Abbeville, not far from the Georgia border, he spoke at a rally of nearly two thousand Republicans at the fairgrounds—until hundreds of mounted Red Shirts began circling and toppling anyone in the way.[16] Eventually, he worked his way eastward, with large and somewhat less rowdy crowds in the towns of Laurens, Newberry, and Lexington. By the end of October, he was back in Columbia, working toward the November 7 election day.

The day of the balloting in South Carolina, marked by a sense of anticipation and excitement, was comparatively peaceful. Many of each political party rushed to vote several times at various polls, and duplicate ballots were not surprising. W. E. B. Du Bois later reported that in rural areas particularly, "there was cheating, intimidation, bribery, and repeating in voting . . . , and Negroes were kept from voting." One local observer explained, "United States troops were posted at a large proportion of the polls and places where trouble or overt intimidation was apprehended. . . . Both parties turned out in full force, and stayed at the polls all day. Guns were brought by both parties, and concealed in houses near many polls, but the troops would not allow any to be shown." However, he noted, "in counties terrorized by the whites, white bravadoes rode from poll to poll, and voted time and again. Hundreds of Georgians and North Carolinians crossed the borders and joined in the work."[17]

• • •

The results for the South Carolina gubernatorial election and for many state senate and house seats were equivocal, contested, recounted, and debated for many weeks to come. The State Board of Canvassers (five elected state officials, all Republican) reported that Rutherford B. Hayes had won South Carolina's seven electoral votes over Samuel Tilden with a margin of about nine hundred popular votes. Initially, this was not disputed by Democrats. However, when the board reported Republican victories in all but two statewide races and announced that this outcome was due to reversing results from counties with reports of intimidation and fraud, the battle of the ballots was on. The state supreme court jailed the board of canvasser members; a panel of Republican circuit judges let them out. The sitting Republican legislators held fast in Columbia, and the Democrats set up a rival body as their House of Representatives. Each party inaugurated its candidate as governor. The coming weeks witnessed the odd spectacle of two separate governments meeting in Columbia. The Democrats then decided to send to Washington their own seven electoral votes for Tilden, although these were without the official state certifications that arrived with the electoral votes for Hayes. As a US Senate investigating committee began hearings into reported irregularities in South Carolina, the results of the close presidential race remained in limbo, due to additional voting problems in Louisiana and Florida. Undoubtedly, Greener knew plenty about corruption among state Republican officeholders during the Reconstruction era. Waste, fraud, paybacks, and friendly favors were either alleged, obvious, or both. One analyst of the era pointed out that "the fact that there was corruption at all levels in South Carolina's Reconstruction government cannot be gainsayed." Yet, while a Democratic administration might produce new political faces, it seemed unlikely to practice cleaner political habits. Democratic corruption simply "did not gain as much publicity. . . . So, to many Republicans there must have been little to choose between the Democrats and their own party on the corruption issue. The key issue remained not one of corruption, but one of power."[18] For Greener, who well enjoyed the life of a professor, a librarian, and an influence in the lives of young citizens, the issue was about race. Any future for the integrated university looked grim at best under Democratic power in the legislature and the governor's office.

While arguments ground on about who would be the next US president and the next governor of South Carolina, the university resumed classes, recitations, and examinations. As the closing for the Christmas holiday approached, Greener and eight others—seven African American graduates and two white graduates—were awarded law degrees. Three of the graduates had been born into slavery. Greener was admitted to the South Carolina bar a week later. He would soon make two trips to Washington, DC, to testify first to a US Senate committee and then to a House of Representatives committee about the violence and intimidation he had experienced on the campaign trail. In late January, he and his wife greeted their second child, Mary Louise Greener.[19]

Given the near impossibility of untangling voting irregularities in South Carolina, Louisiana, and Florida, a fifteen-member federal electoral commission (drawn from members of both houses of Congress) had a great deal of power in deciding how to deliver the electoral votes of those key states. Although few disputed that the popular vote was in Tilden's favor, the contested electoral votes in those states would determine the national outcome. Pressures were brought to bear on all sides and from all quarters. Even Confederate cavalry raider John Singleton Mosby personally visited President Grant to offer his services in lobbying for Hayes. Political deliberations dragged on through February and finally were resolved the old-fashioned way: with a deal. The compromise of 1877 was a negotiated settlement with Rutherford B. Hayes. He promised to remove the remaining federal troops from Louisiana and South Carolina, and the electoral commission gave the electoral votes of all three disputed states to him. By the end of February, Hayes, who had lost the popular vote by approximately 250,000 ballots, had won the presidency by one electoral vote. He would soon become disparaged by detractors who called him "His Fraudulency," "Queen Victoria in Breeches," and other names that emphasized his tarnished image.[20]

The University of South Carolina limped along during this period, with student recruitment and necessary planning stalled by its uncertain future. Since scholarship money had not been awarded by the legislature during the months of turmoil, many students simply could not stay on. Faculty, also unpaid, continued in the hope of continued Republican control. When the announcement came of Hayes's election victory, southern Republicans knew nothing about the deal to remove troops and were optimistic about a continuation of Reconstruction. Greener initially regarded the Republican success with a sigh of relief. He sent a congratulatory letter to the new president, complimenting his inaugural speech for its "grave and judicious words," which had "already given hope, confidence and increased strength."[21]

Several weeks later, when Democrats in the House of Representatives were pressing him to make good on his promise to remove federal forces from southern garrisons, Hayes invited Hampton and Chamberlain, still in a struggle for gubernatorial control, to Washington. It was clear to him that Chamberlain would not support the removal of troops and that Hampton might try to somehow keep peace even when they were removed. On April 10, he ordered the troops withdrawn from Columbia. Chamberlain quickly and bitterly conceded that he could no longer govern under those circumstances, and he addressed his Republican stalwarts: "By the order of the President whom your votes alone rescued from overwhelming defeat, the government of the United States abandons you, deliberately withdraws its support. . . . And by the withdrawal of troops now protecting the State from domestic violence, abandons the lawful State Government to a struggle with insurrectionary forces too powerful to be resisted." Two months later, still bitter and now blaming, he claimed his "defeat was inevitable under the circumstances of time and place which surrounded me. . . . The uneducated negro was too weak, no matter what his numbers, to cope with the whites."[22]

The Hampton administration immediately took over the governor's office, Republican legislators in disputed elections conceded, and the majority Democratic legislature replaced nearly all Republican circuit court judges. Democratic control of all three branches of government presided over the end of Reconstruction in South Carolina. Hampton had assured potential black voters that he supported them as "free men" with "free schools and free ballots," but there was now no need to carry through on campaign promises.[23]

• • •

Greener and his colleagues busied themselves during the spring with the final activities of the integrated university, ending the semester with examinations, graduations, and hopeful letters of recommendation for the students who badly needed employment in which they might use their new learning. Professor Fisk Brewer offered a poignant summation of that brief and singular period of racial integration at a state university in the Confederate South:

> The black boy who has solved all the knotty problems in arithmetic, who can explain the cube root and compute the value of partial payments, who has learned the long paradigms of Greek and Latin, and read in the original of Caesar's wars and Xenophon's march, Cicero's patriotic orations and the poetry of Virgil and Homer, is no longer a cornfield negro. He has a platform of common knowledge and sentiment with his white classmate. Either there is no virtue in the humanities, or he has acquired something of true courtesy. He presses his society on no one who declines it. He regards the feelings of others with whom he has any relations. It is now true that most of the advanced students of color now in the University are gentlemen, and deserve to be treated as such.[24]

Mortimer Warren, principal of the integrated and coeducational State Normal School on the campus, succinctly described the last graduation of future teachers from that short-lived institution: "On the 31st of May, we graduated a class of eight young ladies. . . . The exercises took place in the chapel and were listened to by a large audience. There was a feeling of sorrow pervading the occasion impossible to describe." That spring, Governor Hampton signed the diplomas of those eight graduates, as well as those of the three BA candidates who graduated from the university. In a subsequent description of the era, W. E. B. Du Bois was concise and eloquent: "The slave went free; stood a brief moment in the sun; then moved back again toward slavery. The whole weight of America was thrown to color caste."[25]

Greener would soon understand that his experience as a professor at a southern university had been a rare circumstance in many regards. Although a black man surrounded by white colleagues, he was respected and befriended. There was no need for any pandering or pretense on his part and no reason to downplay his eager commitment to opportunities for black youths. His work, in an area generally reserved for white men, utilized his abilities and education, while allowing him to make a positive contribution to fellow black citizens. Such conditions were unlikely to converge again. Greener would ever after refer to himself "a South Carolinian in exile."[26]

CHAPTER SEVEN

Unsettled Advocate

THE DISMANTLING OF PROGRESS toward racial equality happened quickly in South Carolina. After Daniel Chamberlain conceded the governor's race to Wade Hampton, many Republican officeholders and legislators quickly resigned, turning control of the state legislature over to the Democratic majority. The University of South Carolina, where the termination of state funding had left faculty unsalaried and scholarship students unsupported for a number of months, closed its integrated campus to begin plans for reestablishing itself as a small, white, male college. As one new trustee stated, the idea was to create "a Southern Institution" that would reflect "our Southern notions of personal honor and truth." A local newspaper gloated that "our beloved and honored university is freed forever from the Radical and the negro." Greener, who had by April already moved to Washington, DC, to seek employment in the federal government, submitted his formal resignation from the faculty in June 1877. The campus would remain closed for three years. When it reopened for white males only, it initially retained one important feature that Greener had pushed: low or no tuition. As historian Michael David Cohen has observed, "Ironically, the educational legacy of Reconstruction in South Carolina was that a college education became attainable for a wider range of white men."[1]

• • •

The nation's capital was the natural choice of destination when Greener, his wife, and infant daughter retreated from the South. In Washington, public schools had begun to integrate, black men had won common council and board of aldermen seats in municipal elections, and growing numbers of black citizens had joined the ranks of salaried professionals in integrated federal offices. The city could even boast (though some there would have preferred not) the first black president of a predominantly white university: Rev. Patrick F. Healy, the son of a freed slave mother and an Irish father, who was named president of Georgetown University in 1873 and served until 1882.[2]

Conveniently for Greener, Washington also was still home to many of his friends and to his wife's immediate relatives, the Fleet family. The Greeners soon moved to a row house next door to Genevieve's mother, Hermione Fleet, and two brothers in the 1400 block of T Street, NW. Another Fleet brother lived on the other side. The couple relocated to a much more livable city than they had previously known. By 1878, the District of Columbia had been enhanced by the installation of thousands of gas street lamps, numerous new parks, and miles of freshly paved roads.[3]

During Reconstruction, Washington had achieved a reputation as "the center of black aristocracy in the United States," according to historian Willard Gatewood. It was a showcase for black social elites "whose emphasis on family background, good breeding, occupation, respectability and color bound them into an exclusive, self-consciously elitist group." Upper-crust African Americans gravitated to the capital city "because of its educational and cultural opportunities, the availability of white-collar jobs commensurate with their education and aspirations, and the presence of a black social group that shared their values, tastes, and self-perceptions."[4]

Members of Washington's black elite generally had the fairest complexions among multiple gradations of skin color described as "black." As Franklin Frazier observed, this segment of society was populated largely by "upper-class mulattoes" who gave great importance to "family background and color snobbishness based upon white ancestry." The editor of the black newspaper, the *Washington Bee,* claimed, "There is more color prejudice among the so-called colored society of this city than there is among white people toward the colored." The census of 1880 listed the Greener family— by then including son Russell Lowell (born in 1878) and daughters Mary Louise (born 1877) and Belle (born 1879)—as "white," although "black" and "mulatto" also were options, as were Chinese and Indian.[5]

Employment was Greener's initial concern. Although he needed a job to provide immediate income, he also hoped eventually to succeed in private legal practice, public speaking, and writing for publication. With no examination required for admission to the District of Columbia bar, he quickly became a member via a sponsorship recommendation. He could perhaps make use of his legal credentials in private practice, but it was more likely that he could use them in a government job. The federal government had a long and growing tradition of patronage, and job seeking was a frenzied endeavor among hopefuls who scurried from meetings with members of

Congress to audiences with cabinet members and even presidents. Given the sheer numbers—there were nearly sixty thousand civil servants and lobbyists in Washington at the time, with plenty of turnover as politicians came and went—the prospects were fine.[6]

Among Washington acquaintances who might help Greener were South Carolina representative Joseph Rainey, the second black man to be seated in the US Congress, and the well-known and well-placed Frederick Douglass. Douglass had remained silent during the political compromise that put Rutherford Hayes in office in exchange for the removal of federal troops protecting black citizenship in the South. He then landed a lucrative political plum when President Hayes appointed him US marshal of the District of Columbia. Greener wisely resisted commenting about the influential Douglass when many critics carped that "a fat office gagged him." Eventually, Greener managed to arm himself with a letter of recommendation to President Hayes that he obtained from, of all people, Gov. Wade Hampton. Hampton later explained that he "had not intended to give any recommendation of the late administration in South Carolina, but as Greener was a colored man, had voted for Hayes and stumped the state for Chamberlain, I thought I could afford to make an exception in his case."[7]

However, to Greener's misfortune, the Hayes administration soon proved to be of little benefit to either black citizens or federal office seekers. On the race issue in the South, President Hayes acted from his conviction that "the whites have the intelligence, the property and the courage which make power. The negroes are for the most part ignorant, poor and timid." Furthermore, the president believed, naïvely, that in the absence of federal watchdogging, whites and blacks in the South might come together in peace. "My policy is trust—peace," he had said shortly after his inauguration. And after the removal of troops from South Carolina and Louisiana, he reiterated, "I now hope for peace, and what is equally important, security and prosperity for the colored people. . . . The wish is to restore harmony and good feeling between sections and races."[8]

Such Hayes policies and hopes, backed by little in the way of focused action, amounted at best to benign neglect of southern race turmoil. At worst, as one commentator noted, the actual objective of Hayes's southern policy was purely political—aimed at fusing Republicans and moderate Democrats in order to effect "a change in the base of Republican support to make it a truly national party."[9] That never happened, and the monumental failure of any notion of achieving shared peace or prosperity was immediate. New power brokers in southern states quickly grasped the opportunity of federal nonintervention to deny equal treatment and rights to their black citizens. Many of those citizens, especially the well educated, swelled the ranks of hopeful professionals looking for a new start in Washington and other Atlantic Seaboard cities. As a patronage seeker, Greener had ample competition.

Government job hunters were undoubtedly also disappointed with Hayes's determination to reform the civil service into a more nonpartisan workforce and to greatly curtail congressional patronage appointments. The president was particularly chagrined that in his first six months of office, during a scramble for jobs, "some bad appointments have been made; some removals have been mistakes. . . . All this I must try now to correct."[10] Nevertheless, the president did employ patronage to appoint southern Democrats to office in an effort to expand his Republican base and encourage a conservative wing. He also retained his power to make diplomatic appointments, and Greener had his eye on the position of US minister to Haiti. That appointment, however, went to John Mercer Langston, a successful black lawyer and former Howard University dean, vice president, and acting president. President Hayes briefly thought of Greener for "one of the consulships in South Europe,"[11] but that possibility never materialized. The best Greener could do upon arrival in the nation's capital was to accept a temporary clerkship in the US Post Office Department. Even when he was elevated several months later to a first-class clerkship at the US Treasury Department, however, he continued to struggle financially.

Although government pay was generally very low, the work was rarely arduous. The federal workday at the time was typically from 9 a.m. to 3 p.m., and overtime or completing assignments at home were nearly unknown. Greener discovered he had plenty of time to engage in additional endeavors. One of these was a vigorous campaign for back payment from the state of South Carolina for "deficiencies" occasioned by uncompensated faculty work during the final embroiled months of the 1876–77 academic year. To that end, he had met with Wade Hampton in Washington just before the resolution of the disputed gubernatorial election. At that time, Hampton had assured him that if Democrats won control of the state government, they would approve the back pay. Later, when nothing had been done, Greener wrote to Hampton and noted that anything short of paying what was owed seemed "contrary to your sense of equity, and surely not in accord with the assurance given me by your excellency in the interview I had the honor to have with you when you were here." He again campaigned for the money due him when he returned to Columbia in June to formally resign, just weeks after the university had closed indefinitely. Upon his return to Washington, he wrote letters to members of the board of trustees of the then-inoperative university. He had been "partially provided for" with $386.66 through state comptroller warrants, but he insisted he was still owed for the month of October 1875 and four months during the busy summer and fall campaign season of 1876.[12]

The situation looked hopeful when the trustees recommended to the new legislature that the professors of 1876–77 be paid for three-fourths of the fiscal year. Greener continued writing to other influential contacts in Columbia as the actual pay failed to materialize. It was not until March 1878 that the South Carolina General Assembly passed an act to authorize back payments for professors, naming for specific sums nine professors, a librarian, and two janitors—but not Richard Greener. Greener and others surmised that his part in campaigning for Governor Chamberlain, as well as racist sentiments in the newly Democratic state legislature, had prompted one or more legislators to cross his name off the list, costing him $1,500. Indeed, he eventually discovered that a newly elected Democratic state senator from conservative Newberry County, Confederate Army colonel James N. Lipscomb, had struck him from the list of payees for just those reasons.[13]

· · ·

Not for the first time, Greener swallowed his pride and approached his Philadelphia cousin, Isaiah Wears, for a loan to make ends meet. He also added to his Treasury Department work in 1877 by accepting an instructor position in the Law Department at Howard University, where an acquaintance of his from Oberlin, John H. Cook, had recently become dean. At the same time, he was determined to pursue private legal work by joining Cook's law practice as a junior partner. But that meant buying equity—about $600 worth—and immediate cash was something Greener never seemed to have on hand. In his request to Wears, he railed against the withholding of his back pay from the University of South Carolina, explaining that without that he did not have the funding for the partnership. Such a legal practice was "the one thing" he had been "looking forward to for ten years," and he was "utterly heart sick at the prospect of letting this chance go." If he could see through his plans to represent black citizens in litigation, war claims, and real estate, he would finally be in his "real life work."[14] His lengthy and poignant appeal paid off. Wears eventually came through with a loan, and the firm Cook & Greener, Attorneys and Counselors at Law, came into being. Greener continued his job at the Treasury Department and his instructorship at Howard University.

Financially, the Howard Law Department operated autonomously from other areas of the university, barely surviving on student fees. Most students had government jobs, and their numbers fluctuated greatly during the 1870s. By summer 1878, Dean Cook resigned. Greener became acting dean and then dean. With little money for a faculty of only two or three part-time instructors and with classes held in a borrowed room on university grounds far from the center of town, student enrollment had dropped precipitously. It didn't improve when Greener arranged for temporary use of a room in a bank building downtown. And the problem was still unaddressed when Greener missed seven weeks of the fall 1879 term to travel through the Midwest on behalf of the movement for southern blacks to emigrate westward. In the summer of 1880, the university executive committee (of the board of trustees) terminated the services of the law faculty. They then quickly regrouped, appointing a new dean and faculty within a few months. Some speculation circulated about possible personality clashes or dissatisfaction with Greener's performance as dean, but it has never been verified. Greener, perhaps not wanting to invite questions about a job loss, later noted in a Harvard alumni publication that he had served at Howard from "December 1877 . . . until 1880."[15]

Continually seeking opportunities to be heard on race issues and to make his mark on the national scene, Greener wrote to his Harvard classmate Thomas Ticknor, asking about contacts at the *North American Review*: "Can you gain me an admission to its columns on the southern situation from a negro's point of view? . . . If not in the *N.A.R.* is there a chance in *The Atlantic*?" Later, after oratorical successes in Washington and beyond, he wrote confidently to Isaiah Wears in Philadelphia: "I know my own worth, the strength of my pen and my voice and the character of my determination."[16]

Greener did soon get the opportunity to air his views on race to a national audience in a lengthy essay, "The Intellectual Position of the Negro," published in *National Quarterly Review* (July 1880). Part history lesson and part advocacy, the essay reminded readers of the accomplishments of black citizens on three continents over more than three centuries, including scientists, philosophers, priests, politicians, and authors. Greener was also quick to critique authors who had recently questioned the achievements of his race in print: "Rhetorical finish is exhibited where foundation is lacking, and damaging assertions are promulgated, not only without verification, but so easily controvertible by the mere novice that it would seem a waste of time to prove their untenable nature." He singled out an article in the *North American Review* by James Parton, "Antipathy to the Negro," as "a glaring example of the prevalent inaccurate and hasty way of disposing of matters pertaining to the Negro and his interests in this country." Greener's essay illuminated a race that produced "talents, virtues, services and abilities, notwithstanding the illiberal prejudice, the prevailing ostracism and the lack of opportunity afforded us to demonstrate our claim to humanity."[17]

After leaving Howard, Greener proved to be a man of many talents as he continued to balance multiple roles. Although his law partnership ended when Cook died in late 1878, he continued with his own practice. He also lectured widely, generally in Maryland, Pennsylvania, New York, and Washington. The range of his subject matter is shown in lecture titles like "The Great Pyramid: Its Age, Builders and Purpose," "Socrates as a Teacher," and "The Academic Life," and he also spoke about current issues faced by blacks in the South. Young, energetic, and speaking to largely black audiences, he quickly became accustomed to an enthusiastic reception. Of his pyramid lecture, one newspaper reported that "he maintained his high reputation for scholarship and erudition" and "made a dry and technical subject luminous with information and illustration. . . . His defense of the negro race and his enumeration of its magnificent achievements was very fine and provided much applause."[18]

When he addressed a mass meeting of Washington's Irish citizens on Irish land questions, Greener quipped that he had been "called upon to add a little color to the Irish question" and was applauded in the press as the "most eloquent and interesting speaker" of the evening. Reviewing his speech at an anniversary celebration of the ratification of the Fifteenth Amendment to the US Constitution, the *Baltimore American* reported that Greener gave an "eloquent address" on black progress that "kept his audience in continual laughter." He also delivered stirring eulogies—first at the funeral of celebrated abolitionist William Lloyd Garrison and later upon the deaths of abolitionists Wendell Phillips and Henry Garnet.[19]

After establishing himself locally in Washington and Baltimore, he connected with other prominent black Republicans to stump for the party in New York, Ohio, and Pennsylvania during 1879. Politically astute and aware that recognition for his service to the Republican cause might come in handy for patronage positions, Greener waited only a few hours after election results were final to send congratulations to James Garfield on his 1880 presidential victory. He didn't hesitate to couch himself as a representative of his race who had assisted the campaign.

> In the hour of the triumph of the party you represent, permit me to tender the hearty congratulations of the young colored republicans of this country, who look forward to your administration as their fathers looked up to Abraham Lincoln after The Proclamation. Some of us value you no less for your scholarship and lofty aims than for your undoubted patriotism and consistent republicanism. . . .
>
> We, who have humbly labored for the cause you uphold in this contest, are assured that it is safe in your keeping.[20]

He signed his letter "Sincerely and Fraternally Yours, Richard T. Greener" and was soon appointed to Garfield's inauguration planning committee. It is possible that had Garfield not been so soon the victim of an assassin's bullet, Greener might have benefited from a patronage appointment. Although he railed against the time it took to deal with job seekers, Garfield was known for taking care of his friends. He quickly appointed several prominent black citizens to high-level posts, including Douglass, Langston, and Blanche Bruce.[21]

In addition to his Department of Treasury job, his legal work, and his public speaking and writing, Greener quickly became a busy joiner of causes and clubs. He was appointed to a "Committee of 100" to arrange a citywide reception for Ulysses S. Grant on his first return to the capital since his presidency. He also helped to organize a Scottish Rite black freemasonry society and the Negro American Society in 1877, and he served as recording secretary in a Knights Templar Gethsemane Commandery and in the Banneker Historical Society. Still very closely aligned with the South, he was president of the local South Carolina Republican Club and a representative from South Carolina in the Union League of America. When asked about his past, he continued to identify himself as a "South Carolinian."[22]

The Negro American Society, launched at a meeting of ten influential black citizens of Washington, DC, hoped eventually to have branches throughout the nation to "promote the culture, material progress and educational interest of the colored people of this country." Greener became the society's president and helped push through a constitution, draft rules of membership and meeting, and organize a large community commemoration of the 108th anniversary of the Boston Massacre. Although the ambitious group ultimately disbanded operations, perhaps expiring under the weight of many meetings about the organizational structure and location, it gave Greener an opportunity to demonstrate his growing commitment toward pride of race. He was increasingly active in proclaiming his determination that "the Negro in America was not to lose his identity by absorption with the dominant race, but to endeavor to do something *as a Negro*." To that end, he argued in a letter to the *Christian Recorder* that the term "Negro," denoting a race, was "certainly more appropriate than 'colored,' that weak euphemism which means nothing or anything." Preferring the term "Negro American," he insisted that "African American" was simply inaccurate, since "many Africans are not Negroes. Some Negroes are Americans by birth and some are African by birth." The "Negro," he urged, "must rise by making that name respectable, aye eminent if possible, in every domain of art, science and literature—the region where genius wins respect, even if it be as flat-nosed and thick-lipped as the Lybian [*sic*] Sphinx."[23]

* * *

Although generally in sync with other black activist leaders of his day, Greener broke with the renowned Douglass in a dispute that would risk his standing with influential black friends and expose differences between older abolitionists and eager young civil rights activists. The rift began when black citizens in the South—especially Louisiana, Texas, and Mississippi—realized that resounding Democratic political victories in southern statewide elections of 1878 meant an end to any hope for a black voice or vote in those regions. Many then began moving West in mass—to Missouri, Kansas, and beyond—in search of good jobs and the freedom to exercise their rights as US citizens. Soon, their plight (How to get there? How to settle there?) became a cause for other (especially northern) blacks and some whites who wanted to help. The "Exodus Movement" was born.[24]

Greener immediately jumped on board the emigration cause, joining such prominent advocates as Garrison, Langston, Phillips, and Sojourner Truth, and he soon became secretary of the National Emigration Aid Society. Serving with him on that group's National Executive Committee were notable men from thirteen states, including four US senators. But not all prominent black activists agreed with the exodus idea, especially not Frederick Douglass. The celebrated orator lectured blacks that gaining the ability to enjoy full and equal rights was just a matter of time, since "the Fourteenth Amendment makes him [the black man] a citizen, and the fifteenth makes him a voter." Greener cautioned, however, that conditions in the South—such as violence, fraud, poverty, and oppression by the Ku Klux Klan—would endanger the welfare and negate the rights of black citizens for many years to come.[25]

There was some reason for Greener to believe he might equal or even best Douglass in a head-on debate about black emigration westward. He was a widely sought-after speaker whose oratorical skills were evident from newspaper accounts and audience responses. The Harvard stamp, along with the "professor" title and the Howard law deanship, didn't hurt either. And, he had done his homework on the issues by living in the South and meeting frequently with southern congressional members and his South Carolina acquaintances.

The first publicized debate between the two black activists occurred in the spring of 1879. It took place in the Hillsdale area of Washington near the Anacostia River, giving Douglass a home-court advantage: His twenty-one-room home and estate, Cedar Hill, was only a mile away. Speaking before an audience of black and white local residents, Douglass, widely respected and referred to as "the lion of Anacostia," also had the advantage of lengthy experience. Tall and muscled, with the great head of hair that marked his enormous presence, he commanded any stage. Douglass characterized his approach to the exodus argument as one of reason and Greener's as one of emotion. Claiming that the "premature surrender" to emigration only "strengthens the argument of the inability of the colored people to take care of themselves," he concluded that the valuable labor black workers provided, so necessary in the agrarian South, would eventually gain them increased political and economic strength.[26]

Greener, who was the exact age of Douglass's youngest son, didn't shrink from directly engaging his impressive opponent. He detailed the violence against blacks in the South that went unchecked by local police forces and the legal rights that went unenforced by courts. He noted that Douglass might not understand these matters because he was safe in his home within sight of the Navy Yard, which had monitors on guard. He also reminded the audience that black southerners themselves favored the idea of emigration: "Those engaged in it know much better than we and much better than Mr. Douglass who has never been South." When Douglass's argued that blacks might not be treated so well in Kansas and Missouri, Greener produced a letter from the governor of Kansas stating that the majority of the thousands of immigrants so far had found steady employment. He reasoned, "Why should not the negro go West? Irish, Hebrew, German and Swedish colonies are going out from New York and the East almost daily."[27]

While no particular winner or loser was declared, Greener enjoyed favorable press for his debating abilities, such as the *National Republican* newspaper headline, "Professor Greener Ably Sustains the Flight of His Race from Southern Oppression." Wisely, Greener stopped short of making severe attacks or instigating any lasting conflict, and the exchange ended cordially, with both men agreeing to discuss the matter further on a future occasion.[28] The opportunity came several months later, when Greener and Douglass were scheduled to present their sides on the exodus issue at the annual meeting of the American Social Science Association (ASSA) in Saratoga, New York. Douglass, however, wanted no debate; rather, he preferred only that papers be prepared and read. When he saw press accounts that indicated debate might happen, he decided to back out three days prior to the scheduled date. A disappointed Greener heard the news when he arrived in Saratoga but determined that he could at least use his skillful oratory to highlight the need for black emigration from the South. Eighty-four-year-old Francis Wayland, former and formidable Brown University president and presiding ASSA president, read the paper sent by Douglass.

Douglass's paper reiterated his argument that blacks did not help themselves by taking a defeatist attitude, even though "the unjust conduct charged against the late slaveholders is eminently probable." Still, if southern blacks would just hold tight, they would find that the ongoing need for their labor would ultimately result in more humane treatment. He maintained that the situation of the time was "exceptional and transient" because the black man had "the permanent powers of government on his side" and President Hayes was "still liberal, just and generous toward the South."[29]

Greener's argument, keenly developed for the largely northern white audience at the meeting, described in detail the circumstances confronting southern blacks since Reconstruction—they lived amid "southern barbarity and lawlessness." He continued, "Negro representation went first; next the educational system. . . . Majorities were overcome by shot-gun intimidation or secretly by tissue ballot. Radical office holders were forced to resign, robbed of their property by 'due process of the law,' and driven North. The jury box and representation the negro was forced to give up; but after enduring all this, he found himself charged exorbitantly for the most necessary articles of food. His land was rented to him at fabulous prices. His cabin was likely to be raided at any time."[30]

On the idea that southern whites would eventually capitulate to black demands, due to their need for black labor, Greener pointed out that such labor—generally connected to cotton, rice, and sugar—would remain cheap and menial as long as there continued to be more willing blacks in the South than were needed to perform it. Recalling one of Douglass's arguments, he concluded, "We are assured that there will be misery and want resulting from this 'ill-timed' movement. . . . The crucial test, however, is whether there will be more misery and want by migrating than by remaining; we think not."[31] His speech, applauded long and loudly, inspired University of Rochester president Martin B. Anderson to rise and offer a statement of approval.

Greener and others involved in the National Emigration Aid Society turned their attention to urging government and philanthropic aid for black citizens who wanted to emigrate—especially many who had piled up in St. Louis and elsewhere on their way west but had no means to continue on. Happily for Greener, whose many and various endeavors were testimony to his ongoing attention to networking, this work put him in contact with many influential white politicians and supportive black leaders. His commitment to the cause was only strengthened by his travels in the fall of 1879 to Missouri, Illinois, Kansas, and Iowa. There, he gave speeches, met with exodus participants and state officials, and assessed the chances for black employment and well-being. Tens of thousands of southern blacks moved to the Midwest between 1870 and 1880, traveling by riverboat, train, wagon, or foot; nearly fifty thousand arrived in Kansas alone during 1879 and 1880. Others went to Missouri, Ohio, Iowa, and elsewhere. Many were destitute when they left and destitute when they arrived, and these refugees were aided by Greener's Emigration Aid Society, the Freedmen's Relief Association, local churches, and improved opportunities for employment.[32]

Democrats in US Congress and some state legislatures, fearful of shifting political balances as thousands of Republicans moved into the Midwest, waged fierce political campaigns against the exodus movement and its aid organizations. This effort undoubtedly helped to stem the tide of departing southerners after 1879. As the emigration bubble subsided at the close of the decade, emigrating blacks either became absorbed into the economies of Midwestern states or grew discouraged and returned to the South. Greener and others were able to slow the pace of their aid work. A third child—their second daughter, Belle Marian—had been born to Greener and his wife while he was on his fall trip to the Midwest.[33] When his deanship at Howard ended, it was time to work on building up his law practice.

• • •

Greener quickly found that legal work for a new black attorney in town was anything but steady, as was the collection of fees when work did show up. Black clients, especially in trial work, were either destitute, difficult to defend, or both. James Stone, noted in the press as "a yellow man," was typical of such clients when Greener partnered with A. K. Browne to defend him in a well-publicized local murder case. The accused's initial lawyer had deserted him in the midst of pretrial investigations that failed to support Stone's denial that he had slit his wife's throat in front of several witnesses. Greener and Browne tried for an insanity defense but in the end got nowhere. Their client was unable to pay, found guilty, and hanged.[34]

In a more intriguing case, and one that certainly elevated his legal reputation, Greener defended a well-known North Carolina black activist against extradition from the District of Columbia back to his home state. Samuel L. Perry, a former slave, was a schoolteacher when he and neighboring black citizens became frustrated with their treatment by whites in rural Lenoir County, North Carolina. They heard of better opportunities in Kansas, and Perry volunteered to travel there at his own expense to check out the possibilities. On the way, he was delighted to encounter the people of Indiana. There he found that "his people could find ready employment and Christian treatment," so he arranged to start his own small exodus movement with a group of blacks from North Carolina. Later, he went back for another group of emigrants and then another. About three thousand black North Carolinians settled and began working in Indiana, and Perry spent much of his time in North Carolina helping others to move.[35]

This exodus created problems for local white farm owners, who had always counted on cheap black labor. According to a *New York Times* reporter, "Perry was attacked by all those methods peculiar to southern civilization . . . and was finally forced by threats of personal violence to remove with his family from the State of North Carolina."[36] One of those attacks occurred when he was charged in 1880 with forging a $45 school warrant nearly two years before. With the help of friends, he posted his $100 bail, and the forgery case was dismissed at trial as false and malicious. But it was enough to motivate Perry to move to Washington, DC, to avoid further persecution and possible violence.

Soon, however, a dentist from Lenoir County, George K. Bagby, showed up with documents from the governor of North Carolina requiring Perry's extradition as a fugitive from justice and citing the old forgery case. But the extradition process server wasn't only a dentist. According to press accounts, Bagby's racial prejudice was well known, and he had been involved in a number of incidents against black citizens in his area. Black activists in Washington, including Greener and Frederick Douglass, heard about the case. Greener, who soon joined veteran Washington defense attorneys Samuel Shellabarger and John Wilson in the extradition hearings, well understood the dangers facing black activists in southern states. He pointedly asked Bagby about the existence of the Ku Klux Klan in Lenoir County, and he wondered why the governor would send Bagby, instead of a sworn officer of the state or local government, on the extradition errand. After much testimony and press coverage, District of Columbia Supreme Court justice Andrew Wylie, suspicious of political motives and possibly wary of the potential for violence against Perry, determined that "the state of North Carolina would not suffer if Perry should not be returned." He ordered no extradition, explaining that "the duty of the Judge is to examine as to the crime, and, if satisfied that there was none, to discharge the accused."[37] The *New York Times* reported that the attempted "revenge upon a leader in the negro exodus" was "a good example of Bourbon malevolence" in North Carolina.[38]

· · ·

The Perry case marked the waning of Greener's active involvement in the exodus movement. Eventually, however, he would be able to take some comfort in Douglass's reversal of opinion on the issue. After finally visiting

South Carolina and Georgia in 1888, Douglass reversed his earlier position and proclaimed that he could "welcome any movement" for the black people of those states "which will take them out of the wretched condition in which I now know them to be. . . . I give my hearty 'God-speed' in your emigration scheme."[39] Greener's stance on emigration would eventually soften as well. By 1884 he would determine that, given the larger population of blacks in the South, "it is to the negro's interest to remain at the South, and even to encourage his Northern brother to come there also. . . . A century hence, he will be the ruling power at the South."[40]

Greener had been careful to make no lasting enemies among influential black leaders. He had even joined his debate opponent Douglass in New York and Ohio during 1879 to give stump speeches on behalf of Republicans running for office. Their joint efforts for the Republican Party continued for several years.[41] With widening gaps between recently successful and still oppressed blacks, however, Greener faced a tricky balancing act in promoting responses that reflected his own views, those of the divergent elements in the Republican Party, and those of blacks in wide-ranging circumstances. Similarly, his various interests and activities, often uncompensated, resulted in ongoing financial difficulties. Yet, his work at the Treasury Department eventually yielded greater personal satisfaction when he served as law clerk to the first comptroller of the Treasury, Judge William Lawrence, from 1880 to 1882. A former US congressman from Ohio, Lawrence presided over scores of Treasury legal decisions that were edited for publication by Greener.

The Greener family expanded again, to three daughters and a son, in December 1880, with the birth of Ethel Alice.[42] Residing in the same block as his mother-in-law and other Fleet family members supported family stability, and the pace and economy of the nation's capital supported Greener's professional opportunities. Still, he understood that he was well short of reaching his full potential in legal practice, government service, political influence, or national black leadership. He had a hand in all those areas but seemed unable to achieve clear prominence and a steady income in any one of them.

CHAPTER EIGHT

A Violent Attack and Hopeless Case

IME SPENT WORKING, speaking, writing, and campaigning for racial justice left little opportunity for anything else. Greener was making a well-regarded name for himself but barely managing a bit of home life with his family and some correspondence with friends. Yet, he was determined to maintain a connection with the young black men he had guided during the short-lived integration of the University of South Carolina. One of those, Johnson C. Whittaker, had achieved an appointment to the US Military Academy. Greener mentioned his former student in an 1877 congratulatory note to Cadet Henry Ossian Flipper, the first black graduate of West Point.

> I felt a thrill of pleasure here the other day when I read your name as the first [black] graduate from the Academy. I take this opportunity of writing you again to extend my hearty congratulations, and trust your future career may be as successful as your academic one. "My boy" Whittaker has, I am told, been rooming with you, and I trust has been getting much benefit from the association.
>
> I am your friend and well-wisher,
>
> Richard T. Greener[1]

Greener had encouraged his "boy" Whittaker to try the sub-freshman preparatory program at the University of South Carolina in 1874. Whittaker then moved quickly to full admission and success at the top of his class. Finally, he won an appointment as one of the earliest black cadets at West Point. He would soon be asking his former professor for help and legal counsel.

• • •

During the latter years of Reconstruction, when a number of blacks and liberal white "carpetbaggers" were serving southern states in the US Congress, a few black students received appointments to the US Military Academy at

West Point. Fewer still passed the entrance examination after arrival, and very few—only three of the first twenty-three appointed—graduated. James Webster Smith from Columbia, South Carolina, successfully passed the entrance examination in 1870 and was the sole black cadet at the academy for his first two years. He was hazed, ostracized, tricked, and taunted to an extent that spoke volumes about unchecked racial prejudice at West Point. He fought back in many scrapes and quarrels with fellow cadets. After a dismissal that was reduced to a suspension by President Grant, he completed four years. He was dismissed again when he failed to pass his final exam.[2]

Flipper, a tall, slender cadet from Georgia, took a different tack, remaining quiet and determined through insults, isolation, and bigotry. In his 1878 autobiography, *The Colored Cadet at West Point,* he described the beginning of his four lonely years: "When I was a plebe those of us who lived on the same floor of the barracks visited each other, borrowed books, heard each other recite when preparing for examination, and were really on most intimate terms. But alas! In less than a month they learned to call me "nigger," and ceased altogether to visit me. . . . In camp, brought into close contact with the older cadets, these once friends discovered that they were prejudiced, and learned to abhor even the presence or sight of a "d—d nigger." Flipper, whose discriminatory treatment came from his fellow cadets rather than West Point officers, decided that he would simply view himself as "above the rabble and their insults. . . . To stoop to retaliation is not compatible with true dignity, nor is vindictiveness manly." His patient suffering was remarkable, and he recalled as he reached his final year: "To me it was to be not only an end of study, of discipline, of obedience to the regulations of the Academy, but even an end to isolation, to tacit persecution, to melancholy, to suspense."[3]

His final year was also an opportunity for Flipper to become a role model to his new roommate, first-year cadet Johnson Chesnut Whittaker. A slightly built, light-skinned young man with a freckled face, Whittaker was a mixed-race former slave from the heart of cotton-growing country in Camden, South Carolina. His mother had been the house slave of Mary Boykin Chesnut, later famous for her Civil War diary. His father had decamped during Johnson's infancy, and the mother and children transitioned from slave work to paid domestic work after the war. Greener, proud of the unlikely scholar's academic success at the University of South Carolina during Reconstruction, had suggested Whittaker to South Carolina congressman Solomon Hoge as a nominee for an appointment to the US Military Academy. He also helped with Whittaker's preparation for his entrance examination.[4]

Newspapers around the country had anticipated and then covered Flipper's commencement. On June 14, 1877, beneath the shadow of the maple trees in front of the central administration building on campus, the seniors took their seats; the other classes stacked their arms and stood around the square. The *Christian Recorder,* published by the African Methodist Episcopal Church, reported that "Lieutenant H. O. Flipper was the only cadet who received the cheers of the assembled multitude at West Point upon receiving his parchment. How the fellows felt who wouldn't associate with him, we do not know."[5] It is possible that the celebratory outburst reflected northern sentiments about southern attitudes toward racial equality. Flipper's graduation also marked Whittaker's new status as the only cadet of color at West Point. A reporter for the *New York World* soon noted his lonely presence.

> As you are aware, there is at present a colored, or partly colored, cadet in the Freshman Class—Whittaker by name. This poor young mulatto is completely ostracized not only by West Point society, but most thoroughly by the corps of cadets itself. Flipper got through all right, and, strange to say, the cadets seem to have a certain kind of respect for him, although he was the darkest "African" that has yet been seen among the West Point cadets. Flipper had remarkable pluck and nerve, and was accorded his parchment—well up on the list, too—at last graduation day. He is made of sterner stuff than poor Whittaker.
>
> . . . When I asked a cadet today some questions concerning the treatment of Cadet Whittaker by the corps, he said: "Oh, we get along very well, sir. The cadets simply ignore him, and he understands very well that we do not intend to associate with him."[6]

On his first day at West Point, Whittaker was greeted by a fellow cadet with, "Are you the nigger that's coming here?" He quickly noticed that no cadets would sit beside him in the mess hall, and none would respond to his requests to pass food or drink to him. In his second year, he wrote to his former roommate, Flipper, noting that he was being "treated bully" by most officers and faculty. But, he added, "As I am sitting in my room on third floor, sixth 'div,' a kind of sadness creeps over me, for I am all alone."[7]

Whittaker adopted Flipper's playbook to deal with his ostracism. Stoic and shy, he spent his time reading his Bible, writing letters to his mother, occasionally chatting with some black servants, and studying. He stayed quiet amid social isolation and various pranks, and did not respond to a threatening note nor an insulting poem, "Nigger Jim," in a cadet publication. During two vacation periods, he visited a friend in New York; he stayed with Richard Greener in Washington during another. He survived academically until January of his junior year (1879), when he failed an exam and was found deficient by the academic board. West Point superintendent John M. Schofield, a decorated Union general in the Civil War, determined that Whittaker and two academically deficient white students should be dropped back to repeat a year instead of being dismissed.[8]

• • •

At six o'clock in the morning of April 6, 1880, Whittaker failed to report for reveille. The cadet officer of the day, George R. Burnett, was ordered to go to Whittaker's room, where he found Whittaker unresponsive, lying on the floor in his underwear. His feet, bound together at his ankles, were tied to his iron bed; his wrists were wound tightly with belting and secured in front of him. His ears were mutilated and badly bleeding, with pieces of one lobe cut off. One hand had some cuts, and blood was on Whittaker, as well as on the bed and bedding, a wall, and elsewhere. Burned paper, pieces of a broken mirror, and bunches of Whittaker's hair littered the floor.

That much was a matter of general agreement. Everything else about the situation—How much blood? How tight the bindings? How unconscious was he?—would become points of great national contention and speculation for many months. And of course: Who did it? The intrigue soon escalated to become one of the most widely puzzling and publicized mysteries of the nineteenth century.

When Burnett left to get the officer on duty at the guardhouse, two other cadets came into the room and watched over Whittaker. They offered no assistance and did not try to untie his hands or feet. The duty officer, Major Piper, at first thought Whittaker was dead but then found a pulse. By the time the academy surgeon, Dr. Charles T. Alexander, arrived, eight cadets were ranging through the scene. The doctor thought Whittaker's pulse seemed too regular for a totally unconscious man; when he tried to get a response, Whittaker simply mumbled over and over, "Please don't cut me." As Alexander ministered to the wounds, other officials arrived. Eventually, Whittaker was able to slowly sit up and even talk about three masked intruders, seemingly fellow cadets, who had broken in during the early morning hours, cut him, tied him, and warned him to stay silent. He mentioned a note he had found in his room several days earlier. It read, "You will be fixed. Better keep awake," and was signed by "A Friend." Lt. Col. Henry Lazelle, commandant of cadets, ordered Whittaker's clothes to be washed and the room to be picked up.[9]

As word of the incident spread, stalwart West Point defenders and some skeptical onlookers immediately floated the notion that the victim was to blame. Soon, that idea ballooned into the belief that the victim was the perpetrator. Colonel Lazelle, who submitted his immediate report of the incident to the superintendent, General Schofield, speculated that Whittaker had himself written the note of warning, mutilated himself, tied himself up, and faked unconsciousness.[10] His view was widely shared by most who worked at the military academy. The four officers appointed by General Schofield to sit as a court of inquiry (a three-man tribunal and a recorder) regarding the case were all West Point faculty members, as was Whittaker's appointed representative for the occasion.

General Schofield, eager to insert himself as offstage director of the upcoming inquiry process, wasted little time in making his own views public. In an interview with a *New York Times* reporter one day before the first court of inquiry meeting, he stated, "We have found nothing whatsoever to justify us in suspecting any of the cadets." Rather, "the general sentiment among officers and cadets at West Point is that Whitaker [*sic*] himself was the author of the alleged outrage." Schofield claimed, "There are several discrepancies in the boy's story which seem to cast doubt over its truth." Downplaying the ear mutilation as superficial, he also remarked about the tight hand and ankle bindings: "He might have had an accomplice." The alleged motivation was that Whittaker wanted to avoid a June examination in philosophy so he could "gain a commission in the Army without graduating."[11]

Beyond West Point, there was less agreement about victim blame or guilt. Even Charleston's conservative *News and Courier* reported that "some of the leading officers at West Point discredit the statement that Whitaker [*sic*] committed the act." The article took exception to the idea that Whittaker wanted to avoid academic examinations in June, pointing out that a cadet with academic problems would already be under some sort of warning or sanction. It concluded, "As yet no one is justified in charging that he did the deed, for there is no evidence proving that fact. . . . There is no doubt that there is a strong feeling in certain quarters at West Point against the colored cadet."[12]

Richard Greener received a desperate letter from Whittaker in which he described the situation as a "heinous plot engaged in by no others than cadets." Whittaker asked his former teacher to come to West Point, and Greener immediately took leave from his Treasury Department job to be on hand for most of the court of inquiry meetings in the academy library. He was called to the stand several times as a witness.[13] Another who attended, the outspoken race activist Rev. Justin D. Fulton of Brooklyn, was so moved by the obvious impossibility of a fair hearing that he immediately wrote to US Secretary of War Alexander Ramsey.

> I went yesterday to attend the investigation of the case of the colored cadet, J. C. Whittaker, in the U.S. Military Academy and, judging from what I observed, I am convinced that the young man is not likely to have a fair trial. . . . The story of the boy impressed me and others not prejudiced, as being straightforward and truthful. There seems to be a disposition to make out a case against him. He is there quite alone and isolated. This nation owes to the black race a debt for services rendered in the past, notably during the late war, and it cannot afford to now let this young man (the only representative of four millions of loyal citizens in the U.S. Military Academy) be the victim of Southern hate or prejudice. I therefore think that the honored Secretary of War could do no wiser or better thing than secure the best of legal talent for the young man's defense.[14]

The reverend would prove a savvy analyst of the situation. The investigation dragged on and included rumors of cadets heard plotting to get rid of Whittaker, as well as testimony from a local tavern keeper, a milkman, and handwriting experts who tried to match the handwriting in the warning note to that of Whittaker. Both houses of the US Congress debated the affair, drafted resolutions to investigate, and considered special committees and subcommittees to examine conditions at West Point. President Rutherford B. Hayes and his cabinet sent Martin Townsend, US district attorney for northern New York, as an observer and adviser. Townsend would also become somewhat of an informal counsel for Whittaker and was "obviously convinced of the black cadet's innocence and critical of West Point's handling of the case." Unable to make much headway in that direction among West Point inquiry officials, however, he departed before the final weeks of the inquiry.[15]

After about six weeks, the inquiry concluded with what one Pennsylvania newspaper simply described as "the finding that Whittaker warned himself, tied himself and mutilated himself."[16] Schofield's appointed recorder, West Point captain Clinton Sears, had concluded for the tribunal that the testimony showed Whittaker had planned and executed his own attack. The three West Point faculty who comprised the court of inquiry agreed, as did much of the press and the general public.

The previously skeptical *Charleston News and Courier* now supported the court of inquiry. Reflecting the views of many white southerners, its editors maintained, "The mistake is in attempting to make 'an officer and a gentleman' out of such material. Flipper, who scraped through, was no better than Whitaker [*sic*], and his coming to grief is only a matter of time." A well-regarded national journal, the *North American Review*, printed a lengthy article by West Point professor Peter Michie that extolled the greatness of the US Military Academy, boasted about its color blindness, and ranted at its doubters: "The bodily injury to Cadet Whittaker is practically nothing, but the Academy has received wounds which are still fresh and bleeding." Yet, the media, like the country, was not at all united on the issue. *Harper's Weekly*, the *New York Tribune*, the *Washington National Republican*, and others found the inquiry conclusions questionable and the treatment of blacks at West Point abhorrent.[17]

Whittaker, who had attended and testified at the inquiry, had little time and even less focus for studying for his upcoming examinations. He wrote to Greener after the inquiry decision, "My heart droops in despair and life seems almost a burden."[18] Not surprisingly, after various examination processes, including oral testing in philosophy by Sears, recorder at the inquiry, and Professor Michie, author of the *North American Review* article, an academic board found Whittaker deficient.

Shortly after the announcement of academic deficiency, Greener wrote an open letter "to the colored people" that was published in the *Philadelphia Christian Recorder*, the *Washington (DC) People's Advocate*, and elsewhere.

West Point has at last completed the last act in the conspiracy against Cadet Johnson C. Whittaker. Fearing the Secretary of War would override their partisan, unjust and flagrantly prejudiced report, they have descended to covert methods and found Cadet Whittaker deficient in Philosophy, so as to recommend his dismissal from the Military Academy before their report could be examined. The colored taxpayers and voters ought to be heard throughout the country denouncing the farce of a trial accorded to the colored cadet and demanding from the President of the United States that a commission as a 2nd Lieutenant in the regular army be issued to cadet Whittaker.[19]

Whittaker was put on leave of absence until the US Department of War could review the report of the court of inquiry. President Hayes, due to the negative publicity for West Point, began to consider ways to reorganize the academy or at least do some housecleaning among its leadership. With only a few months left in office before James Garfield would assume the presidency, Hayes's options were to restore Whittaker to West Point, let the academic dismissal stand, or do something in between those extremes. He first replaced Superintendent Schofield with General Oliver O. Howard, who had served in the Civil War, then as commissioner of the Freedmen's Bureau, and finally as president of Howard University (1869–74).[20]

Eventually, Hayes agreed with Greener, Whittaker himself, Howard, and others that Whittaker should have another day in court—this time by a court-martial of ten members convened outside the academy in New York City. Many believed this tribunal, with only four West Point graduates among its ten representatives, was the only way to truly clear Whittaker of all guilt. Many others viewed it as a set-up by those who favored Whittaker. Varied press reports throughout the country reflected the controversy. It was "a scheme to vindicate him through a court martial" by a president who had always had "sympathy for the youth," the *Washington Post* maintained. The *Memphis Daily Appeal* dubbed it "the Court Martial which is trying to find out who did or not cut the coon's ears." Yet the *Press and Daily Dakotaian* of Dakota Territory insisted that "the original court of inquiry was a one-sided affair into which much of the prejudice of color entered."[21]

Greener, who had written a letter to Secretary of War Ramsey outlining the legal bases for a court-martial, later would credit his "legal demand" as the key to "establishing the precedent that a cadet at the United States Military Academy is an officer of the United States Army" who therefore can be tried by court-martial. In actuality, a number of West Point cadets had been subject to courts-martial in the past. Among those were Edgar Allan Poe, who in 1831 deliberately disobeyed all orders and rules to assure a trial, a guilty verdict, and a dismissal from the academy. Another cadet, George Armstrong Custer, class of 1861, was tried by a court-martial for conduct that had encouraged a physical brawl between other cadets, but his sentence was reduced to a reprimand. Additionally, as one legal analyst has written, "Cadets and midshipmen have historically been viewed as a form of officer."[22]

• • •

The first meeting of the court-martial took place on January 20, 1881, in the Army Building of New York City. Greener was Whittaker's associate defense counsel. His defense counsel was Daniel Chamberlain, former governor of South Carolina, who had built up a lucrative law practice in New York City. Although a Republican and proponent of black rights in his southern politician days, he was now decidedly not a supporter of President Hayes and was quickly becoming politically independent. By the late 1880s, he would become a candid white supremacist, "increasingly anti-black and anti-Republican" according to historian Richard Nelson Current. Nevertheless, Chamberlain was a skilled lawyer, and it is possible that Greener, who had visited New York City in late December, had urged him to lead Whittaker's defense.[23]

Leading the prosecution was Judge Advocate Asa Bird Gardner, an army major in the Civil War and New York native, who later changed the spelling of his name to Gardiner. He was assisted by Captain Sears, the recorder in the earlier court of inquiry. The charges against Whittaker were "conduct unbecoming an officer and gentleman," stemming from an accusation of self-mutilation, feigned unconsciousness, and falsification of the warning note; and "false swearing to the prejudice of good order and military discipline," related to the accusation of lying under oath at the previous inquiry. After preliminary formalities on the first day, the trial was postponed by two weeks after Chamberlain appealed for more time to review the three thousand pages of court of inquiry documents that he had only received a few days earlier.[24]

When the court reconvened in February, familiar witnesses from the earlier court of inquiry reappeared, as did familiar questions and answers. The atmosphere was more intense, however, and the defense counsels were far more aggressive than the examiners at West Point had been. Whittaker took the stand and repeated the testimony he had given previously, as did other cadets and officers. The cadet's motivation was again an issue. At least one West Point professor, Peter Michie, who taught the cadet's difficult natural philosophy course, testified that he had not viewed Whittaker as particularly likely to fail. Handwriting analysts paraded through for nearly three weeks to discuss authorship of the warning note, with those for the defense contradicting those for the prosecution. Chamberlain was overruled when he contended that the use of Whittaker's earlier letters, which had no bearing on the case, should be inadmissible even for handwriting-comparison purposes.[25]

Greener and Chamberlain hammered away in cross-examinations, determined to shake testimony about faked unconsciousness, superficial wounds, self-bound hands and feet, and, most importantly, the impossibility that a West Point cadet would ever do harm to another cadet. Finally, in a small victory, the defense counsels did get one officer to admit that a cadet who had done such a thing would probably lie about it. Another agreed that the court of inquiry had been conducted on the theory that Whittaker was the sole perpetrator of all aspects of the assault. By bringing in lawyers from other cases that had relied on the prosecution's handwriting authorities for analysis, Chamberlain and Greener were able to demonstrate the fallibility of the experts.[26]

During a welcome recess in early March, Greener traveled back to Washington, DC, to attend the inauguration of President James Garfield and related festivities, likely also managing some networking for patronage appointment possibilities in the new administration. Another break came later in the month, when the secretary of war granted permission for the trial to move out of its cramped and poorly ventilated room to the new US Court House and Post Office. In April, during the defense stage, Greener himself took the stand to testify about the bloodstains he had seen in Whittaker's room in May—by his estimate, the blood was much more copious than the prosecution witnesses had indicated. He also demonstrated that Whittaker's record and grades indicated no sign of deficiency. Whittaker was again called to testify, as were new handwriting experts who determined that Whittaker could not have written the warning note, medical authorities who testified against the faked unconsciousness idea, and three of Whittaker's former University of South Carolina professors, who spoke about his high academic standing and character.[27]

After four months of tedious proceedings that eventually slipped out of press coverage, Chamberlain gave a lengthy summation that included an attack on the alleged motive: Why would a cadet superficially wound himself in April in hopes of being deemed unable to take an exam in June? Chamberlain poked holes in much of the prosecution's case. For the prosecution, Major Gardner similarly discredited the defense. He disputed the handwriting experts produced by the defense, emphasized inconsistencies in Whittaker's testimony, and insisted that any ostracism was just a matter of cadets choosing their own friends. Finally, he also managed to slip in his personal reminder that "negroes are noted for their ability to sham and feign" and are "endowed with cunning."[28]

The ruling of the court-martial, which would next go for approval to army Judge Advocate General D. G. Swaim, and then to President Garfield, was made public just a few days after the closing arguments, on June 10, 1881. The court-martial found Whittaker guilty on both counts and recommended the penalty of dishonorable discharge, a one-dollar fine, and a year in a hard-labor penitentiary. Six of the ten members, however, signed an addendum recommending cancellation of the fine and imprisonment.

Variously labeled in the press as "the self-constituted champion of the 'oppressed cadet'" and "the clever young negro lawyer," Greener had long felt that Chamberlain's defense strategy unnecessarily downplayed the reality of racism at West Point. But since Chamberlain did most of the witness examination and all of the final summary, there had been little Greener could do to change that direction. It is likely that he did not entirely trust Chamberlain on race questions, an area in which the ex-governor was becoming steadily more equivocal. In correspondence with Garfield shortly after his election to the presidency, Chamberlain had advised that he should drop southern Republican leaders who had been part of Reconstruction and "embrace those who had esteem for southern whites."[29]

Greener quickly returned to Washington to continue his own legal work and his Treasury Department job. The *Washington Post* sniped, "Prof. Greener has all along been a clerk in the Treasury Department; he is in the First Controller's office and draws each month the snug little sum of $100. . . . He has steadily drawn his salary, though for several months absent from his post of duty championing Whittaker's cause."[30]

By unfortunate coincidence, one of Greener's legal activities was to provide assistance and advice at a distance to lawyers handling another court-martial case—that of Henry O. Flipper. After his pioneering West Point graduation, Flipper was at first detailed only to army construction duties. Finally, however, he became a cavalry officer and then a commissary officer at Fort Davis, Texas. There, he was expected to keep army cash in his own quarters, and he eventually found some of that cash missing. Flipper was accused, court-martialed, and acquitted of the theft, but he was deemed guilty nonetheless of conduct unbecoming an officer and gentleman. After his dishonorable discharge in June 1882, he worked in engineering in Texas, Mexico, and Venezuela. Greener had once again found himself on the losing side of a hopeless case.[31]

Still on leave from the academy, Whittaker remained in limbo—a state no doubt lengthened when President Garfield was shot three months after his inauguration. He lingered, bedridden with infection, over the summer and died in September 1881. Greener, who had felt guarded optimism with a final review of the Whittaker case in the hands of President Garfield, was less certain about the views of the new president, Chester A. Arthur. During the wait, Greener reestablished a social life and family life with his wife and four young children in Washington.

Finally, in December, Swaim submitted his report to Secretary of War Robert Todd Lincoln, the slain president's son. It was a scorching denunciation of the environment at West Point, and it refuted the findings on all charges. More importantly, it concluded that only the superintendent of the US Military Academy had authority to call a court-martial; since this one had been called by President Hayes, it had operated outside the law and was declared void. While Secretary Lincoln studied the report for several months, he asked the US attorney general about the admissibility of the Whittaker letters used as evidence beyond handwriting analysis. They were ruled inadmissible.[32]

President Arthur took little time to decide. In March 1882, he ruled in agreement with Swaim and Lincoln that he would not approve the court-martial findings against Whittaker, citing especially the issue of material evidence that should not have been admitted. Still, US Military Academy officials held one remaining trump card. With the blessing of Secretary Lincoln, they exercised their right to discharge Whittaker on the basis of his academic deficiency stemming from the 1880 examination.[33] Whittaker was a free man, but he was no longer a cadet or a future officer.

Given his recent national renown, it was perhaps not surprising that Whittaker next took to the lecture circuit. His debut in Buffalo, New York, in 1882 met with a "small but appreciative audience," who listened as he recounted "the story of his grievances in a calm, dispassionate, logical, and interesting manner." A *Buffalo Commercial Advertiser* reporter concluded, "No one, unless it be a West Pointer, a Southerner, or an aristocrat, can listen to him without having his sympathy excited for the persecuted youth." Throughout the summer of 1882, Whittaker traveled to Atlanta, Baltimore, Philadelphia, Washington, DC, and elsewhere to tell his story. At a South Carolina appearance, the local paper echoed the surprise of many in the audience who found him to be "almost white" and "well educated."[34]

In time, Whittaker became a faculty member at Avery Normal Institute, a secondary and teacher preparatory school for black students in Charleston, South Carolina, and then at the South Carolina Agricultural and Mechanical Institute, a black land-grant college. Later, he was a teacher and principal at a high school in Oklahoma City. Much later, in 1995, he became a second lieutenant in the US Army. Sixty-four years after his death, President William Jefferson Clinton awarded Whittaker a posthumous commission, announcing, "We cannot undo history. But today, finally, we can pay tribute to a great American and we can acknowledge a great injustice."[35]

• • •

Still invigorated from the lengthy courtroom drama, Richard Greener decided to return to his longtime ambition of pursuing a life in law, literature, and oratory. Having already left the Howard Law Department, he now resigned from the US Treasury Department. Still open to taking a nice patronage job on the side, he hoped to earn enough for the comfortable support of his family in the meantime. This next chapter of his life started auspiciously with a new accolade. Monrovia College in Liberia awarded him an honorary Doctor of Laws (LLD) degree for "distinguished services rendered his race in literature and education."[36]

While Greener had never shied from controversy, the debates he had previously entered into were generally foreseeable polarizations about racial issues and/or partisan politics. Only on the subject of black migration had he dealt with splintering within his race or political party. Now, however, controversy was almost inescapable for a frequent lecturer and writer on topics that included race relations, education, politics, and international issues. As the Chinese Exclusion Act worked its way toward President Arthur's signature in 1882, Greener wrote a letter to the *New York Globe* in support of limiting Chinese immigration. Unlike African Americans, Greener asserted, the Chinese were an "alien class." Many, if not most, prominent blacks and black newspapers disagreed with him, viewing the exclusion of Chinese as bigotry that appeared all too familiar. Well-known black lawyer Augustus Straker, outspoken among those who disputed Greener's position, wrote, "The opponents of the Chinese are opponents of the negro. Human rights must not be based on color or condition."[37]

Greener must have known he would draw fire from fellow blacks with a lecture to the Bethel Literary and Historical Society of Washington, DC, titled "Mohammedanism vs. Christianity." In that talk he suggested that Islam might be better than Christianity for Africa's native blacks—much to the consternation of many of his black friends and associates. Later, he objected to a National Colored Convention planned by some prominent black men. Pessimistic about the possibility that any such meetings would result in positive change, he saw the national convention as the opportunistic work of a small group of big insiders—"men who have rarely shown interest in our race outside of retaining themselves in office." He determined that the race would be better off "if the negro could get rid of his black leaders and his white philanthropists." After all, what had they done for bright young black men like Whittaker and Flipper or for the black boys who could no longer study at the University of South Carolina? Greener undoubtedly was discouraged when he made the point that meetings of leaders rarely seemed to translate into action; he also made some long-term enemies among those black leaders.[38]

Fortunately, nobody seemed to dispute Greener's eloquence and intellect. He typically drew large audiences and kept them interested, even though his speeches often ran longer than an hour. If there were several speakers, he might speak first and leave almost no time for the others. Not all his speeches were about race or politics. A genuine man of letters, he spoke on a wide variety of topics, sometimes offering exhortations, as in a lecture called "Success as Duty," given at Bethel Church in New York City. His most common theme was past and future achievement among black Americans. He spoke at the Congregational Church in Washington, DC, on Benjamin Banneker, the self-taught black astronomer, mathematician, and surveyor. At the Philadelphia Musical Fund Hall, he extolled African American achievement in "The Educational, Industrial, Mechanical and Political Progress of the Colored People of the United States," arguing that prejudice would disappear as blacks worked hard and educated themselves. He joined with Frederick Douglass and others in oratory and writing concerning the preservation and strengthening of the endangered Civil Rights Act of 1875. The Supreme Court decision in 1883 to strike down the act, with its provisions for equal access to and use of public places and facilities, was an occasion for more Greener oratory, written opinion, and interviews. To a *New York Evening Post* reporter, Greener maintained that the decision was "no credit to the statesmanship, to say nothing of the legal learning, of the Supreme Court, knowing as they must what it cost to reach the point of equality we occupy at the present time."[39]

Throughout 1883 and 1884, Greener politicked and orated up and down the East Coast and beyond. Speaking in schools, churches, and public halls, he stumped for local liberal and black candidates and roused audiences to the cause of racial justice in North Carolina, Virginia, Washington, Philadelphia, Baltimore, New York, and Ohio. In 1884, he was the commencement speaker and guest of Booker T. Washington at Tuskegee Institute in Alabama. He visited relatives and friends on many stops, including his Andover and Harvard buddy, Horace Deming, now a busy lawyer and well-known Republican in Brooklyn. When the *North American Review* published a symposium issue on "The Future of the Negro," Greener's essay on the subject was in good company with pieces by Frederick Douglass, Joel Chandler Harris, two US senators, and others.[40]

Nevertheless, Greener's professional situation was far from ideal. He had built a fine reputation and extensive network of well-placed individuals, but his law practice continued to struggle for business. With his cousin, Isaiah Wears, and some black businessmen, he founded and became president of an insurance business, the National Benefit and Relief Association, which brought in some additional income. Still, he could barely keep up with the needs of a large family, travel, and an active social life among Washington's black elites. After his extensive Republican Party campaigning during the summer and fall of 1884 in eight states, he might have hoped for a lifeline in the form of a high-level government appointment. But that possibility disappeared with the November election of Democratic president Grover Cleveland.

Washington no longer seemed as promising for a black man of intellect and ability as it once had been. The Republicans had attempted some fusion with moderate white Democrats in the South but had still lost ground in the US Congress and in patronage jobs. Legalized racial discrimination, as indicated by the Supreme Court decision to strike down the Civil Rights Act,

Greener (*right, second from top*) in 1883, at thirty-nine years of age. Here he is de-
picted among African American leaders Frederick Douglass (*center*), Robert Brown
Elliott, Blanche K. Bruce, William Wells Brown, Rev. Richard Allen, J. H. Rainey,
E. D. Bassett, John Mercer Langston, P. B. S. Pinchback, and Henry Highland Garnet. Courtesy of Library of Congress.

was increasing. Perhaps nothing brought this home to Greener so much
as his application to the Washington, DC, Harvard Club. He and Robert
Terrell, a black cum laude graduate of Harvard in 1884, applied for membership at the same time. At a January 1885 meeting their memberships were
denied—for no other possible reason than their African American ancestry.

There was some negative reaction about the decision in the press, and two club members resigned: US representative John D. Long and US senator George Hoar, both of Massachusetts. A *Boston Daily Advertiser* editorial, charging that color was the only reason for the blackballing, fumed, "How a man can get through Harvard College and accumulate in the four years' stay so little sense that he could be guilty of such an act of stupidity as certain members of the Harvard Club at Washington have committed, is past the comprehension of the average intellect." Ironically, Greener had earlier been a speaker at a New York City Harvard Club dinner, where he drew loud cheers and applause when he praised Harvard's expectations that alumni would be "democratic in their aristocracy, catholic in their liberality, impartial in their judgment, and uncompromising in their convictions of duty."[41]

Greener's mounting frustrations finally erupted as a tirade against the Republican Party. In an open letter published via the Associated Press in June 1885, he attacked Republican leaders as "bosses" and charged that the party had been "inviting defeat for eight years by its arrant cowardice, truculency, and exultation of little men with big ambition, no heart and contempt for principles." He added, "The negro is not responsible for its blunders, timidity or consequent defeats." He had clearly decided that the party had left him and abandoned the cause of racial justice, and he didn't mind burning some bridges to let the party leadership know it. Greener and many other Republicans thought that party attempts to capture white southern voters and to build a more moderate base in general were at the root of election losses in 1884. Some, like black activist and well-known journalist T. Thomas Fortune, bolted from the party. Others, like former US senator and secretary of state Hamilton Fish, blamed the party. Greener, at least outwardly, was in the second category. He knew that with a Democratic president in the White House and influential Republicans stung by his insults, he had no foreseeable future in politically sensitive Washington, DC. Tired and testy, he freely commented on what he viewed as the capital's "fetid and vitiated political and social atmosphere." He badly needed a change of venue. For once, his timing would prove excellent.[42]

CHAPTER NINE

Monumental Plans

WILLIAM RUSSELL GRACE was accustomed to thinking big. He left his home in Ballylinan, Ireland, at age fourteen to travel to New York City. He returned two years later but soon traveled to Peru to work as a ship's chandler and then to build his own business. As a wealthy shipping magnate and committed philanthropist, he had nearly no political experience when he became the first Roman Catholic mayor of New York City in 1880. Few knew that when he was nominated, he was not a US citizen but had entered the country easily by being classified as a seaman. A quick naturalization by a friendly judge granted him citizenship shortly before his inauguration. Considering himself an independent Democrat, Grace managed some reform of Tammany Hall machine practices, but he did not run again in 1882. His reelection in 1884, haunted by the unusual naturalization that got him labeled the "alien candidate," was soon followed by two momentous events: the arrival in his city of 214 enormous crates that contained the Statue of Liberty, and the death of his hero, Ulysses S. Grant. Mayor Grace decided immediately that New York City should be the final resting place of the widely, if not unanimously, adored general and former president. And he was determined that there should be an appropriately colossal mausoleum. The mayor acted on that conviction more than immediately. A full week before Grant died, Grace wrote to Grant's son, Frederick, asking him to come to New York City to "confer" about a "site" in Central Park.[1]

There were other potential locations for the president's remains. West Point Cemetery at Grant's beloved US Military Academy and Arlington National Cemetery both seemed likely. But at neither of those could his widow Julia one day be buried by his side, something both Grants dearly wanted. General Philip Sheridan pleaded with Frederick Grant for burial at the Soldier's Home in Washington, DC, "in keeping with the grandeur of the character of the man whose remains are there left to repose." Other possibilities were St. Louis, Missouri, and Galena, Illinois, places Grant had lived prior to the Civil War. In New York City, he and Mrs. Grant had settled in a brownstone on the Upper East Side in 1881. On the day of Grant's death, Mayor Grace hurriedly telegrammed and then dispatched a representative to the Grant family to offer land set aside in one of the city parks for burial. Frederick replied by telegram: "Mother takes Riverside; temporary tomb had better be at the same place."[2]

Grace gathered a committee of mostly wealthy and/or influential New Yorkers, and, less than a week after Grant's death, brought its eighty-five initial members together to launch the Grant Monument Association (GMA). He invited Richard Greener to join the group and act as its secretary at that first meeting. Undoubtedly, he had been informed that Greener had known Grant, having met him first in 1868, when Grant visited Harvard, and again on several occasions when Greener appeared with delegations to the White House arguing for civil-rights legislation. Greener was the only black member in a group that included familiar names like John Jacob Astor, Alonzo Cornell, Cornelius Vanderbilt II, John P. Morgan, Hamilton Fish, Charles and William Steinway, Joseph Pulitzer, Arthur Dodge, and Chester A. Arthur. At the first meeting, the group decided on a nineteen-member executive committee for immediate work, a nine-member committee on organization, and a much larger and national general committee. They voted for Chester A. Arthur to be chairman and Greener secretary of the Grant Monument Committee (later, the Grant Monument Association), and they agreed on the purpose of building "a national monument in the City of New York worthy of the illustrious dead soldier and patriot and worthy of the city itself." Later, the group would incorporate with thirty-three trustees, including Greener. Erect and slender, with closely clipped hair, moustache, and beard, he fit in well with successful New York businessmen.[3]

Grant's funeral, held in New York City on August 8, 1885, testified to his immense popularity at home and abroad. Sixty thousand marchers, most of whom had fought in military campaigns, processed by an estimated 1 million spectators as they accompanied the coffin to Riverside Drive and 122nd Street, where it would rest in a brick vault until the monument was erected. By this time, Greener was already up to his elbows in setting up the association office at 146 Broadway, drafting fundraising materials, managing correspondence, and interacting with committee members. Always scrambling for personal income, in December he began supplementing his GMA salary with a second job, an appointment by Mayor Grace as an examiner for the New York City Civil Service Board.[4]

• • •

Initially, Greener's wife and children did not move to New York with him. Genevieve Greener's extended family in Washington was still needed to help with seven-year-old son Russell Lowell and daughters Mary Louise, Belle Marian, and Ethel Alice, ranging from four to eight years old. A fourth daughter, Theodora Genevieve, would be born in February 1886. Greener also wanted time to clear some debts, a goal facilitated by Genevieve and the children living with her mother. Once that was done, with his $200 monthly income (about $5,000 in today's dollars), the family might live somewhat comfortably in New York City. His insurance-company venture had begun to falter, although it still advertised into late 1886, and he now closed down his Washington law practice. He was optimistic about the future and pleased to report to Isaiah Wears that he was finally in work that was "about something big enough for me to handle."[5]

Black residents of New York City at the time typically lived in Brooklyn or upper Manhattan. Greener settled into rental lodging in a house in the small village of Sea Cliff on Long Island. As in other eastern cities, New York's black citizens were stratified into upper-class elites, generally from old families, and working-class strugglers. Societies, churches, and education were important to the socially prominent, and their wealth was more comfortable than vast. When Greener arrived, one of the most notable New York black elites was his former student and sometime nemesis, T. McCants Stewart, a well-known Brooklyn lawyer and Democratic Party leader who was the second African American to be appointed to the Brooklyn Board of Education. Although state legislation of 1873 and 1881 forbade racial discrimination in New York public accommodations, transportation, and amenities, many businesses managed to discriminate through giving black citizens poor service or offering them substandard facilities. Public schools in Manhattan theoretically made no distinction between black and white students, and separate schools for black students were abolished in 1884. However, in practice, as historian Seth Scheiner noted in 1965, "Negro children were usually limited to a few schoolhouses that were predominantly Negro."[6]

The GMA set its fund-raising goal at 1 million dollars, with $100,000 goals along the way. The first of those milestones was met in November 1885, and

Greener was relieved when it was reached just in time. Shortly after that, he was delighted to write to Isaiah Wears that he had paid off a large portion of his debts and would be financially clear by early 1886. He also reported thoroughly enjoying his new work: "Never have I felt more hopeful, and at no time have I done harder or more consecutive business work; and yet I seem to thrive on it."[7]

Greener wrote fund-raising appeals to be placed in newspapers throughout the country, posted in church bulletins, circulated through offices, and read at club meetings. A letter went to consular officers in foreign countries who might be able to appeal to Americans living abroad. Black organizations, churches, and individuals responded well to targeted requests. However, there was substantial resentment among individuals who viewed New York as an inappropriate location for Grant's final resting place or who felt that the City of New York and its wealthy citizens should pay for the monument themselves. The *Evening Register* of South Bend, Indiana, published a letter sent to Greener that stated, "The feeling is pretty general in the West that as the Empire State secured the remains of General Grant over the protest of nine-tenths of the United States, she is duty bound to place a monument over the grave of the grand old commander at her own expense." An editorial in the *Clay County Enterprise* of Brazil, Indiana, advised that "not a dollar of help be sent to the millionaire city from Indiana."[8]

Enthusiasm for honoring Grant's legacy was the largest asset to Greener's fund-raising work, but it was also the largest impediment. While it enabled the project to quickly launch with impressive sums from deep New Yorker pockets, it also inspired schemes by the dozen from citizens who wanted to help by contributing their own artwork to be sold, their own poems to be read, or their own benefit performances to be held. Greener spent many hours dealing with correspondents and visitors whose ideas ranged from possible to preposterous. Editors of a weekly journal, the *Judge,* proposed a contest for competitors to list all the words made from the question, "Who will be our next President?" The winners, the journal, and the Grant Monument fund would share the proceeds from entry fees. A clock builder and a puzzle maker wanted investment money in exchange for a share of their eventual sales.[9] Among the ideas that did get implemented were a benefit vocal concert at Madison Square Garden amphitheater, a benefit fair at the Metropolitan Opera House, collection boxes at the New York state capitol in Albany, and the sale of souvenir items from Grant's funeral.

Nationwide excitement for the fallen hero also bred competition from other cities for contributions to their own local Grant memorial efforts. Chicago started a committee of its well-heeled citizens to plan a Grant sculpture near Lake Michigan; Ft. Leavenworth, Kansas, formed a committee for a local Grant monument; Leland Stanford's generous contribution to a Grant monument effort in San Francisco led him to refuse an appeal from his New York friends; and Cleveland, Ohio, citizens raised money for a monument to President Garfield. Curiously, a man from Atlanta requested the GMA donor list for use in his fund-raising for a monument to the former vice president of the Confederate States of America. Closer to home, the City of Brooklyn was raising funds for a "Soldiers' and Sailors' Monument," which would incorporate figures of Lincoln and Grant.[10] Additionally, benevolent citizens everywhere were being asked to contribute to nationwide efforts to aid victims of the 1886 earthquake in Charleston, South Carolina, and the 1889 flood in Johnstown, Pennsylvania.

Although contributions slowed after the early months of GMA work, Greener continued to be heartened by small victories. Donations arrived from Paris, Amsterdam, and Hamburg, indicating the reach of Grant's popularity. US representative Abraham Dowdney of New York introduced a bill for a contribution of $250,000 to the monument through the US Department of War. Greener maintained that if it passed, the GMA could raise the remainder needed "in a few months," and he thought that a congressional contribution would "put at rest the objection that a mausoleum at Riverside was simply a local monument." At the same time, a US Senate bill proposed allocating $250,000 for a Grant monument in Washington, DC.[11]

When he wasn't dealing with fund-raising, Greener was addressing design and siting issues for the future monument. GMA representatives felt they had selected a "manifestly commanding" part of Riverside Park, on high ground at 122nd Street. Some local architects and landscapers, however, wrote to argue for a site farther to the east. Residents began volunteering design ideas by mail to GMA offices; these were time-consuming to deal with, as they generally required discussion and thoughtful written responses. Greener had been able to hire some clerical staff, but that assistance was reduced in late 1886 as a cost-saving measure.[12]

• • •

With his Civil Service Commission job and his GMA work, Greener had nearly no time to carry on his activities on behalf of his race or his political pursuits. He did try to continue writing, and in 1886 he authored an article that appeared in the *Southwestern Christian Advocate*. In it, he addressed the issue of discrimination within his race, particularly the matter of "pure blood" and "mixed blood" African Americans. While he maintained that whites were more prejudiced against those with darker skin, he pleaded for unity within and among all "colored people" to help in steadily overcoming this prejudice. It is possible that Greener's thoughts on this issue had been sparked by his own treatment by some fellow blacks skeptical of his commitment to the race because of his light skin and his professional associations with whites. An article in a black newspaper, the *Christian Advocate*, noted that Greener thought some blacks unnecessarily had "a chip on their shoulder" and advised that "if the professor's face were several shades darker, or [if he] were to be observant, he would soon learn that the chip theory is not necessary."[13]

Editors of the *Washington Bee* had frequently criticized Greener for being friendly with white politicians of influence while speaking out for the black race in public lectures and published writing. One article warned readers that he "wants to run with the hounds and hide with the hare." In fact, Greener did enjoy many notable white friends and companions in New York, particularly at Harvard alumni dinners at posh restaurants, where he might catch up with his old roommate Horace Deming and chat over fine wines with Harvard faculty and graduates.[14]

While Greener's writing and speaking on race issues became infrequent after his move to New York, his political work ceased altogether. His disillusion with the Republican Party as it pulled away from active support of black Americans was matched by his knowledge of the racist activities of southern Democrats. Once an eager campaigner for Republican candidates, he took no active part in the local or national election races of 1886 or 1888.

Greener managed to spend holidays and vacations in Washington, and he found himself generally happy with his growing family. All the children seemed healthy and bright, and Greener boasted that, at seven years old, Russell Lowell wrote him letters "worthy of a boy of twelve." Sadly, another son, Charles Woodman, born in the summer of 1887, died at three months old. Shortly afterward, during Christmas vacation in Washington, daughter Theodora Genevieve, not quite two years old, was christened at the Fifteenth Street Presbyterian Church by the Greeners' good friend, Rev. Francis Grimké. At the end of that holiday season, Genevieve and the five children moved to New York City.[15]

The Greener family's initial residence was near Columbus Circle, only a few years prior to the arrival of its Columbus statue in 1892 and just a block from the southwestern corner of Central Park. Within a year they would move six blocks farther west and later to West 99th Street. With four of the five Greener children now in school, Genevieve had more time to meet neighbors and begin to make some friends. In neighborhoods that were not noted for black residents, many of these friends likely would have been white, and they may have considered the light-skinned Greener family as more multinational than black. Similarly, Greener's GMA associates were white businessmen, artists and architects, and city government employees. Greener occupied a rare position. In 1890 black residents of New York City comprised only 1.4 percent of the total population, and not quite 2 percent of those who were working were classified as "professionals." Greener joined the Commonwealth Club of New York, a group of influential white New Yorkers that had been organized by Deming, his old friend from Andover.[16] More than ever, Greener was working in the divide between black and white. He was committed to working for black civil rights through speaking, writing, and political involvement. But, he also badly wanted to help see the Grant Monument through to completion, which, along with his civil-service job and other activities, had placed him strictly among white friends and colleagues.

He knew there was talk. With his light skin and white friends, he was open to criticism from the black press and black activists that he was, at best, being too cozy with whites and, at worst, trying to pass for white. He wondered why Francis Grimké and his wife, race activist and talented teacher Charlotte Forten Grimké, had visited New York but not found time to see the Greener family. He wrote Grimké that he would have been especially glad to see him "because of some absurd and silly talk which I fear has caused some of my good friends not to call on me." In the same letter, he was careful to mention mutual black friends and concerns, and to emphasize that his work for the Grant legacy, as well as some writing underway, kept him devoted to purposes "not unconnected with the race."[17]

Greener's life became fuller than ever when he began evening tutoring of private students preparing for college. Financial worries continued to plague him, especially after he invested in a business venture and, as he explained to his cousin Isaiah Wears, "lost a little sum." He shared that he was "chagrined" by his inability to manage his finances adequately and be-

Richard T. Greener, circa 1890, at about age forty-six.
Courtesy of Harvard University Archives.

wildered that "my house expenses come right up to my income, no matter what that is." His "whole life" seemed to him "one of continuous struggle, aspiration, some success, but very little money." He noted that he and
Genevieve spent any free time at home rather than socializing, although he
did sometimes attend local ward meetings of the Republican Club. Finances
got even tighter in the fall of 1888, when his mother, Mary Ann Greener,
died in Cambridge. Inexplicably, there is no evidence that she ever met her
son's wife or children. Greener traveled to Boston to arrange transfer of her
body to New York for burial. Those costs prompted Genevieve to approach
Wears for a loan without her husband's knowledge, an act that infuriated
Greener. However, he knew there was no alternative way to deal with new
expenses. As he had done in the past, he accepted Wears's loan but told
his cousin that, had he had known about his wife's request, he would have

vetoed the idea. Indicating marital friction, he admitted that such oppo-
sition to his wife's intentions, however, would not "ordinarily amount to
much."[18]

. . .

By 1888, with far from enough funds raised, the trustees of the GMA decided it was time to get a design in hand for exactly how the monument
would look. They announced a competition and ultimately received sixty-
five design submissions from throughout the United States and Europe. A
panel of judges narrowed the field down to five designs that they proposed
for cash prizes and final review by the GMA executive committee. When
that committee found none of the five suitable, they gave the cash prizes
but reopened the design competition. This time they invited only five distinguished architects from New York City and Philadelphia and gave them
much tighter guidelines, including a five-month submission deadline and a
maximum project cost of $500,000. The architect selected in late 1890 was
John H. Duncan, whose submission called for a neoclassical design that
used granite from Maine, marble from Massachusetts and Italy, and stained
glass from Tiffany & Co. Duncan had been selected about a year earlier
for the design of the triumphal arch that became Brooklyn's Soldiers' and
Sailors' Monument. His design for Grant's tomb included elements of burial
memorials of great historic leaders, such as Les Invalides in Paris and the
tomb of Emperor Hadrian in Rome.[19]

Just after Duncan's selection, the idea of unburying Grant to rebury him
somewhere other than New York surfaced in the press and elsewhere. US
representative Charles O'Neill of Pennsylvania proposed a resolution that
"Congress desires the removal of the remains of Ulysses S. Grant. . . . and
their interment in Arlington National Cemetery." The ensuing debate was
mostly ridiculous and only occasionally sublime. The New York delegation
was particularly incensed, with Representative Roswell Pettibone Flower
leading the charge: "This is a revolting precedent. . . .Why not ask that
the bones of Franklin Pierce, Andrew Johnson, and all the rest of our ex-
Presidents and heroes be brought here in order to strengthen the present
boom in real estate?" New York representative John Raines added, "You
cannot break into a graveyard with a joint resolution of Congress [laughter
and applause]. . . . It is a ghastly, and I had almost said a ghostly, imperti-
nence." A letter from GMA officers, including Grace and Greener, read into

the *Congressional Record*, reiterated that the Riverside Park site for Grant's remains was "the spot approved of by him, dedicated by the City of New York, and accepted by his family." Congress soon after adjourned for the Christmas recess, and the issue of the final resting place was finally put to rest.[20]

The initial fund-raising goal had been pared down, and the deadline for completion had been extended. Greener, who had lost his municipal civil service job when a new Democratic mayor took office in 1889, was able to devote more time to GMA activities. He was optimistic about fund-raising prospects once the design was publicized and talk of a different burial location was squashed. "There is not the least doubt that we shall have whatever money we need as soon as we can go to the people with our design," he claimed. Although less than half the necessary $500,000 was in hand, Duncan's design inspired the GMA to move forward with a groundbreaking ceremony in the spring of 1891 and the beginning of work on the foundation. Ten thousand people attended the groundbreaking, accompanied by salutes from Navy ships on the Hudson River, military formations, songs, prayers, and oratory. Brigadier General Horace Porter, vice president of the Pullman Company and former Union Army aide-de-camp to General Grant, fulfilled the "orator of the day" role with a nearly one-hour speech. A week later, Grace was able to announce that another $50,000 had been raised for the monument fund.[21]

The GMA members, and especially the executive committee, had long represented a fragile balance of political sentiments and struggles for influence. In particular, representatives of the Grand Army of the Republic (GAR) wanted more influence than they were getting while Mayor Grace presided over the group. Eventually, their faction managed to vote in two new members of the executive committee and tip the balance toward the Democrats and the GAR. Exasperated at the maneuvers used to get the new members voted in, Mayor Grace resigned from the association in November 1891. Soon, association vice president Hamilton Fish also resigned. Several others who supported Grace followed suit. Greener now found himself vulnerable amid calls by newly influential members for all association work to be voluntary. He was able to argue for a delay in the termination of his secretarial salary, but only until February 1892. It was little consolation that, in announcing Greener's resignation soon after his paycheck ceased, the black weekly *New York Age* noted Greener as "one of the most eloquent

Afro-Americans . . . and one of the best critical scholars the race has produced."[22]

The new association president was the expansive orator of the groundbreaking, Brigadier General Porter. He immediately attacked the job with
the determination he had brought to the Battle of Chickamauga and the
Battle of the Wilderness. Following central-office cost-cutting, he enlarged
the group of GMA trustees, including familiar names like Andrew Carnegie, Augustus Juilliard, Elihu Root, and Charles Tiffany. Most importantly,
he figured out a way to actively involve thousands of workers throughout
the city by developing a committee system that reached into "all the mer-
cantile and commercial business interests and all the professions and trades
in our city." Noting that the time for "piecemeal" approaches was past, he
explained, "Each one is separate and distinct from the others, and if each
will organize an auxiliary committee to assist in reaching every firm and individual in its particular branch, there will be no working at cross purposes
. . . and the result will be rapidly reached." Porter and others at the GMA held
scores of meetings with representatives of hundreds of business and trade
groups to urge them to appoint a committee chair and committee members
who would be responsible for each group's contributions. Among the groups
tapped in this way were millinery workers, pharmacists, perfumers, tele-
graph operators, electricians, gold pen manufacturers, diamond importers,
insurance agents, stevedores, opticians, produce sellers, electricians, and
lawyers. Representatives of each group stayed closely in touch with GMA
representatives through depositing contributions, receiving printed materials, and reporting contributor names and numbers.[23]

An additional boost for fund-raising occurred on the seventieth anniversary of Grant's birthday, April 27, 1892, when the monument cornerstone was
laid. At the ceremony, tens of thousands of people looked on as President
Benjamin Harrison held a gold trowel to the task. By June, GMA president
Porter was able to announce the receipt of $350,700 in new cash and sub-
scriptions. Greener would remain on the GMA board of trustees throughout his life. At the dedication of the completed monument in 1897, however,
while General Porter was "at pains to mention everybody who contributed
to the success of the enterprise," he "ignored the African American population" in general and "the splendid and enduring work" of Greener in
particular.[24]

CHAPTER TEN

Off White

ICHARD GREENER WOULD SOON refer to his years with the Grant Monument Association as a period when he "had disappeared beneath the waters." He had spent only limited time advocating for his race in print or in speech during those years, but he still longed to be viewed as a (or perhaps "the") prominent nationwide voice in those arenas. In the meantime, surviving by stringing together tutoring stints and small legal assignments quickly proved nearly impossible. Greener's financial situation as the head of a household that now included five children (ages six to fifteen) was so gloomy that even friends of friends—people he'd never met—became concerned. One of those, Ellen Collins, wrote to her friend Booker T. Washington. Although she did not personally know Greener, she was quick to note, "I understand he looks almost white, his wife also." That reminder likely did not impress Washington, who was already familiar with Greener. She also mentioned his Harvard education, his profession as a lawyer, and his current state of being "hard pressed for a living." Perhaps Washington's Tuskegee Institute might "happen to need more workers"?[1]

Although there is no evidence that Washington gave the query much thought, nearly two years later he did ask his associate Thomas J. Calloway about Greener and, given Calloway's reply, probably about rumors of Genevieve Greener passing as white. Calloway replied that Mrs. Greener "is colored and never passed for anything else while here [in Washington, DC]. It is understood here that she associates only with whites in New York. They are poor and in very straightened circumstances."[2]

That nothing much came of job-seeking activities by and for Greener was indicative of a confluence of changes in political winds, race relations, and economic realities. Timing, of course, rarely seemed to be on Greener's side. Shortly after he left the Grant Monument position, the Panic of 1893 ushered in a severe depression that affected employment in most sectors for at least four years. Greener's chances of a federal patronage appointment would have been rosiest when Benjamin Harrison took office in 1889 and began naming new postmasters, clerks, diplomats, and others. Harrison, who had served as a colonel in the Union army, was committed to the Republican agenda in general and to expanding rights for African Americans in particular. Presidential historian George Sinkler concluded, "Harrison exerted greater leadership in matters of race, no matter how unsuccessful, than any of the post-Reconstruction presidents." He repeatedly proposed federal funding for black education and federal voting rights enforcement for African Americans who were being subjected to all manner of racist rejection and intimidation at the polls. But he was repeatedly rebuffed by the US Congress in his attempts to "secure for all our people a free exercise of the right of suffrage and every other civil right under the Constitution and laws." By the time Greener left the GMA, it was too late to tap the president for any appointment. Harrison was winding up his first—and only—term in office with substantially less popularity than he'd had at the outset.[3]

Grover Cleveland, who returned to the White House in 1893 as the only president to serve two nonconsecutive terms, was a highly unlikely source of patronage for Greener or other liberal Republicans. A New Jersey native and then New York resident, he had sidestepped Civil War service by hiring a Polish immigrant to take his place in the Union army. As president, he was committed to reforming civil service in the direction of merit appointments rather than political rewards, and he had no use for the idea of federal protection of African American voting rights. As if to underscore that message, he appointed white supremacist Hoke Smith of Georgia as his Secretary of Interior. The national depression and subsequent strikes that marked his second administration did, however, help to assure that he would be the only Democratic president in a stream of Republicans that started with Abraham Lincoln and ended with the election of Woodrow Wilson.[4]

• • •

While in New York, surrounded by white notables guiding the GMA and by white colleagues at the city's Civil Service Board and in state Republican politics, Greener had seen his reputation as an activist for his race wane substantially. He now seemed part of an old guard, as many of those with whom he had been identified were aging. The most celebrated of the group, Frederick Douglass, would die in early 1896. The younger generation had begun to attract attention when Booker T. Washington, the forceful founder of Tuskegee Institute in Alabama, catapulted to national celebrity with a speech in Atlanta in 1895. Eventually dubbed the Atlanta Compromise Address, it did not support the necessity of desegregation or black civil rights but emphasized the idea of individual black responsibility for hard work and learning as a route to economic advancement. By advising blacks that "we shall prosper in proportion as we learn to dignify and glorify common labor," Washington took a tack that would divide African American opinion for many years. Historians later generally agreed with Philip Foner and Robert Branham, who suggested that the Washington perspective "was welcomed with relief by many whites as evidence of black acceptance of the order of white supremacy and an indefinite deferral of full-citizenship rights." Regardless of his "submissive philosophy," Washington was often viewed as the successor to Douglass in terms of prominence.[5]

Historian C. Vann Woodward pointed to the last decade of the nineteenth century as the period that sealed the end of the possibility of racial justice and the dominance of racial prejudice for many decades to come. According to him, three realities of the time supported Jim Crow segregation, lynchings, voter disfranchisement, and Ku Klux Klan terrorism: "the complacency of a long-critical North, the propaganda of reconciliation, and the resigned compliance of the Negro." Black citizens found themselves in two different camps: those attracted to the idea of a more "humble and menial role," as outlined by Booker T. Washington, and those committed to the demand for equal rights.[6]

How Greener would fit into the changing landscape of activism was an open question. His professional network was now largely white, and any well-paid work he might find suited to his education and intellect was likely to keep him in a largely white sphere. Yet, his personal aspirations still leaned firmly toward black activism through writing and speaking. T. Thomas Fortune, editor of the highly regarded black newspaper, the *New York Age*, wondered why Greener, "one of the most eloquent African Americans in the country," with a record of "effective campaign work for the Republican party," had been unable to secure a government job that amounted to "more than a clerkship." However, historian Rayford Logan found that in the federal government "an infinitesimal number held the top 'Negro jobs,'" such as "register of the treasury, recorder of deeds, minister to Haiti and minister to Liberia." Instead, "most were in the menial and custodial categories, but a few held clerical jobs." As an African American out of work, Greener faced a decidedly uphill struggle.[7]

Fortune also commented on Greener's withdrawal from race-related activities while in New York and speculated that it stemmed from either his failure to secure plum appointments or his sense that "the race had failed to sustain him as it should have done." Others, however, felt Greener had failed to sustain his race. Such controversies later broke into print in black newspapers when Greener's former University of South Carolina student, T. McCants Stewart, attacked Greener's limited recent Republican political work and sparse race activism in an article published in the *New York Age.* Greener's lengthy reply, published in the *Indianapolis Freeman,* was angry enough to be titled "T. M'Cants Stewart Flayed." He not only defended his actions but condemned Stewart, concluding that his attacks were "despicable, worthy only of a cowardly nature. . . . His last utterance is the subterfuge of a weak mind and a cowardly spirit, attempting to hide guilt and rehabilitate his wretched past by slinging mud at me."[8]

Regardless of his attempts to set the record straight, some of Greener's fellow blacks persistently accused him of becoming too friendly with New York whites, deserting the Republican political cause, and even trying to pass as white. Hoping to correct such rumors once and for all, Greener eventually wrote to powerful Cleveland African American businessman and politician George A. Myers.

> I am free to challenge any man to produce an instance, *one,* where during my residence in New York I ever failed to act, or use my influence, for the race. Every negro on the Grant General Com[mittee] was put there by me alone. Everyone invited to take part in the public affairs connected with the Monument, breaking ground, laying corner stone, etc., was designated by me. . . . True, I did not take much part in public meetings because I had hard work to attend to and besides, was connected from 1885 to 1890 with the Civil Service Board which forbade an active participation in politics. If I had been a democrat, why was I not for Cleveland in '92, a man I knew personally and favorably . . . ? But I was for Harrison and took part and went down with the party as I did in 1884.[9]

Although Greener's protest may have seemed overly strident to Myers, the two men soon forged an agreeable relationship in working toward the presidential election of William McKinley.

• • •

Having moved to a predominantly white New York City neighborhood near the upper west end of Central Park, Greener managed to cobble together a small law practice and some business ventures. Still committed to race issues and their political underpinnings, he soon busily involved himself in various clubs, meetings, and speaking engagements. During the five years following his work on the Grant Monument, he presided over an anti-lynching meeting in Providence, Rhode Island; lectured at the Washington, DC, Bethel Literary Society; became vice president of the Riverside Republican Club; served with a group of prominent New Yorkers on the Committee of Thirty, formed to reorganize and rejuvenate the city's Republican Party; undertook the vice presidency of the northeast section of the National Federation of Colored Men; and headed planning for a thirty-year memorial of Abraham Lincoln's death to be held at Cooper Union. He served as an alternate to the New York Republican State Convention of 1894, and he continued active involvement in the American Missionary Association, the New York Alumni Association of Phillips Academy, Andover, and the board of trustees of the Grant Monument Association.[10]

Greener's writing—mostly of lectures and articles—was far more prolific than its publication during the years following his resignation as GMA secretary. However, several of his articles did appear in the *Cleveland Gazette,* the *Indianapolis Freeman,* and the *New York Herald.* In 1894 he sent an upbeat letter to his Philadelphia cousin, Isaiah Wears, detailing his plans for several more writing projects and reporting happily that his son Russell Lowell, called Lowell, was a freshman at the College of the City of New York, while his daughter Mary Louise was attending the Girls' Normal School in New York City. His daughter Belle Marian was expected to attend Teachers' College the following year.[11]

A major breakthrough in Greener's literary career finally occurred with the publication of his eloquent and creative approach to race relations, "The White Problem." Published in the national monthly journal, *Lend a Hand: A Record of Progress,* in May 1894, the essay drew widespread attention and applause. As scholar Martha Nussbaum concluded more than a century later, it expertly managed "to turn around and study as pathology what white culture has taken for its own normalcy and superiority. Greener pillories the tendency to see white behavior as unproblematic and what deviates from those customs as 'a problem.'"[12]

Greener deftly proclaimed that white bigotry, blaming, superiority, and self-interest were at the root of problematic race relations—thus reversing widely held assumptions among whites that problems stemmed from various deficiencies within those of other races. He marched dozens of accomplished and celebrated black citizens across the thirteen pages of his article, cataloging their achievements in the Revolutionary War, the War of 1812, and the Civil War, as well as in science, literature, music, and politics. He noted that a "difficulty with the white problem is the universal belief that somehow the Negro race began its career with President Lincoln's proclamation." As evidence, he offered black citizens active well before the Civil War, including 1770 Boston Massacre hero Crispus Attucks; Benjamin Banneker, who calculated information for the only almanacs printed in the mid-Atlantic states in the late eighteenth century; early nineteenth-century Baptist leader Thomas Paul; Washington, DC, businessman Isaac Carey; and coeditors of the first black newspaper Samuel E. Cornish and John Russwurm. Pointing especially to black service in wartime, Greener insisted, "No sneer of race, no assumption of superiority, no incrusted prejudice will ever obscure this record, much less obliterate it, and while it stands, it is the Negro's passport to every right and privilege of every other American."[13]

To dispel any notion that only benevolent white leaders were responsible for eventually bestowing emancipation and some civil rights on black citizens, he reminded his readers that there was "nothing which tended to unshackle the slave or remove the clogs from the free colored man, in which he was not the foremost, active, intelligent participant, never a mere recipient." Among later exemplary black leaders, he named Booker T. Washington, W. E. B. Du Bois, educator and classical scholar William S. Scarborough, college founder Joseph C. Price, and others, maintaining that these and all other members of his race considered themselves American citizens first and black citizens second. In a final twist, he concluded that, unlike the problematic white citizens, black citizens were actually saved by their race "from illiberal prejudices, from over-weening race-pride, from utter disregard of other races' rights, feelings, and privileges, and from intellectual narrowness and bigotry."[14]

As Greener had undoubtedly hoped, the article made a large splash. A headline in the *Cleveland Gazette* announced, "The White Problem: Professor Richard T. Greener's Splendid Effort Attracting Much Attention." Later, the same paper reprinted the essay in full. Booker T. Washington was among those who wrote approving notes to the author. Greener responded immediately, clearly wanting Washington to understand that his commitment to racial activism had never truly diminished: "I have never been idle, in this line, although I have not had my say over my own signature. . . . perhaps it may be found in time that my pen has not been idle nor my influence lost." He also told Washington of his intentions for further publication. Perhaps hoping to build more outlets for his work, he asked Washington to consider enlarging his Tuskegee Institute paper to become "a vehicle of news, for the race as well as Tuskegee."[15]

As always, the indefatigable Greener continued to have many irons in the fire, although few of them were lucrative or long lived. He was still susceptible to the siren call of investment in supposedly good business deals, and word of such possibilities abounded in New York City. At one point, he became the president of the Dominion Pulverizer Company, which was co-owner of a rock crusher called the Luckenbach Pulverizer. However, there is no evidence he profited by it. With four white associates, he helped organize and then became president of the General Development Company, a gold-mining operation in Nova Scotia. That, too, seems not to have prospered in the long run. In 1895 he applied for the position of assistant district attorney for the City and County of New York at a salary of $7,500, but he noted law practice and Republican political campaign work as his only endeavors since working for the Grant Monument Association. He later withdrew his application, possibly due to his busy political involvements and his desire to broaden his racial activism.[16]

After attending the first National Conference of Colored Women of America in Boston in 1895, Greener participated in the National Convention of Colored Men in Detroit. D. Augustus Straker, a friend of Greener's who had served in the South Carolina legislature during the closing years of Reconstruction, was the key conference organizer, but Greener became "the pivotal leader of the meeting." He took on responsibility for securing the group's full inclusion of black women as voting delegates, and, perhaps even more important, he successfully worked to assure that the primary purpose of the conference was to shape the demand for full rights and just treatment for black people, rather than encourage the push for individual economic self-help and betterment as set forth by Booker T. Washington. The final conference address, drafted by Greener to the US Congress, left no room for doubt about what he considered to be necessary action, stating, "We do not acquiesce in the dictum that we must trust to time and to the pleasure or disposition of our enemies to grant rights." It proclaimed "the opening of a militant period of our race in this country." Greener was applauded in the press as "the leading spirit of the present Conference of Colored Men, at Detroit, Mich., where a National Federation was organized."[17]

• • •

Recognizing that he needed to continually fend off rumors of his political desertion of black causes and his overly eager relations with whites, Greener was careful to keep in touch with influential black friends and acquaintances. These included lawyer and diplomat Archibald Grimké, former University of South Carolina student and noted Republican Whitefield McKinlay, journalist and historian John Edward Bruce, and others. Perhaps hoping for tighter ties to the black establishment, he asked Grimké to use his influence at Lincoln University to help him obtain an honorary Masters of Arts degree at that institution at the 1896 commencement exercises. In a later letter seeking endorsement from Booker T. Washington for a federal appointment, he was careful to remind Washington that "in each National [Republican] campaign from 1872 until and including 1896, with the exception only of 1888, I have been an active worker. . . . In the last campaign, as in 1892, I went in and earned my spurs anew."[18]

Greener got his chance to move beyond defending himself to doubters when he was appointed by the National Republican Committee as assistant manager of the Colored Bureau for the presidential campaign of William McKinley. He would operate out of the Western Colored Bureau office in Chicago. Even the *Washington Bee,* the weekly that enjoyed stinging blacks who didn't seem black enough, applauded him in this position as "one of the most gifted speakers in this country and a man of ability." While Greener had some responsibility for general strategy, correspondence, and arrangements, it was clear to Republican National Chairman Marcus Hanna that his oratorical skill would be most helpful. Hanna not only created a new presidential campaign funding approach by tapping businesses and wealthy businessmen, he also understood political strategy. Crowds were more likely to be roused by Greener and other top orators than by McKinley himself, who possessed a less stirring podium voice. This was particularly important in light of the highly regarded rhetorical agility of Democratic nominee William Jennings Bryan.[19]

Soon Greener was working out of an office in Chicago and addressing crowds in Missouri, Indiana, Illinois, Kentucky, and Tennessee. At some events, he spoke to white audiences as well as black. At a county fair in Rockford, Illinois, he estimated that the twelve thousand who attended his speech were "all white, but about 20 colored." He told Wears, "My success in speaking has been good. I am now booked for the next four weeks ahead." Although he was "up to the ears" in work, he claimed to be in high health and spirits and to "enjoy the western life and ways."[20] The nearly four months he spent in the Midwest were some of the best of his life.

It was not surprising that McKinley won handily with 271 of the 447 electoral votes. The Democrats had not managed to overcome the depression that had intensified on President Cleveland's watch, and the party split between traditional Democrats and its candidate's populist wing. William Jennings Bryan's moralistic lectures and revivalist style were not for everyone, while Hanna seemed to come up with a strategy for everyone. He raised and spent record amounts of money, ushering in political-campaign priorities that would continue into the next two centuries.[21]

Back in Washington, Greener happily joined the whirlwind of postelection fervor that soon included the inaugural ceremonies and parade, the "colored balls and receptions," and side trips to Baltimore and Mt. Vernon. "I began to forget what I came for," he told his friend, Lewis Latimer, the noted black engineer and inventor. What he came for was the vigorous job seeking that marked the start of every new presidential administration but became especially frenzied when there was a switch in executive-branch political parties. By his own estimation, the competition was fierce—"about fifty candidates for every office held by a colored man, or likely to be held or which has been held."[22] The job-seeking activity meant trolling throughout various federal offices for endorsements from influential individuals, then standing in line to make appointments or even meet with elected officials and staffers who controlled patronage decisions, and finally waiting and more waiting.

Greener actually enjoyed the hunt and considered himself particularly eligible for a diplomatic appointment to Haiti or for the position of District of Columbia recorder of deeds. In his favor was his record of campaign work and President McKinley's positive attitude toward black voting and black opportunity. As one historian noted, McKinley would build an "extremely generous patronage record for blacks." Although Greener didn't view his prospects a "lead pipe cinch" for either of the spots he had in mind, he told Latimer, "My line is in, however, and with some bait on it, whether enough to catch a fish, Heaven only knows." Eager for an endorsement from

Washington, who had quickly become the black leader with the most influence among whites, Greener appealed to him twice for "my first draft
on our friendship since 1884." First, he asked Washington for "a letter addressed to the President, stating how long you have known me, and what
your opinion is of my character, fitness and training." A week later, he added
"I should take it as a favor, should you see the President, to say a good word
for me."[23]

A diplomatic post began to look better and better to Greener for a number of reasons. His marriage was faltering under the strain of his absence
from home in New York City during much of 1896 and 1897, as well as from
the continued absence of a steady income. During the years following his
GMA work, Genevieve surely would have preferred that he find reliable
employment in New York City. Historian Heidi Ardizzone has concluded
that an additional marital stress was "the question of racial identity" that
arose because "Genevieve, and probably her children as well, were already
working, going to school, and socializing in contexts where they were presumed to be white." Greener, in turn, saw Genevieve's enjoyment of the
New York white world as at least somewhat responsible for his own reduced
standing among influential blacks. The couple opted for separate domiciles
in 1897 and would never again live under the same roof. When Greener was
in New York, he lived what he called "a very lonely and unsatisfactory life."
Using his office as his residence, he reported, "It makes me bitter to even go
about here. . . . I attend simply to business, go nowhere except to the P.O.,
libraries, and parks."[24]

Further motivation for Greener to seek a foreign posting may have been
rooted in the continued sniping from some of his own race about his commitment to issues of racial justice, his ambiguity as a mixed-race citizen, his
many white friends and associates, and other similar notions and activities.
Scholarly theologian Alexander Crummell, who had grown particularly
grumpy in his old age, had known Greener for at least a decade when in
1897 he founded the American Negro Academy, a group dedicated to African American educational and intellectual achievement. He managed to
block Greener from membership in the organization because, as he insisted
to a friend, Greener "has been a white man in New York and turned his
back upon all his coloured acquaintances." He elaborated, "I have no objection to his being a white man; but I do object to his coming back to our

ranks and then getting on my negro shoulders to hoist himself, as a negro, into some political office."[25]

Washington Bee editor W. Calvin Chase enjoyed attacking Greener (among many others) in print, often referring to him as "Dick" Greener. When Greener addressed the Bethel Literary Society, Chase wrote that he "spoke in a general manner, not selecting any particular subject." That complaint was mild for Chase, who expressed a marked distaste for the light-skinned citizens of his race. In another issue, reporting on a lawyer who viewed Greener as a leader, Chase charged that "Mr. Jones doesn't know Greener as well as *The Bee* and the people of Washington. He is a national failure of the first water." Oddly, another article in the same issue, titled "Greener a Leader," applauded Greener's lengthy history of leadership in Republican Party campaigns. When Greener was rumored to be a candidate for a public-school superintendency in Washington, Chase charged that "Mr. Greener is not a success as a teacher. . . . The people in this city would not tolerate Mr. Greener as superintendent of Public Schools."[26]

In January 1898, the job seeking seemed about to bear fruit when President McKinley sent appointments to the Senate for confirmation, including Greener's as US consul to Bombay (Mumbai), India. After a fairly quick confirmation, he set about lobbying for his salary, which was ultimately set at $2,000 per year. Even the irascible Chase published a fairly laudatory article about the appointment. Reprinted from the *Brooklyn Daily Times,* it proclaimed, "The appointment of a prominent and distinguished Afro-American to such an important post as the Bombay Consulate, where he will be brought into constant official relations with the British authorities, is a distinctly new departure." Noting that the appointment extended the "field of official service for capable citizens of African descent," the article suggested that there was minimal racial distinction in India "between the dark scholar and gentlemen who derive their lineage from Hindoo or from African sources."[27]

Greener, however, was soon conferring with State Department officials and influential Republicans about the possibility of a different, perhaps even better, diplomatic appointment. Years later, he explained that "just as I was getting ready to go [to India] the plague broke out. . . . I concluded that I would prefer to serve the Lord and the Republican Party in a healthy climate." Yet, if nothing better came along, he decided he would go to Bombay.

"The more I read about Bombay, the more I am inclined to go," he wrote to Wears: "The fact is, I need a change of scene." He would soon get that change. In May 1898, President McKinley appointed him to the US consul post newly created in Vladivostok, Russia. He was quickly confirmed and given a $500 raise without ever officially occupying his first consular appointment. Although located in a multinational city, he would be the first black consul in what was considered a white country.[28]

CHAPTER ELEVEN

Our Man in Vladivostok

THE BREAKAWAY WAS COMPLETE. Greener's journey from life as he had known it took him first to Chicago to visit some distant relatives, then through Seattle and on to Tacoma, Washington. There he boarded a steamship heading out of the Puget Sound and across the Pacific Ocean. At sea in weather that varied from "abominable" to "charming," he managed to thoroughly step out of his past.[1] At fifty-four, he was no longer functioning as a father or husband. In fact, his family members would soon distance themselves from him and his color, changing their names in order to pass as white. The racial activist, eager lawyer, political campaigner, stirring orator, and respected professor were also shed. During his passage to Japan and then on to Russia during the summer of 1898, Greener gladly embraced the role of a US representative traveling to a place where there had been no previous official US presence.

Greener characterized his nearly three-week voyage as "in many respects an eventful one for me," but that was a great understatement. He had the comforts of a large stateroom, the dinner "seat of honor" at the captain's right, an attentive young servant, and a multinational group of fellow passengers available for games of whist and poker. Particularly pleasing to him, he was addressed as "your honor" and "consul." Even better, he was able to report that "no question of race has come up—thank God—that damnable American ghost."[2] By winning a diplomatic appointment overseas, Greener had reached the career summit of top black leaders of his time. But his appointment was unique in sending him to a largely white country—a place where he would be presumed to be white.

The crew and passengers represented many nations; they were mostly from Japan, China, and Great Britain. Greener welcomed assumptions that he was simply an American of mixed ancestry, rather than an African American. Nevertheless, when he wrote to his friend Whitefield McKinlay, he worried that his new racial identity might be precarious: "Since I have been at sea, from sun and tan, I am one of the blackest fellows on board, except a few of the deck crew. . . . But, my blood is good and the red is in my cheek and on my hands, so I manage to pass. I look narrowly at times to see if I can observe any special attention to myself, but thus far if felt, it is not exhibited by look or act."[3]

Greener managed to learn some Chinese and Japanese words and phrases during the passage, and he became friendly with a Japanese clergyman who had just finished theological studies in the United States. The State Department had planned for Greener to spend two weeks in Yokohama to learn consulate duties and processes, but, somewhat characteristically, Greener decided to instead "see Japan and learn my duties when I reached Vladivostok."[4] He planned a tour, and, with his shipmate friend as interpreter, he spent several weeks living among the Japanese, touring towns and countryside, and making "some valuable acquaintances and dear friends."[5] He called on American consuls in Tokyo, Kobe, and Nagasaki before he traveled by steamer to Vladivostok, with stops at several Korean ports.

Greener's post in Vladivostok could be viewed accurately as either a "Siberian exile" or an appointment "of great significance." A port town in southeastern Siberia on a slim finger of land closely neighboring Korea, China, and the Sea of Japan, Vladivostok was at once a remote fortress and a growing commercial crossroad. As a back door to Eastern Europe, it would soon benefit from the completion of the Trans-Siberian railroad, which had started construction at Vladivostok in 1891, and as a fishing and shipping center, it could boast year-round access facilitated by machinery that cut harbor ice, allowing ships to get to port. Historian Allison Blakely noted that "Vladivostok, in its capacity as a channel of information alone, was not an isolated post."[6]

In a dispatch to his superiors in Washington, Greener described Vladivostok as reminiscent of a "western town," with hilly streets, little foliage, a new brick city hall, a Greek Orthodox church, and "hotels springing up in every direction."[7] Although Russians were the majority of the town's citizens, Chinese, Japanese, and Korean resident nationals were well represented. There also was a noticeable number of French and German citizens and even a small American colony. A 1900 census reported 38,000 residents in Vladivostok and predicted ongoing rapid growth. In addition, thousands of seasonal workers, mostly from China, crowded into the city each year.[8]

Greener seemed to thoroughly enjoy his initial impressions as a stranger in a place where he estimated no more than three people in the town spoke both fluent Russian and English, where postal and telegraphic service was unreliable and slow, and where a Russian military presence was constant. He could, however, enjoy the natural beauty of hills rising almost immediately from the harbor, the Bay of the Golden Horn, forming what one observer described as "a spectacular embrace of hills and sea [that] creates Vladivostok's natural relief." Scenic attraction provided a backdrop for cultural diversity in a city noted as "Russo-European in Asia, settled by Russians, Germans, and Scandinavians, on land ceded only in 1860 from China."[9]

To his disappointment, Greener immediately suffered a reduction in rank. The Russian government had determined that Vladivostok was not yet a place meriting foreign representation at the consular level. Instead, Greener would be classified as the US commercial agent to Vladivostok. The US State Department recalled his consular passport and sent him a new one as commercial agent.[10] Eager to quash any impression that he had been demoted, he explained to his cousin Isaiah Wears that since the Russians classified Vladivostok as a military fortress, and "only Russian authority is recognized," no foreign consuls were approved. He was quick to add that he really still had "all consular power" and "all the [foreign commercial] representatives are called indifferently consul and commercial agent."[11] Over the coming years he would continually push officials in Washington to convince the Russians that he should have the consular title, but his efforts were to no avail—and likely to the detriment of personal goodwill toward him within the State Department. Even when he requested approval to perform minor consular duties, such as issuing passports to Americans in Vladivostok, he was rebuffed.[12] The assistant secretaries at the State Department had no interest in using up diplomatic chips with the Russians by making such requests.

In fact, commercial agent was not at all an insignificant position in an area that could only increase in market importance and opportunity. President McKinley, moving away from protectionism to embrace Open Door trade, hoped that Russia and China would become expanded trading (or at least importing) partners. More committed to the integration of foreign policy and foreign trade than any previous US president, he argued, "It should be our settled purpose to open trade wherever we can, making our ships and our commerce messengers of peace and amity."[13] Secretary of State John Hay was especially eager to get Russia and Germany to soften their protective policies. Vladivostok was then a free port and soon to benefit from a new cross-country rail system. Greener was well positioned to take a visible role in creating expanded commerce for American goods in Siberia and beyond, and he immediately went about surveying possibilities and writing frequent and lengthy reports on his findings.[14]

. . .

During his first few months in Vladivostok, Greener stayed at three different hotels and found it "difficult to say which is worse." When he explored outside the center of town, on several occasions he accidentally walked too close to concealed Russian fortifications and was immediately stopped by gun-pointing soldiers. He also occupied himself by sending reports back to the United States, calling on commercial agents from other countries, and looking for a suitable rental office from which to represent US interests. When Greener discovered that the Russian governor general of the district that included Vladivostok spoke French, he sent him a message in that language. The two then met for nearly an hour of French conversation about American commercial prospects in eastern Russia. Limited in political acumen concerning international diplomacy, Greener also apparently asked him if he could check with his contacts in St. Petersburg about the possibility of allowing consular level appointments in Vladivostok.[15]

During his early explorations, Greener surveyed the commercial establishments and trading practices of other foreign countries and found that goods from Denmark, Finland, Germany, France, Japan, and China were all represented. His immediate conclusion was that US goods could find a market but only if the goods were "substantial." He determined that anything delicate or fancy would not be suited to the "beefy men and women" of Siberia.[16] After about six weeks in the area, he wrote an enthusiastic thirteen-page letter to a third assistant secretary at the State Department to catalog the opportunities for American commercial investments. He emphasized the little-known reality that the port was open all year, with channels cleared by ice-breaking vessels when necessary.[17] Greener determined to make the most of the job he was dealt, and "seeing himself as the principal agent for expansion of American business to Siberia, he attempted to take full advantage of this chance to advance American interests and, of course, his own."[18]

By the start of 1899, the new commercial agent had somewhat settled into his new life and work. No longer moving from one hotel to another, he found lodging with the family of a Russian military officer. The wife spoke French, so communication was not a problem for him. A second boarder was Japanese and had some connection with the Japanese diplomatic corps. Greener noted in a letter to his Philadelphia cousin, "We have a very pleasant family, and I am picking up a few, very few [Russian] words and phrases." He also had rented office space, and on December 22, 1898, he had raised the American flag for its first official appearance in Siberia.[19]

• • •

A regular correspondent to friends and relatives, Greener was pleased when he began receiving letters from the United States, generally about eight weeks after they were mailed. Of his immediate family, only his twenty-one-year-old daughter, Mary Louise, a teacher, wrote to him in Vladivostok. When Greener had left for his Siberian post, his son, Russell Lowell, twenty years old, was at City College in New York. His daughter Belle was a student at Teachers' College, which had just affiliated with Columbia University. Two other daughters, Ethel and Theodora, were seventeen and twelve years old. Before his departure, at a contentious meeting with his wife, Greener had refused to provide any support of his children past their eighteenth birthdays. Genevieve, living with her children as a single parent on the Upper West Side in New York City, began working as a piano teacher.[20]

Still angered about some attempts his wife had made the previous year to block his consular appointment to Bombay, Greener hoped that Genevieve would divorce him in his absence. He wrote to his cousin, "Mrs. G. has shown she cannot live with me and for me alone. She has ample grounds now, on which to secure a divorce. . . . She has made friends in New York, at my expense, and by disparagement of me to an extent I can never forgive. . . . I am firmly resolved never to live in the Fleet family any more."[21]

Soon, however, the Fleet family name was barely associated with members of Greener's family. Genevieve Ida Fleet Greener variously renamed herself Genevieve Van Vliet Greene or simply Genevieve Van Vliet. In the 1900 US Census of New York City, she was Ida Green, age forty (which would have meant she was fourteen when she married Greener). She and her children were listed as white, as were all other residents of their eight-unit building on West 99th Street. Perhaps most indicative of a determination to fully break with Richard Greener, the youngest daughter, Theodora, who had been given the feminine form of Greener's middle name, Theodore, was now listed simply as Jenevine (a possible misspelling of Genevieve). Russell Lowell became Russell da Costa Greene, and Belle took the name Belle da Costa Greene.[22] Claiming Portuguese or Spanish ancestry to explain dark hair and eyes was not unusual for individuals with African American ancestry who wanted to identify as white.[23] Greener was the only one in his family who identified as African American when he was in the United States. For the rest of them, the process that had begun with acquiring white friends and neighbors, and continued with others' assumptions that they were white, was now complete. At a time of increasing segregation and shrinking opportunity for black citizens, this family had slipped across the color line.

• • •

Greener's job consisted of a great deal of reporting, and he expanded that both in terms of geography—sometimes reporting on conditions throughout all of Russia—and his assigned scope of work in commercial matters. For example, in an annual report on education for the US Department of the Interior, he included news of a new female medical college in St. Petersburg, as well as greatly increased spending on education throughout Russia. His information, undoubtedly gathered from available newspapers and Russian government documents, was lengthy and detailed in the extreme. The new Oriental Institute in Vladivostok, which taught seven foreign languages, particularly impressed him.[24]

Within five months of his arrival, Greener compiled an extensive overview of Siberian trade, listing the volume of all foreign goods that had come into the port for the past two years. Not surprisingly, iron and "railway materials" were high on the list. While American imports were only a fraction of the trade—well behind those from Germany, Norway, Japan, England, and other areas of Russia—Greener suggested that there were good opportunities for materials for new electric systems and water works. He warned against offering "cheap goods," which were already sufficient, but insisted that "superior goods bearing an American mark would find a ready sale among the better classes." He also suggested that such trade would benefit from sending qualified agents for marketing purposes: "An agent speaking German or French, if not Russian, is worth a thousand circulars."[25]

Later reports included details and analyses related to trade prospects in canned goods, timber, grains, coal, cotton, farm machinery, and minerals. Among the ideas he transmitted to State Department contacts were suggestions about the "establishment of a regular American steamship line between the Pacific coast and Vladivostok; a department store featuring American goods; an American mineral water industry involving a Russian partner; and the introduction of California fruit products in to Siberia."[26] In a lengthy report on the growing importance of Manchuria and its commercial conditions, Greener noted a demand for American goods such as "prints, canned goods, watches, musical and cuckoo clocks, steel, fancy goods, and novelties." He warned that American ventures in mining, fishing, or agriculture were unlikely to succeed due to "expensive formalities to be complied with," but he reported a good market for American appliances and agricultural equipment.[27]

Outside of conducting business related to his commercial appointment, there is only limited evidence that Greener associated much with Vladivostok's small American community—numbering perhaps thirty permanent residents. Charles and Sarah Smith, the owners of Vladivostok's small American store, were joined in 1894 by Sarah's brother, Frederick Pray. Frederick's wife, Eleanor, a native of Berwick, Maine, was an avid diarist and prolific letter writer during her thirty-six years in Vladivostok. Strictly Victorian in manner and conservative in opinion, she particularly objected to any hint of flamboyance, self-promotion, pushiness, or casual manners. Not surprisingly, she thought little of Richard Greener. Among the issues she fumed about were that he played poker, he bragged, he drank, and he once wore a pink shirt. Only a few weeks after Greener arrived in Siberia, Mrs. Pray wrote:

> The crowning stroke came last Friday—there was a long article in the *Dalnii Vostok* about this same Mr. Greener, a regular cheap politician's puff, which could have been dictated by no one but himself! . . . Among other things in this article were the facts that he was a close personal friend of both [President William] McKinley and [Secretary of State William] Day. . . . He informs everyone he meets that he speaks several languages, and then to back up his statement, he usually drags in some French phrase. . . . He goes swelling around town with a flag, about four inches long, pinned with an eagle to his waistcoat, and a flag pin in his tie, so of course everybody knows who he is.[28]

Even secondhand gossip was fair game. Mrs. Pray was quick to write her sister-in-law that she had heard that "Mr. Greener got himself into disgrace at the opening of the pawn shop, and we are all glad of it." Apparently, with a slip of the tongue, Greener had extended "greetings of the American Republic to the Russian Republic," while the Russian Empire was still in full swing. He then proposed a toast to the health of the tsar but was stopped when another attendee insisted it was his, not Greener's, place to propose the toast.[29]

Nevertheless, on at least some occasions Greener managed to pass muster. In 1899, Mrs. Pray wrote of a tea party where "Mr. Greener was there and we really had a very pleasant tea. I read four choice selections from Marie C. which were without doubt beautiful." And, he again managed to receive credit from Mrs. Pray for getting the American colony together to send condolences to Mrs. McKinley upon the assassination of the president and for continually apprising US State Department officials on the conditions of Americans in Vladivostok during the Russo-Japanese War.[30]

Undoubtedly, Mrs. Pray and others were indignant when it became apparent that Greener was cohabitating with a young Japanese woman, Mishiyo Kawashima. Kawashima had worked for a Russian diplomatic family—first in Nagasaki, Japan, then in Washington, DC, and eventually in St. Petersburg, Russia. Originally, from the small village of Kita Arima Mura, near Nagasaki, she was on her way home to Japan, via Vladivostok, when she met the American commercial agent. According to her granddaughter, this meeting was actually their second, as they had first been introduced in Washington.[31] Kawashima spoke Russian, English, and Japanese, and it is likely that she assisted Greener a great deal in his efforts to gather information from Russian and Japanese reports on commercial interests. In 1901, when they were very much together, Greener hired twenty-three-year-old Kawashima as "messenger at the Commercial Agency."[32] Her younger sister, Suyo-san, was a young widow who also joined them in Vladivostok for a time, possibly hoping to find a new husband. Kawashima traveled back to her native village to give birth to each of the three children she had with Greener—a daughter and two sons—between 1900 and 1906. Some residents in Vladivostok assumed that Kawashima was Greener's wife, while others understood him to still have a US wife.[33] In any case, Kawashima was with him long enough to be viewed as his common-law wife.

Greener managed to earn kudos from the many visiting Americans who arrived to examine commercial prospects in the region. George Newhall of the San Francisco Board of Trade wrote that through Greener he got "a start among people [he] would not have met otherwise." An agent of

Otis McAllister and Company extolled Greener's "worth and ability" after Greener introduced him to key contacts throughout Vladivostok, and William Whiley of the Sperry Flour Company wrote of Greener's influence in that city and his clear demonstration that "the United States government really wanted to help its citizens in trade." US Consul to Nagasaki Charles B. Harris wrote, "Every once in a while, someone comes along and says, 'That man Greener up in Siberia, is all right.'"[34] Historian Michael Mounter concluded that although Greener did not have the resources "to run his office in Vladivostok on a comparable level to the other commercial agencies in the city," he cultivated good contacts with key authorities "by working harder than other commercial agents."[35]

• • •

In late 1899 a Chinese secret society, referred to as Boxers by western nations, began an uprising supported by the Chinese Dowager Empress. Ritualistic and fanatical, the Boxers railed against foreign elements in China, especially foreign missionaries. During the uprising that continued through the first half of 1900 in Peking, Tientsin, and the countryside, there were riots, street fighting, and massacres. Foreign legations within China closed down, under siege until allied forces (largely Japanese, Russian, German, British, French, and American) managed to battle their way toward Peking and win a nervous armistice, eventually followed by a treaty.[36] The Chinese commercial agent in Vladivostok asked Greener to look after his country's interests and people there while he returned to China during the rebellion. As thousands of foreign troops flooded into China during the summer of 1900, thousands of Chinese citizens left for greater safety on the Siberian coast. Greener assisted in their relocation and served on a committee raising funds for Chinese victims of the uprising. Two years later, the Chinese government awarded him the Order of the Double Dragon for his assistance to Chinese merchants and citizens during the crisis.[37]

Feeling increasingly confident of his abilities in representing US commercial interests and more, Greener continued to advocate for either consular status at Vladivostok or a promotion to consul at another place. Although his record may have merited such advancement at a time when merit was becoming somewhat more important in consular service assignments, he decided to use a combination of political pull and personal push to launch a climb up the diplomatic ladder. Understanding that other regions of Siberia were becoming more important than Vladivostok, he noted to his friend McKinlay that he had "telegraphed [New York senator Thomas C.] Platt, [Massachusetts senator] Henry Cabot Lodge and others and announced myself as a candidate for reappointment and promotion as Consul General for Eastern Siberia." He mentioned that he had also written to Booker T. Washington, whose close relationship with President Theodore Roosevelt might help Greener, and he asked McKinlay to help "get him [Washington] actively interested" and to also approach several others on his behalf. To his primary State Department contact, Herbert H. D. Peirce, he insisted that "persons well informed here" believed "there can be no objection to the establishment of a Consulate General for Eastern Siberia. . . . My work here and my original endorsements for a place under the State Department would seem to warrant my promotion and enable the department to take a step in advance in Eastern Siberia."[38]

Greener's determination for diplomatic career advancement reflected not only his impression of his own worth but also his reluctance to return to the United States during a time of increasing racial discrimination. He had left on the heels of the Supreme Court commitment to "separate but equal" in the *Plessy v. Ferguson* decision, which effectively promoted all manner of discrimination. As he told Wears, he viewed himself as "an officer of a Government powerless, or indifferent to my protection at home. Here I am virtual commander of any naval force to protect me or any American interests. At home, in the satrapy of D.C., I could be murdered at will for my political opinions."[39] While angling for a promotion, Greener also worried about being recalled altogether, as he felt there might be "a move to edge 'the brother' out" of any but "certain undesirable" diplomatic assignments.[40] Although that notion was not completely unfounded, and an informal quota system for black government appointments was generally evident, President Roosevelt was reluctant to remove any McKinley appointments while serving out the assassinated president's term—instead waiting to do so until he won his own presidential election in 1904.[41]

Greener would soon get a chance to demonstrate his diplomatic abilities well beyond promoting US commercial possibilities. Asian countries were quickly becoming a source of political contention as well as commercial importance among many nations. China held the key to many of Russia's expansion plans since its government had granted permission for Trans-Siberian rail service to pass across Manchuria. Manchurian timber and mining possibilities attracted the attention of nearby Japan and Russia, and they both courted Chinese concessions. Russia's growing economic domination of much of Manchuria gave her what one later analyst viewed as "a base of operations of incomparable strategic value for economic and ultimately political penetration of intramural China."[42] The Korean peninsula was also an area ripe for expansion, and Russia was determined to thwart any foothold of Japanese influence on the Asian continent. The large Russian military presence at Vladivostok and, through an agreement with the Chinese, at Port Arthur to the southwest was particularly worrisome to Japanese maritime elements, and European nations—especially England, Germany, and France—were eager to maintain the balance of power that had served them well in Asia, or to best one another in making their own inroads in China.

Antagonisms among the nations festered and finally exploded when Japanese forces launched a sneak attack on the Russian naval unit at Port Arthur in February 1904. The Russo-Japanese War did not immediately spill into the "important but vulnerable city of Vladivostok," but with Japanese governmental officials quickly removed from Russia, the United States was asked to have its representatives oversee Japanese interests.[43] Much of Greener's work in this regard related to seeing that Japanese citizens could make their way home, which was especially tricky amid disruptions and general chaos in banking, housing, and transportation. By his own estimate, he managed to arrange passage for 1,500 Japanese to safely return home before hostilities began, while protecting some who remained.[44] He also helped arrange for the Japanese diplomatic premises in Vladivostok to be used by Red Cross nurses and patients, and he aided in providing the Japanese government with names of ships and sailors lost or seized in the area.[45] Japanese officials sent several notes to the State Department during 1904 to communicate their "cordial appreciation" for actions taken by the US commercial representative in Vladivostok.[46] In the absence of a British presence in Vladivostok, the US Department of State asked Greener to represent British interests as well.[47]

Greener quickly determined that his new responsibilities, as well as the significantly increased cost of living in Vladivostok, should merit an increase in his pay. Not surprisingly, he fired off a letter to Second Assistant Secretary of State Francis Loomis, detailing his hardships and requesting an immediate $500 raise for himself, as well as increases for his messenger, interpreter, and clerk.[48] There is no evidence that any such action was taken or even seriously contemplated. Foreign commercial agents were advised by the Russian government to vacate Vladivostok in May 1905 during a bombardment by the Japanese fleet and disruptions in communication and other areas by Russian worker strikes. Greener went north to the city of Khaborovsk and lost contact with the State Department for at least part of the time that he was there.[49] Throughout the summer, President Roosevelt worried that if the Russo-Japanese war did not soon end, the Japanese would permanently take Vladivostok, the railway through Manchuria, and much of eastern Siberia.[50] However, by early September he managed to help mediate (in Portsmouth, New Hampshire) the peace treaty that ended the conflict. Greener was ready to resume his post at Vladivostok by October.

Perhaps to his surprise, and certainly to his dismay, Greener found upon his return to Vladivostok that plans for his official recall from diplomatic service had been underway for many months. As early as April 1905, a Washington, DC, newspaper had erroneously reported that he had already been replaced by Thornwell Haynes. Ironically, Haynes, who had been a commercial agent in Europe, was the author of a glowingly complimentary biography of South Carolina's dogmatic white supremacist governor, Benjamin Tillman.[51]

Although the reasons for Greener's recall against his own wishes were not altogether clear, a combination of many factors were at work, some possibly related to his race or his personal characteristics, but others related to the politics of government appointments. When President Roosevelt won the election of 1904, most McKinley diplomatic appointees understood they would likely be replaced. As Joseph H. Choate, ambassador to the Court of St. James, wrote to Roosevelt, "I have always regarded my tenure of office as limited to the term of the President who appointed me. I assume that every Ambassador and Minister now in office will tender to you their resignation before [your inauguration on] the 4th of March." Laurits Swenson, minister to Denmark, wrote that President Roosevelt felt "after the present incumbents had been allowed to serve eight years or nearly so, they had been given their fair share, and there ought to be a change. . . . he naturally had prominent friends whom he felt like recognizing with these places."[52] Blakely pointed to Greener's Vladivostok post as the "most promising of all his attempts at finding a place for himself in public life."[53] However, Greener would have been quite naïve to view such a highly political appointment, more than two decades before the foreign service was organized on a merit basis, as a career pathway.

It certainly did not help Greener that Third Assistant Secretary of State Peirce was tasked with an Asian inspection tour during late 1904 and early 1905. Peirce attacked the assignment as a man with an axe rather than a scalpel. His scathing report about irregularities and local unpopularity regarding Shanghai consul John Goodnow was soon followed by negative reports on five other US consuls in the region, including those in Singapore, Hong Kong, and Yokohama. President Roosevelt quickly requested the resignations of all six men.[54] A highly unfavorable report about Greener in Vladivostok was perhaps inevitable.[55] Although Peirce never actually traveled to Vladivostok, he did not hesitate to file a stinging report to Department of State officials based on hearsay.

> Everywhere throughout the East I received unfavorable reports of Mr. Greener, our commercial agent at Vladivostock [*sic*]. His habits are said to be extreemly [*sic*] bad. The Department has many times had occasion to complain of his manner of treating his pecuniary obligations and of the insolence of his attitude toward it. It is his habit to treat the instructions of the Department with contempt and utterly to disregard them. . . . The impression I gathered from persons who have had the opportunity of observing conditions on the spot is that Mr. Greener's presence in Vladivostock in his present official capacity is unfortunate.[56]

Greener also faced some criticism within the State Department and in the US press for failing to go through appropriate channels at the US embassy in St. Petersburg before allowing the empty Japanese diplomatic premises in Vladivostok to be used by the Red Cross. However, it was likely that wartime circumstances made it impossible for him to communicate with St. Petersburg much of the time, and, when informed of the issue, Japanese minister Kogorō Takahira wrote that his government had no objection to such use. Nevertheless, the conservative *Washington Times* reported nearly a year later that Greener, "one of the few colored men in the American consular service," had used "undiplomatic procedure."[57]

One person who seemed not at all disappointed about the idea that Greener would be recalled from Vladivostok was Booker T. Washington. Always, according to his biographer Louis Harlan, "inordinately involved in politics, and particularly the politics of patronage," he relished the opportunity created by Greener's recall. It fit well with his "overarching goal to enhance his own power by getting Roosevelt to appoint the men he wanted, so that he could reward friends and punish enemies among the black leadership."[58] Although Greener had called upon Washington for support from time to time, there was no evidence that Washington considered him truly a friend. In late 1904, Washington asked Roosevelt to appoint a Mr. Tibbetts "as a consul or something." He then reported to his friend Samuel Laing Williams, a black lawyer in Washington, DC, that President Roosevelt mentioned that Greener would likely be recalled because of "incompetency and several other troubles." Washington had then proposed Williams as a replacement, but Roosevelt felt Williams better suited to a diplomatic position "in a warmer country."[59] Later, Washington wrote to Secretary of State Elihu Root to suggest two other men for Vladivostok, "if you still have in mind putting a colored man in the position."[60]

Regardless of the political machinations of Washington and others, the new US commercial representative appointed to Vladivostok would be twenty-five-year-old Roger S. Greene, who had grown up the son of missionary parents in Japan, graduated from Harvard, and served as an interpreter and then US vice consul in Kobe. He arrived in Vladivostok in November 1905 but did not take over as commercial agent until recognition was received from St. Petersburg in December. Four months later, just before Greener reached the United States, Greene was promoted to the rank of US consul, with a salary 40 percent higher than the commercial-agent pay.[61] One of his early dispatches captured the changes that had taken place since Greener's appointment to Vladivostok: "Now express trains are running to Europe and express steamship lines are attracting through travel from China and Japan. . . . There is a Chamber of Commerce, a large foreign trade, and three or four times as much shipping."[62]

President Roosevelt may have determined that the Siberian port had become too important for a strictly political appointment—and perhaps especially for a black political appointment. Japanese racist sentiment also may have somewhat influenced Roosevelt, who claimed he "favoured Japan" and wanted "to advance her interests" in eastern Asia.[63] Minister Takahira made a cryptic, and perhaps telling, comment in a brief letter to Secretary of State Root. After a paragraph informing Root of Greene's anticipated departure date from Japan for his new post in Vladivostok, he added "grateful appreciation of the Imperial Government of the prompt and friendly action taken by the United States Government in meeting with our desire."[64]

Roosevelt well understood that Greener's appointment had broken the previous pattern of sending black diplomats only to Africa or Latin America. He soon reestablished that tradition with three 1906 black consular appointments—songwriter and poet James Weldon Johnson to Venezuela, physician James Garneth Carter to Madagascar, and newspaper manager William J. Yerby to Sierra Leone.[65] However, historian Louis Harlan noted that overall "the Roosevelt administration steadily reduced the number of black presidential officeholders" and concluded that the most significant explanation for this reduction was "the loss of black voting power. A disfranchised people obviously had no votes to trade for political appointments."[66]

Greener remained in Vladivostok until the spring of 1906. When he finally headed back to the United States, he left not only his diplomatic post but also his Japanese family—Mishi Kawashima, a daughter, and two sons. Kawashima did not want to leave her family members in Japan, and she understood the United States as increasingly racist. At sixty-two years old, Greener had diplomatic experience, good professional contacts, and a working knowledge of two additional languages, Japanese and Russian. He departed with some hope that he might find a position that would return him to the Asian continent.[67]

CHAPTER TWELVE

Closure in Black and White

EARLY IN THE MORNING of April 18, 1906, the earth heaved and split, mountains shifted, and buildings careened off their foundations. The San Francisco earthquake and subsequent fires, occurring just after Richard Greener arrived back on US soil in that city, might be viewed as symbolic of his difficulties to come. He did not personally suffer the effects of the earthquake, but he reported losing correspondence and other treasured belongings he had brought back from Siberia. Fortunately, he had left many other personal effects, including his beloved collection of books, with the relatives he had visited in Chicago just before departing for Vladivostok.[1]

As he made his way eastward and southward, the sixty-two-year-old unemployed former diplomat would confront a country squarely in the grip of Jim Crow segregation, racially motivated burning and lynching, and disfranchisement of former or potential black voters. Historian C. Vann Woodward noted that amid a national reform agenda aimed at corporate greed, machine politics, and boss rule, "the typical progressive reformer rode to power in the South on a disfranchising or white-supremacy movement." With convoluted rationalization, southern politicians determined that solidarity among whites was necessary to advance progressive democracy and could happen best by barring black citizens from political, social, and economic involvement. During Greener's years in Russia, Jim Crow segregation laws in South Carolina had extended to first- and second-class railroad cars, waiting rooms, streetcars, steamboats, and numerous other areas. The state's white-supremacist governor, Benjamin Tillman, had won a victory for racism by securing a voter-registration requirement of "intelligence" that now allowed local officials to easily exclude black voters. He proudly boasted that he viewed blacks as "akin to the monkey" and "ignorant and debased" as a race. Even so, a combination of nostalgia, curiosity, and opportunity compelled Greener to travel at least twice to South Carolina in the first years of his US homecoming.[2]

• • •

When Greener stepped onto the University of South Carolina campus in 1907, thirty years had passed since his last tumultuous year as a professor there. His old residence, Lieber House, looked little changed as he strolled by it and headed across the green. There, the stately brick facade and wide columns of the library remained as impressive as they had seemed during Greener's assignment as university librarian. Inside, a friendly assistant librarian greeted him and asked if he were a visiting professor. He mentioned quickly only that he had been a professor "a long time ago." His light skin and gray hair did not reveal his part in integrating the university during Reconstruction. But someone did remember him—an aging worker busily shelving books from a ladder. Robert, who had years before helped Greener in reorganizing and cleaning the library, climbed down and rushed to shake his hand. Quickly turning his head away from the assistant librarian, Greener whispered in Robert's ear, "No names!" When the assistant librarian wondered how he knew Robert, Greener simply explained, "I met him when I visited the library years ago. He evidently has a good memory!" He had successfully dodged the possible embarrassment of being evicted as a black interloper among an all-white faculty and student body.[3]

Greener's visits to South Carolina in 1906 and 1907, while he was living primarily in Washington, DC, contrasted sharply with his experiences during the state's integrated Reconstruction era. Now, traveling with black friends, he found that "everywhere the signs of caste appear, 'colored lunch,' 'white lunch,' 'waiting room for colored.' Inside the cars, 'white' stares at you from the one; 'colored' grins at you in the other." He would later conclude to his friend Francis Grimké that both races were to blame: "There is the air of superiority on the one side, and the quiescent acceptance of inferiority on the other." Later, from New Orleans, he complained again that "the dodging, subterfuges, and evident quiet, contented complaisance of negroes and mixed bloods fills me with indignation." For himself, he would have none of it. Instead, he relied on his light skin and confident demeanor in segregated situations like streetcars: "Invariably, I boldly walk up front and avoid the screen [dividing black and white sections]. . . . Only three times have I condescended to take the rear." For Greener, such action was not a subterfuge of passing for white but rather simply a way of refusing to suffer cruel humiliation: "My blood kindles every day at this persistent, petty degradation of race, while all the Americans pratering [*sic*] of liberty and freedom are walking by on the other side."[4]

Greener's traveling companions at various points on his first southern trip after Vladivostok included Kelly Miller, a brilliant mathematician and educator who had been the first black student to attend Johns Hopkins University; Greener's old friend and former student Whitefield McKinlay; and brothers Archibald and Francis Grimké, well-known intellectuals and black activists who were Charleston natives. The group toured together in South Carolina for about a week and was entertained at various homes with teas, luncheons, and dinners. They joined South Carolina Agricultural and Mechanical Institute president Thomas Miller, once a University of South Carolina law-school classmate of Greener's, as honored guests at the commencement at Avery Normal Institute, a highly regarded Charleston college for black students. Greener apparently had lost none of his oratorical luster. At an Avery Alumni Association meeting, he "delivered an able and eloquent address which was listened to with closest attention," and at graduation exercises at the Hospital Training School for Nurses, he made a speech "sparkling with wit and filled with well-chosen words." When Greener returned to Washington, he sent a donation of $125 to the nurse training school to start an endowment fund.[5]

On a second trip to South Carolina the next year, Greener stopped in Greenville and Columbia before continuing to Charleston. He visited old friends at two adjacent black colleges in Columbia, Benedict College and Allen University, and gave a lecture, "Travels at Home and Abroad," which drew an audience of nearly five hundred students and local citizens. A particularly poignant reunion took place when he then made his way South and was greeted in the town of Orangeburg by Johnson C. Whittaker, the former West Point cadet who was by then a professor at the South Carolina Agricultural and Mechanical Institute. In Charleston, he gave lectures at three different churches for the benefit of the Hospital Training School for Nurses. Titled "The Negro as Seen in High Development Here and Abroad," the lectures were preceded by music and exhibits of the latest technology: moving pictures. The *Charleston News and Courier* reported of his first lecture that "for nearly an hour he held all by his eloquence" and concluded it was "one of the best ever delivered to a colored audience in Charleston. The lecturer is a favorite among the intelligent colored people of this city and invariably draws large crowds."[6]

• • •

Touring and lecturing undoubtedly created a welcome respite from Greener's work in Washington, DC, where he was busy trying to restore his reputation and perhaps revive his professional future. Convinced he had been "treacherously undermined" in Vladivostok, he estimated that he spent his first two years back from Siberia "seeking redress for the trick played upon me." Greener had begun hearing about charges of his misconduct, probably stemming from the negative Peirce report, as soon as he arrived in Washington in May 1906. He immediately wired Booker T. Washington, master of a large information network about black citizens, to insist that he could refute any accusations. Washington replied that he was glad to hear that "all of the statements which have been circulated regarding you are entirely false" and suggested Greener should have a heart-to-heart talk about the matter with Secretary of State Elihu Root. Greener may or may not have realized that Washington had been a key conduit in 1905 for eagerly spreading the word "from headquarters" that Greener was "head over heels in debt," as well as in "the drink habit." Given wartime communication problems in Siberia, Washington seemed intentionally derogatory when he wrote to a correspondent, "Greener would not answer the [State] Department's letters."[7]

Although Greener tried five times in five months to schedule a meeting with Secretary Root "to reply to any and all reflections upon my private character," he continued to be rebuffed.[8] While it was important to him to refute unfavorable fallout from the Peirce inspection report, it was also possible that Peirce's investigation was not the reason for his recall but rather a way to provide support for a recall that was going to happen anyway. The political cards had been well stacked against Greener's continuance: He was the appointee of a previous president; the Russians were especially unfriendly to Americans who had been supportive of Japan during the Russo-Japanese War; and the Japanese, purported to be prejudiced against African Americans at that time, may have known about Greener's ancestry. However, the State Department apparently did take the communications from Greener and/or his supporters seriously enough to at least seek another opinion in the matter. This time, it was the new American consul to Vladivostok, Roger Greene, who was asked to "investigate the rumors about the personal and official conduct and standing" of his predecessor. He also was alerted that Greener claimed that the negative reports were possibly the result of a case of mistaken identity, since there had at one time been another man in Vladivostok with the same last name.[9]

Greene, determined to be neither petty nor personal, chose his words carefully in his investigation report. He explained that the "principal objection on the part of residents here to Mr. Greener's conduct was that though a married man he kept a mistress, a Japanese woman by the name of M. Kawashima." He then noted a "strong feeling" among some that Greener was "unnecessarily familiar" with American prostitutes who were sometimes in town. And he mentioned that some local residents objected to "somewhat unusual personal habits, in regard to dress, etc." Greene verified that another man with the name Greener had been in Vladivostok but was there only for a short time and was not well known by many people. While he concluded that it appeared that "Mr. Greener's official standing was not high," he found no dereliction in performance of duties, and he emphasized that Greener "was here during a very difficult time, when, on account of the sympathy for Japan expressed in America, the Russians were inclined to regard Americans with dislike and mistrust."[10]

Continuing to push for a way to defend himself, Greener was able to marshal some help from New York senator Thomas Platt. However, Secretary Root would not budge when Platt wrote him that Greener thought he was "not confronted with specific charges" and that "it is but fair he should be given an opportunity to refute any accusations." Instead, Root reminded Platt that Greener's case, as a presidential appointment confirmed by the US Senate, did not fall under procedures that might apply to career appointments. He insisted that the change made in Vladivostok was simply to achieve "a more satisfactory performance of the duties of the position."[11]

Greener's frustration over being unable to combat allegations and rumors about his work and character was only the beginning of his postdiplomatic trials. He soon got word that the Japanese were awarding honors to US diplomatic representatives in Russia for service during the Russo-Japanese war, but, regardless of his administration of Japanese interests in Vladivostok during that time, he was not one of the honorees. Worse, Greene, who arrived to replace him after the war had ended, was among those being decorated for wartime activities.

Again, Greener turned to friends in high places to look into the matter. He asked Sen. Henry Cabot Lodge to ascertain the reason for "this apparent discrimination," charging that the State Department left him off a list, provided to the Japanese, of the names of those US diplomatic officers who had served Japanese interests. "The treatment I have already received at the hands of the Department of State is bad enough," he complained, "but this evident attempt to rob me of any credit for work actually performed merits my protest." When Senator Lodge inquired about the matter, Secretary Root replied that "the Department of State did not designate anyone to receive decorations from Japan, but merely communicated the names."[12]

When it was apparent that the State Department was unwilling to take the matter any further, Greener tried to enlist Booker T. Washington's support in getting him a meeting with President Roosevelt. However, no such meeting took place. The error in honoring Greene instead of Greener was likely a simple mix-up of names by the Japanese. As historian Michael Mounter noted, on at least one earlier occasion Greener had been referred to as Greene in a memo from Minister Takahira. Greener, however, envisioned a more conspiratorial process when he later reflected on it to his daughter Mishiyo: "Japan ran a successor in upon me after the war had closed, and one year after 'decorated him' for service to Japan during the war. He was shrewdly selected having a name so nearly like mine. . . . Even when the Japanese government was informed of the facts, it did not deign to rectify a palpable error, or even thank me, at least, for what I had done!"[13]

Still another distressing event upon Greener's return to the United States was word from Mishi Kawashima that she did not intend to communicate further with him. He was as angry as he was sad, and he sent what he later characterized as "a hasty and indignant reply." He had once hoped that if he could get another appointment in Asia, he, Mishi, and their three children might eventually settle somewhere, "where we would all have been happy together." But, he could no longer fool himself about his chances of reviving any semblance of the life he had had abroad.[14]

• • •

While residing in Washington, DC, and working to clear his diplomatic reputation, Greener also kept an eye on the work of his fellow black citizens in promoting racial equality. W. E. B. Du Bois, then a professor at Atlanta University, had recently gained particular note for his founding (with William M. Trotter) of a civil-rights group, called the Niagara Movement after the location of its initial meeting in 1905. When Greener was visiting Harper's Ferry, West Virginia, during the summer of 1906, he heard a lot about the Niagara organization, which would soon hold its annual meeting there. Uncompromising and activist on the part of black citizens, the Niagara Movement represented a clear split from the accommodation-ist stance of Booker T. Washington and his supporters. Du Bois and his followers, largely educated and intellectual blacks, wanted immediate full and equal rights, including the vote and the end of Jim Crow segregation. Washington viewed the group as "impractical visionaries" who "lacked the capacity to lead."[15]

Greener wrote to Washington from Harper's Ferry just weeks before the scheduled Niagara meeting to suggest that he might be on site to play a con-ciliatory role between the two factions: "Now, I seem to see a chance to be present, as a spectator, and perchance have an opportunity to say a word, in reconcilement of apparently conflicting elements, which at the present time, of all others, ought to be completely in harmony, to be effective." Knowing that he needed Washington's highly influential support from time to time, he took pains to avoid any indication that he might stray from the Washing-ton camp. To that end, he suggested they meet privately somewhere before the Niagara conference to "talk over the situation."[16]

When Washington's devoted private secretary, Emmett Scott, read the letter, he was almost giddy about the potential it presented for secret infor-mation gathering. "Here is a good chance to get a good friend into the inner portals of the Niagara meeting," he scribbled when he passed the letter on to Washington. Washington, who loved the idea of getting inside intelligence and was no stranger to cloak-and-dagger plans, agreed. He asked Greener to come to a "private and confidential" meeting with him in New York City at his hotel on a Sunday evening, even noting that he would pay Greener's expenses. How-ever, Greener, then visiting in Chicago, responded that he thought "best not to see you before the meeting." Clearly, he wanted nobody to suspect he wasn't an objective party at the gathering. Washington wrote to advise Greener to "spare no pains to get on the inside of everything" and to remind him that the Niagara Movement was determined "to defeat and oppose everything I do."[17]

Greener and McKinlay, a close friend of Washington's, traveled together to the gathering in Harper's Ferry. Greener delivered a eulogy to John Brown during the meeting, and he left afterward to attend the National Negro Business League conference in Atlanta, where he was a speaker. Al-though he did go from there with Washington to Tuskegee Institute in Al-abama, there is no evidence that he shared any particularly juicy insider details from the Niagara meeting.[18] Greener needed Washington, with his high-level contacts and talent for promoting favored friends for plum jobs, but he also had no desire to alienate black activists who were more militant in their approaches.

Although still happy to speak out for his race, Greener was increasingly disillusioned about the possibility of making any difference amid the back-sliding that had compromised black citizenship in recent years. White su-premacy in the South, victories for states' rights, Supreme Court protection of "separate but equal," shrinking interest in racial justice among Repub-lican party leaders, and some complacency among blacks themselves all combined to leave him bitterly pessimistic. Even Washington was some-what disenchanted with the New South, where all former Confederate states plus Oklahoma formally installed voting policies that discriminated against black citizens. Greener soon moved to Chicago, where he found he enjoyed life "better than the stifling air and toadying life of the Capital." He summa-rized his frustrations in a letter to McKinlay.[19]

> We are becoming more and more a pronounced "pariah class," and when we evade this palpable fact by an enumeration of our own material advancement, we simply avoid the issue. . . . It is bad enough to see the North toadying up to the un-reconstructed rebel South—worse rebels today than their fathers were— but when a race born since freedom shows all the groveling, "Please kick me" instincts, the heart grows sick and hope dies away. The evil is already done. You and I will never live to see it improved. I would rather be a citizen of despotic Russia than a pariah in such a bastard republic! And I hope before long to say so, and say it loud enough to be heard.

Greener found he had no stomach for further activity in support of Repub-lican election efforts, and he did not campaign for William Howard Taft in 1908. Instead, he told McKinlay, "I preserved my own self-respect by keep-ing quiet. The fact is the negro was not wanted anyway by either side." He was fine, although not thrilled, with Taft's handy victory and viewed him as an improvement over Roosevelt—"the platitudinous, barn storming, seeker after notoriety, who now dominates the Republican party and the nation . . . who has combined the professional reformer with Tammany political methods of the commonest sort." Later he added that Roosevelt had "sub-limated his idealism to ambition" and become "intoxicated with his own verbosity. . . . The last man one could trust to lead any real reform!"[20]

Greener also had finally lost faith in Booker T. Washington as someone to be counted upon for positive influence on his behalf. He chided McKinlay for feeling that his recent lack of political participation for the Republican party would lose him Washington's favor. "My dear boy, don't you know Mr. W. has had 2 ½ years to do something for me, if he had any real interest or dared to speak for one unjustly and barbarously treated, before the Tzar of all the United States?"[21]

Amid his angry pessimism, however, Greener displayed something of a sixth sense about the future: "There is a great work still to be done by the so-called leaders of the race. But office holders will never do it. The race is to be aroused on different lines." He would soon attend the 1909 National Negro Conference in New York City, where delegates supporting the Du Bois call to unbending activism were meeting at a conference of white and black citizens that became the precursor to the National Association for the Advancement of Colored People (NAACP). Greener participated in drafting the conference resolutions. And, he undoubtedly especially enjoyed seeing one of his former University of South Carolina students, William Sinclair, deliver a rousing speech that lashed out at the nation and its leaders for remaining "apathetic, supine, limp," while leadership in the South "inaugurated a condition of semi-slavery."[22]

While his active work on behalf of racial equality was slowed by his age and his discouraged spirit, Greener kept in touch with those who arrived or remained at the forefront of the struggle. He admired Du Bois, as much for his scholarship as his leadership on behalf of fellow blacks. "Thanks for the telling blows you have struck," he wrote in a letter praising Du Bois's 1909 book on the biography and legacy of John Brown: "May you long be able to wield so trenchant a blade." Showing a measure of his own frustration and perhaps to signal his approval of the Du Bois camp, he added, "I have little hope of the mature sycophants today, who are apologizing for their existence, still asking hat in hand for largesse. . . . The White American is not yet freed from his prejudices, cruelties, meanness, hypocrisy!" Du Bois, who knew that Greener had once been friendly with Washington and other conservative blacks, replied to him quickly but tersely, mentioning only that "the fight is an uphill one, but somebody is going to win sometime."[23] As a key figure in the struggles for racial equality, Greener's time had now truly passed.

• • •

Richard T. Greener, 1915, at the age of seventy-one.
Courtesy of National Park Service, Manhattan Historic Sites Archive.

Life in Chicago suited Greener well as he advanced in age. He lived with the Platt family, distant relatives he had discovered during his McKinley campaign work, and in 1909 moved permanently into the home that would be his longest and last place of residence. A roomy three-story house, it was situated near the University of Chicago in the largely white neighborhood of Hyde Park. (Coincidentally, the man who would become the country's first African American president moved into a residence only about a block away nearly one hundred years later.) The widowed matriarch of the Platt family had been especially fond of Greener and more than happy to store many of his belongings while he was in Vladivostok. By the time he came to retrieve them, she had died. Her three adult daughters, Ida, Amelia, and Mary Platt, encouraged Greener to move into their house and stay for as long as he wanted with the trio he called "my dear adopted maiden spinsters."[24]

Ida Platt, like Greener, was a pioneer among accomplished black citizens. She had worked her way through law school to become the first African American female graduate, in 1894, of the Chicago College of Law (now Illinois Institute of Technology Chicago–Kent College of Law). She quickly became the first African American female admitted to the Illinois bar, and by the time Greener arrived, she had her own law practice and a steady clientele. Amelia worked in the Chicago public library and kept Greener supplied with books, magazines, and miscellaneous papers. Mary was a semi-invalid and did not work outside the home, but Greener maintained she was "the household lynchpin."[25]

Greener found he could easily occupy himself with correspondence, speaking engagements, a literary club presidency, active membership in several other literary societies, membership in an anthropological society, writing, and reading. He was able to regularly publish essays in the *A.M.E. Review*. And, with two of the most notable black newspapers located in Chicago, he could easily stay abreast of race issues. The *Broad Ax* had relocated to the shores of Lake Michigan in 1895, after a curiously optimistic start in Salt Lake City at a time when the state of Utah had fewer than one thousand black citizens. The weekly *Chicago Defender* was outspoken on equal treatment and championed the idea of black migration out of the South.[26]

During 1911 and 1912, Greener also finally made a business investment that paid off, buying stock in and becoming an "agent" for the Royal Casualty Company of Chicago and Saint Louis, Missouri. Happily, the value of the stock had doubled—ten cents to twenty cents a share—in the few years of his investment. The Japanese community in Chicago was large enough to put on an annual celebration of the Japanese emperor's birthday, which Greener enjoyed attending. Since he had not been decorated by Japan for his service, he wore to the occasions the Chinese red sash and Order of the Double Dragon decoration he had received from the Chinese government after the Boxer Rebellion. Perhaps most satisfying, more than three decades after he was blackballed from membership in the Washington, DC, Harvard Club, he joined the Chicago Harvard Club.[27]

A regular visitor to the University of Chicago Library, Greener was given access to its collections on the basis of his earlier service as a university librarian in South Carolina. Walking home, he often stopped to watch games at the university ball field or nearby Washington Park. His room and an adjacent library were on the third floor of the house, and he was surrounded by his memorabilia from Siberia, Japan, and China, as well his collection of rare books and artifacts. He managed what he termed "an idyllic sort of life" on a small amount of savings. Although he sometimes thought he should be "more actively employed," he eventually decided that "in our country there is no need of old men, and being no longer young, I am supposed to be retired."[28]

Despite his fading involvement with partisan politics and racial justice, each was a constant source of interest to him. Hoping to write an article with his summary denunciation of the situation, he wrote to McKinlay: "I have been gathering material from my knowledge of Republican tactics so far as the Negro is concerned and find there is an argument to raise, all along the line 1876 to 1910, an indictment, which has never been thoroughly drawn, never presented in all its infinite, selfish, cowardly treachery." He maintained that the Roosevelt and Taft administrations together would "cap the climax" of the story of black citizenship curtailed. Roosevelt struck him as "an ingrate and a coward in his treatment of the negro," and he soon concluded that Taft "knows nothing of the Negro" because "the South owns him body and soul." By the 1912 presidential election, he retreated from his lifelong Republican identity to support a Democrat, Woodrow Wilson. He participated in some local Democratic meetings in Chicago, and in March 1913, he attended Wilson's inaugural ceremonies in Washington. Soon, however, Wilson's southern roots and actions in favor of racial segregation left Greener with only "disgust at the universal hypocrisy of the whole mess, Dems, Repubs, and Progressives."[29]

Greener may have adopted something of a grumpy-old-man response to political leadership, but it was well justified concerning the course of racial justice. Soon after his 1904 election, President Roosevelt's courtship of southern whites had sealed his refusal to use his influence to curb lynching, enforce voting rights, or tackle any number of segregation issues.[30] His 1912 third-party movement, the Progressive Party, was "progressivism for whites only" and designed "to placate Southern white racism," according to C. Vann Woodward. President Taft also would not address either disfranchisement or lynching of blacks in the South, and he solidified his white base in that region by removing many southern black patronage appointees. During his election campaign and while in office, his political strategy required much "catering to southern white prejudices." Likewise, according to historian Richard Sherman, President Wilson was "far too tied to the anti-Negro southerners within his party to challenge the pressures for racially discriminatory policies." Eventually, Greener surrendered all hope, writing to Francis Grimké, "I have no faith in any politician strong enough to have a following."[31]

Frequently asked to appear as a guest speaker, Greener rarely turned down the opportunity and never disappointed. At the January 1911, one-hundredth anniversary of the birth of Charles Sumner, he was the keynoter at Chicago's Ebenezer Baptist Church. Introduced as "the first colored graduate of Harvard," "ex-Consul to Russia," and "the most learned man the Negro race has produced," he was, according to a news report, met with "a deafening applause and waving of handkerchiefs." He extolled Sumner for over an hour and recounted his acquaintance with the Massachusetts senator and other civil-rights activists in some detail. Later, he was a speaker at the Abraham Lincoln birthday celebration at Chicago's Fellowship Club, at the St. Mark's Methodist Episcopal Church lyceum, and at a Frederick Douglass birthday celebration. One of his lengthiest speaking tours occurred in 1914 in and around Cincinnati, Ohio, where for over nearly two weeks he spoke about "travels in the Far East." In 1917 he was a guest and speaker at the fiftieth-anniversary celebration at Howard University, and several months later he delivered the commencement speech and received an honorary Doctor of Laws degree at Wilberforce University in Ohio.[32]

Perhaps his most enjoyable travel was what he called a "pilgrimage" to Phillips Academy, Andover, for the fiftieth reunion of his 1865 class. With him he brought a framed portrait of Ulysses S. Grant to give to the academy. He explained the gift's history in a letter to his friend, the inventor Lewis Howard Latimer: "Grant gave it to [General Philip] Sheridan circa 1867–8; Sheridan gave it to a Mrs. Lawrence of New Orleans (colored), the house keeper who accompanied the family to Chicago. Mrs. L. gave it to one of the sisters of the Platt family, who presented it to me last year." Greener had had it cleaned and set in a new frame, presenting it as the gift of the "Appomattox Class of 1865."[33]

When invited to the 1916 NAACP Amenia Conference in New York, however, Greener responded to NAACP secretary Roy Nash that while he was in sympathy with the group's objectives, he was "past the stage of active cooperation." That meeting, occurring less than a year after the death of Booker T. Washington, was, according to Du Bois, a chance for all parties "to get into close and sympathetic conference" and to reverse the "wedges

Greener (*center, standing*) in 1915, at his fiftieth class reunion at Phillips Academy, Andover, where he presented the portrait of President Grant shown here. Courtesy of Archives and Special Collections, Phillips Academy, Andover, Massachusetts.

of discord between different leaders and different schools of thought" that had been driven by detractors of the notion of equality for all. Attendees included Greener's old friends Kelly Miller, William Sinclair, Mary Church Terrell, and Francis Grimké, as well as Emmett Scott of Tuskegee Institute, Morehouse College president John Hope, Du Bois, and others from both ends of the spectrum from accommodation to activism.[34]

• • •

In the summer of 1916, with World War I raging in Europe, seventy-two-year-old Richard Greener got what he considered "the surprise of my life." A letter arrived from Mishiyo, the teenaged daughter of his union with Mishi Kawashima. She wrote from China, where Kawashima had relocated to join a friend in an import-export business. Greener was thrilled to be in touch, to hear about his daughter and two sons, and to begin a long-distance restoration of friendship with Kawashima. He wrote back, sharing loving memories and great pride in the family: "Your mother has every reason to be proud of her success; but she was always a superior, energetic and resourceful person, and very helpful to me. . . . She had the real samauri [*sic*] spirit." He mentioned that he treasured the photos he kept of the children and some sketches by Kawashima's sister, Suyo-san. In subsequent letters, which he signed "Greener-san," "Papa-san," or "your loving father," he rarely failed to praise Kawashima to her daughter. He recalled her as "brave" and "aspiring," and he reminded Mishiyo that her mother "deserves all the credit from her children. Always be loyal to her." Variously referring to Kawashima as "the little mother," "the dear mother," he sent, through his daughter, a photo of himself to Kawashima, and he received one in return.[35]

Although wartime communication difficulties, including censorship, often stalled their letters and prevented much in the way of enclosures or packages, the father and daughter continued to correspond. He held out some hope for a trip back to that part of the world and a chance to once again see his Japanese family. "I am thinking of going again to Siberia, if the [Russian] Revolution succeeds," he wrote five months after the United States entered the war. "At any rate, I shall visit Japan within a year if matters go right." Always expansive in complimenting and advising his daughter, Greener delighted in her intelligence, her artistic abilities, her enjoyment of poetry, and her practice of English and Chinese. He sent her books and magazines, and she sent him a school essay she had written. He advised her to "attend to your studies and get all the athletic training necessary for rigorous health." And he counted on her, with her broader experience and education, to be "the advisor" of her younger brothers. "For you have been emancipated from mere racialism and have mingled with Europeans of quality. . . . You would never be as at home again with only Japanese as with Europeans. I do not know how you take to the Chinese." There is no evidence that Mishiyo ever knew that her father was considered to be black.[36]

Greener felt he noticed some hereditary similarities between his daughter and himself. They shared an enjoyment of poetry, as well as of reading and writing in general, and both had some artistic interest and ability. Greener had always liked collecting and saving photos, sketches, and various small souvenirs of his travels; he had even kept some British souvenirs from his boyhood voyage to Liverpool. Along with books and magazines, his collections crowded every surface of his study in Chicago. He described to noted historian Carter Woodson a large collection of "negro-mania" he had sold to the New York Historical Society—including an 1827 copy of the first African American newspaper in the United States, *Freedom's Journal,* and an 1830 copy of *David Walker's Appeal to the Coloured Citizens of the World.* He had also collected a 1792 edition of Benjamin Banneker's *Almanac,* a copy of a letter from Banneker to Thomas Jefferson, and a copy of an 1862 report by George Livermore, titled *An Historical Research: Opinions of the Founders of the Republic on Negroes as Slaves, As Citizens, and as Soldiers.*[37]

Little, if any, communication occurred between Greener and his American family after his return from Vladivostok. By then, the "Greene" family was firmly situated as white residents on the Upper West Side in New York City. His son, now known as Russell da Costa Greene, was a 1906 graduate in civil engineering from Columbia University. Twenty-year-old Theodora was also in school, and Mary Louise and Ethel were employed as teachers. Greener's wife was known as Mrs. Van Vliet Greene. His daughter Belle Marian had become Belle da Costa Greene. She had just returned from three years working at the Princeton University Library to take on the responsibility of developing, collecting, cataloging, and generally overseeing all aspects of the new John Pierpont Morgan Library. As Belle became more and more essential in directing that endeavor over the coming years, Russell began a successful career in his field of engineering. He returned to graduate school in 1912, this time to the University of Tennessee to earn a master's degree in mining engineering.[38] He was one of the earliest, if not the earliest, African American graduates of that institution.

Greener was aware that Genevieve and his children were passing as white in New York City, and he was likely chagrined about how that would reflect on him if it were widely known. However, he also understood that at that time any black or mixed-race citizen who could manage to be viewed as white would have greatly increased access to a fine education, professional success, and the rights of full citizenship. The Greene family members, now identifying as white, undoubtedly would not want to risk an association with the father who was well known as black, and their distancing themselves from him was made easier by Greener's many years of absence.

When Greener's Philadelphia cousin, Isaiah Wears, died during Greener's years in Vladivostok, his will left a portion of his estate jointly to Greener and his son Russell. When he returned, Greener discovered he could not get his portion without finding Russell to either share in it or renounce his claim to it. Since he had no desire to personally search for or approach Russell about the issue, he left the matter up to Wears's old attorney, becoming increasingly impatient as it dragged on. Finally, in 1915, after lawyers made adequate but unsuccessful efforts to locate Russell, a Philadelphia court determined that the entire sum, estimated at several hundred dollars (about $5,000 in today's money), could go to Greener.[39]

It is possible that Greener knew something about the work and location of his daughter Belle da Costa Greene. Her biographer, Heidi Ardizzone, noted that her name and work had been mentioned prominently in several *Chicago Daily Tribune* articles in 1912 and 1913, including one full-page story with a large photograph. Additionally, Belle may have visited her father in Chicago in 1914. Belle wrote to Bernard Berenson, her long-distance love, that she had "important personal business" in Chicago and would be meeting someone she had not seen in nearly twenty years. Giving few details, she wrote that the trip might help in "rectifying a very grave wrong and injury" but if discovered "would bring disaster to several people." Greener himself may have come to the attention of his children from time to time through occasional mentions in the press of his speeches or appearances at celebratory functions. In February 1917, his photograph filled the cover of the *Crisis*, the NAACP journal edited by Du Bois.[40]

Greener continued his comfortable, if ever slower, life in Chicago until, on May 2, 1922, he died suddenly in his sleep of what was determined to be "senile arteriosclerosis." He was seventy-eight. The *Chicago Broad Ax* remembered him as "one of the best educated and most prominent colored men in the United States." Even more laudatory, the *Chicago Defender* noted, "As a public speaker he was eloquent, forcible and convincing. . . . We have produced very few men who were more widely and favorably known than Richard T. Greener." He was interred in Chicago's Graceland Cemetery, where he joined such luminaries as Cyrus McCormick, Marshall Field, and Joseph Medill. In a final irony for a life that often played out in an invisible space between black and white, Richard Greener's official death certificate identified him as "white."[41]

The Passing of Richard Greener

HE FIFTIETH ANNIVERSARY of desegregation at the University of
South Carolina was a yearlong celebration in honor of the integration
of the student body in 1963. It began with the appointment of a large
committee appropriately representative of wide-ranging academic areas
and student interests. The committee met and divided into subcommittees.
Subcommittees met and planned a year of seminars, speeches, receptions,
and the like. A memorial garden was installed in a central and well-traveled
part of campus to honor the legacy of the pioneering African American
students whose registration for class marked the success of the twentieth-
century civil-rights era. There was only rare mention in casual conversation
of the first campus desegregation, from 1873 to 1877. Anniversaries of campus racial diversity during the Reconstruction years had come and gone
with little fanfare.

The South is known for remembering—taking pride in its diaries, stat-
ues, reenactments, and museums. But recall is a selective pastime, and the
Reconstruction era, from approximately 1865 to 1877, is one of those periods
that many southerners for many years either denied or denigrated. In its
aftermath, as resegregation took hold and kept its grip through the first half
of the next century, forgetting was easy. Only very recently has Reconstruction begun to gather growing recognition as an important period of vitality
and opportunity that demonstrated possibilities for extending education,
participation, innovation, professional accomplishment, and choice to all
citizens. Historian Eric Foner has reminded us that not only were the Fourteenth and Fifteenth amendments to the US Constitution passed during
Reconstruction but biracial governing bodies of the time also "established
the South's first state-funded public school systems, sought to strengthen
the bargaining power of plantation laborers, made taxation equitable, and
outlawed racial discrimination in transportation and public accommodations." Additionally, Foner continued, "Congress enacted one of the most
important laws in American history, the Civil Rights Act of 1866, still on the

books today," affirming citizenship for those born on US soil and remaining contentious in contemporary political battles.[1]

That Richard Greener became less widely remembered or remarked upon after his death is somewhat understandable. In the South, he represented something to erase from memory. In the North and the Midwest, where he was for decades a notable voice for racial justice, his pattern of achievement was multidimensional and somewhat confusing. He was never consistently linked to an accessible and definitive position like Frederick Douglass's fight for emancipation, Booker T. Washington's ideas about accommodation and economic bootstrapping, or W. E. B. Du Bois's commitment to a talented tenth and wide-reaching activism. Examining his "dilemma," historian Allison Blakely noted that many of Greener's contemporaries viewed him as "the most gifted Negro intellectual of his generation." However, she concluded that his commitment to individualism and intellectual independence too often left him "ambivalent about whether he should attempt to be a leader at all." Additionally, she found that during Greener's active years, a generation earlier than those of Du Bois, his "education and philosophy isolated him from the Negro masses to the extent that he could hardly have hoped to be their champion even if he had wished to be."[2]

Greener himself claimed, "I have never aspired to be a leader. . . . I still believe and preach the doctrine that each man who raises himself elevates the race."[3] His education, abilities, and persistence allowed him to exhibit impressive and varied achievements in oratory, writing, education, law, and government. However, he undoubtedly will continue to be best known as the first black graduate of Harvard College and the first black faculty member at a southern public university.

The complexity of Greener's persona, the difficulties of his own racial identity, and the variety of his contributions complicate attempts at any firm definition of who he really was. There were, in fact, two Richard Greeners, and they were not as simple as black or white. One was a street-smart kid who grew into an assertive black activist and badly wanted to use his emotional commitment and his speaking and writing skills to achieve leadership (or at least great prominence) in promoting racial justice and civil rights. The other was a well-educated intellectual with a preference for literature and law who understood that his best chance for meaningful (professionally and financially) work would likely be through the advantages conferred by whiteness—his own light skin and his network of white friends and contacts. In this sense, his life narrative offers support for Du Bois's theory of "double-consciousness," whereby black citizens were both who they were and how they were viewed by whites. "One feels his two-ness," claimed Du Bois, "an American, a Negro; two souls, two thoughts, two unreconciled strivings; two warring ideals in one dark body, whose dogged strength alone keeps it from being torn asunder."[4]

Greener's attempts to amalgamate his varied identities generally worked only temporarily and were often frustrating and embittering. His Reconstruction professorship, however, was unique in allowing him to live comfortably inside both individualities. With his education, professional abilities, and hard work, he was accepted by the inclusionary liberal white leaders then in power. At the same time, he interacted with blacks in politics, on campus, and elsewhere without any hint of criticism from them that he was too cozy with whites. He never explained why he continued to label himself as "a South Carolinian," identifying with a place known for an abysmal record on race issues. However, the rare opportunity to be at ease with the double-consciousness of both Richard Greeners during that time creates a possible rationale.

Light-skinned, often multinational, "black" US citizens have typically had at least some choices and possibilities not otherwise available to darker-skinned citizens. Greener demonstrated, however, that new difficulties were always on the horizon, especially among activists struggling for racial justice and equal opportunity. When he spent too much time passing for the sake of riding in a better railway car, or learning with whites for the sake of a better education, or networking with whites so as to have a better job, he was pegged as a turncoat by stalwart racial activists. Yet, he was enough of an activist himself to expose white prejudices when he wrote about, spoke on, and campaigned for black citizens and causes. While he admired many white friends and colleagues, he exemplified an observation once made about his cousin, Isaiah Wears: "To him, it was obvious that whites could write about equality, as Jefferson had done, but they never understood what it meant."[5] Then, as now, it was possible for a light-complexioned, mixed-ancestry individual to be too white for blacks and too black for whites.

Greener's life was a precarious balancing act not always successfully executed. When he did well, especially as an educator, orator, and writer, he achieved and deserved high accolades as an important black pioneer and leader—the man who identified a "white problem" and worked to solve it. But he also was easily distracted by imagined and real personal slights, by the brass ring he might just catch with his next job or venture, and by an impatience for recognition and reward. With his ramrod straight posture, neatly trimmed moustache, and cultured vocabulary, he was sometimes taken as an arrogant dandy. With his oratorical skill and energetic commitment to black advancement, however, he could also be viewed as a crucial voice for civil rights and equal opportunities.

• • •

Undoubtedly, Greener's personal life was a source of great pain. It started with losing his father at an early age and ended with losing two families. It is understandable that his wife Genevieve and their five children decided to slip across the color line to a place of far greater opportunity—a gradual process made all the more possible by the Greeners' marital estrangement. As noted by legal scholar and historian Daniel Sharfstein, passing was not synonymous with masquerading, and for many people of light complexion "the real struggle was to stay colored rather than cross over. . . . Being white could be as simple as keeping one's mouth shut." Additionally, before reliable official records of ancestry became readily available, "individuals and communities drew lines for themselves and their neighbors in ways that suited them best, often allowing racially ambiguous people to become white."[6]

It is also hardly unusual for a marriage to fizzle and for the spouses to separate and never see one another again. What seems more astonishing, however, is the termination of contact between the children and their father as they switched from Greener to Greene. According to historian Joel Williamson, part-time passing was accomplished by many light-skinned African Americans in the nineteenth and early twentieth centuries. They were white in their new communities and jobs in the North but were accepted as black again when visiting family members elsewhere.[7] However, with the possible exception of a quick visit from his daughter Belle that may or may not have occurred, Greener seems to have had no contact with his five "Greene" children for the last twenty-four years of his life—a situation that seems all the more poignant in light of his enjoyment in receiving letters from his Japanese daughter. Of note, perhaps, are Greener's own habits with regard to relationships. He formed close and continuing friendships with people like the Grimké brothers, Whitefield McKinlay, the Platt family, and his cousin Isaiah Wears, but there is little evidence that he saw his mother between his graduation from Harvard in 1870 and her death in 1888.

Greener would have been especially proud of all his adult children's accomplishments, as he evidently was of the Japanese daughter with whom he corresponded. His daughter Belle da Costa Greene, who became the highly accomplished and widely known mastermind of the J. P. Morgan Library collections, helped her siblings with college expenses and often had one or more of them, as well as her mother, living at her New York apartment. Her professional achievements and personal contradictions were detailed in a 2007 biography, *An Illuminated Life: Belle da Costa Greene's Journey from Prejudice to Privilege*, by Heidi Ardizzone. Russell da Costa Greene had a successful engineering career, a white wife, and a white country club membership. Daughter Louise married noted speech therapist Frederick Martin and helped him found the Martin Institute for Speech Correction in Ithaca, New York. Another daughter, Ethel Alice, married George Oakley and continued her career in public-school teaching. The youngest, Theodora (Teddy), lost her first husband in World War I, then remarried and lost her son in World War II.[8] Greener would not have the pleasure of passing on to any family members his legacy of outspoken oratory and writing on behalf of black citizens.

The daughter who wrote to Greener after he left Vladivostok became part of a new family when her mother, Mishiyo Kawashima, married a British citizen and became Mishiyo Phillips. The daughter, educated in English schools, took Olive as her first name. She eventually returned to Southeast Asia, and in 1932 married a German citizen in Hong Kong, becoming Olive Knierim. She and her young daughter, Evelyn, spent a great deal of World War II in the Black Forest area of Germany. To travel as freely as possible and avoid persecution, she needed proof that she was not of Jewish ancestry, so she wrote to Harvard officials for word of her father's background. The assistant dean who responded simply noted that evidence in Greener's records "indicate[d] he was not Jewish." He did not mention, and may not have even known, Greener's unique position as the first black graduate of Harvard College.[9] Thus, Olive Knierim never knew her father's ancestry.[10] His granddaughter, Evelyn K. Bausman, was educated in Germany and Switzerland. She eventually moved to the United States with her American husband, John Bausman, who had been Moscow bureau chief for the Associated Press.[11]

Greener's generous Chicago cousin, Ida Platt, was the only African American female lawyer in Illinois until 1920. She continued in law practice, particularly in probate and real estate, until her retirement in 1928, when, at age sixty-five, she married and relocated to England. She died in 1939.[12]

• • •

With all his accomplishments, Greener was greatly constrained by a combination of political and social circumstances from achieving still more. The late nineteenth- and early twentieth-century Progressive Era, with its commitment to public service, fair labor practices, clean cities, busted trusts, and help for the disadvantaged, seemed so promising. But the leaders of the Progressive movement, including several US presidents, were selective

Plaque honoring Greener in central Cambridge, Massachusetts.
Courtesy of Cambridge Historical Commission.

in their causes, and segregation, lynching, and social and economic race discrimination actually expanded during the time—somewhat in proportion to the shrinking black voice at the ballot box. It became clear that the path to real racial equality in the United States would be long and tortuous. Citizens like Greener were essential to that process by pioneering personal instances of achievement and by keeping the cause in the forefront. Du Bois implied that sentiment in 1903 when he insisted that "the Negro race, like all races, is going to be saved by its exceptional men." He named Greener as one of the "talented tenth" who filled that role—"a group of educated and gifted leaders" who struggled for racial uplift "through political organization, historical and polemic writing and moral regeneration."[13]

Greener would have been pleased to view himself as part of a process that eventually witnessed the end of legalized segregation and the passage of federal legislation to protect civil and voting rights. And he would have been delighted to know that his legacy is not at all forgotten and, in fact, may be growing. Seventy years after his death, the City of Cambridge, Massachusetts, honored him with a large descriptive plaque across from Harvard Square as part of the Cambridge African American Heritage Trail developed by the Cambridge Historical Commission. In 2016, the Harvard Foundation portraiture project commissioned a large portrait of Greener as an undergraduate standing in front of his Stoughton Hall residence. In 1994, more than a century after his courtroom defense in the court-martial of Johnson C. Whittaker, Samuel L. Jackson played Richard Greener in the television docudrama, "Assault at West Point." More recently, Greener was the subject of a one-act play commissioned for the University of South Carolina bicentennial celebration. His portrait, by artist Larry Lebby, hangs in the office of that university's president, and the university's board of trustees approved plans for a statue in his honor in a prominent location next to the main campus library.

Finally, there was the find that turned Greener into a national news story in 2012: the discovery of a battered steamer trunk in an abandoned Chicago building. The documents inside, long surmised to have been lost in the San Francisco earthquake of 1906, included Greener's Harvard diploma, University of South Carolina Law School diploma, and license to practice law in South Carolina. Now restored, the items are currently at the Pusey Library of Harvard University and the South Caroliniana Library of the University of South Carolina—appropriate locations for treasured possessions of a man who proudly called himself a son of Harvard and a South Carolinian.

ACKNOWLEDGMENTS

I am fortunate that many friends and colleagues accompanied me on the journey that became this book, and I am certain I cannot adequately thank them. The first to contribute and encourage was my friend and collaborator in past research and writing, Professor Carolyn B. Matalene. She initiated the idea of a Greener biography and then supported my efforts with her always expert suggestions, research, chapter reviews, feedback, and mixed-metaphor detection.

Likewise, I could not have undertaken this project without the aid of a 2002 PhD dissertation by Michael Robert Mounter. His thorough research concerning Richard T. Greener created an invaluable guide, and I have cited his work frequently in this volume. Closest to the subject and more helpful than any biographer has a right to expect, was Greener's granddaughter Evelyn Bausman, who opened her house, her files, and her memories to me. She shared her discerning and objective perspectives and checked relevant chapter drafts against her own collections for accuracy. I am ever grateful to her and to her husband, the late John Bausman.

From the start of the project, I received timely answers and needed support from the tremendously responsive professionals at Johns Hopkins University Press. Senior Acquisitions Editor Elizabeth Demers was immediately encouraging, and Managing Editor Juliana McCarthy, along with Meagan Szekely, continued to guide my work and smooth all processes. Julia Smith added her copyediting expertise and patience. Additionally, I have been extremely fortunate in receiving the assistance and advice of my friend John S. McCormack, whose capacity for editorial detail is boundless and who created the index with extraordinary patience and expertise. Another deeply appreciated friend and academic collaborator, Anna Janosik Cooke, skillfully managed the task of pulling together various sources into a comprehensive bibliography.

Colleagues at the University of South Carolina encouraged and advised me often as this project developed. Professors Christian Anderson and Lydia

Brandt, leaders of the university's efforts toward a Richard Greener memorial statue on campus, offered valuable feedback and ideas. Others whose interest provided vital impetus included University President Harris Pastides, Dean of Libraries Thomas McNally, Chief Diversity Officer John H. Dozier, University Architect Derek Gruner, Dean of the School of Music Tayloe Harding, and colleagues near and far, including John Thelin, Linda Eisenmann, Jack Newell, Iris Saltiel, Lisa Berger, Bob Luke, Vivian Gallman Derienzo, Fritz Hamer, James Hudgins, Jane Przybysz, Jancy Houck, Robert Weyeneth, Willie Odom, Telesia Davis, Bernard Powers, Kenneth Frierson, Jay Dowd, Joe Neary, and Jeannie Weingarth.

My research depended on the guidance and good graces of librarians and archivists, whose work is vitally important to all scholars of history. I owe a special debt of gratitude to those at the South Caroliniana Library of the University of South Carolina: Henry Fulmer, Elizabeth West, and the other highly expert staff members who managed to quickly retrieve primary materials even amid the renovation of their wonderful building. Paige Roberts, Director of Archives and Special Collections at Phillips Academy, Andover, made every relevant document and image accessible in record time. Similarly, I thank the helpful professionals at the Pusey and Houghton Libraries at Harvard University, the Moorland-Spingarn Research Center at Howard University, the Manuscript and Newspaper Divisions of the Library of Congress, the New York Public Library, the Addlestone Library and Avery Research Center at the College of Charleston, the South Carolina Historical Society, and the Ulysses S. Grant Monument Association. I also thank Steve Strachan, Dan Jones, and Audrey Bashaw for aiding my access to NewsBank digitized newspapers.

At home and beyond, numerous friends have been good-natured enough to ask about and listen to tales from my research many, many times. For that, I appreciate Joan, Judy, Janice, Karen, Fred and Micki, Krystina and Stan, Isabelle, Chris and Jo, Pete and Lenore, Lynn, Laurie, Cindy and Doug, the "Edisto Beach ladies," Lonna Reynolds, Bret Cohen, Britt Haxton, Les Janka, and all my pals who care. Extra gratitude goes to my immediate family members: my sister, Emilie Egan, and my children, Adrienne and Brett Reynolds. Finally, I have a special kind of appreciation for a cat named Nudge, who faithfully sat near my computer—sometimes on the keyboard—during most of the writing process.

NOTES

Abbreviations

HL-CS	Charles Sumner Correspondence, Houghton Library, Harvard University, Cambridge, MA
HUA	Harvard University Archives, Pusey Library, Harvard University, Cambridge, MA
HUA-FM	Harvard College Faculty Minutes, Harvard University Archives, Pusey Library, Harvard University, Cambridge, MA
HUA-TH	Thomas Hill Papers, Harvard University Archives, Pusey Library, Harvard University, Cambridge, MA
LOC-TR	Theodore Roosevelt Papers, Library of Congress, Washington, DC
LOC-WM	Whitefield McKinlay Papers, Carter G. Woodson Collection, Library of Congress, Washington, DC
MSR-AG	Archibald Henry Grimké Papers, Moorland-Spingarn Research Center, Howard University, Washington, DC
MSR-FG	Francis James Grimké Papers, Moorland-Spingarn Research Center, Howard University, Washington, DC
MSR-JS	Joel S. Spingarn Papers, Moorland-Spingarn Research Center, Howard University, Washington, DC
MSR-JW	Jacob C. White Collection, Moorland-Spingarn Research Center, Howard University, Washington, DC
NA-DS	Numerical and Minor Files, US Department of State, 1906–10, National Archives, Washington, DC
NA-DV	Despatches from United States Consuls in Vladivostok, National Archives and Record Service, Washington, DC
NPS-GF	Grant Family Papers, Manhattan Historical Site Archives, National Park Service, New York, NY
NPS-GMA	Grant Monument Association Records, Manhattan Historical Site Archives, National Park Service, New York, NY
NYPL-JB	John Edward Bruce Papers, Schomburg Center for Research in Black Culture, New York Public Library, New York, NY
PAA	Phillips Academy Andover Archives, Wendell Holmes Library, Andover, MA
QB-LL	Lewis Howard Latimer Collection, Queens Borough Public Library, Long Island Division, New York, NY

RTG   Richard Theodore Greener
SCDAH-WH   Governor Hampton Papers, South Carolina Department of Archives
                and History, Columbia
SCHS   South Carolina Historical Society, Charleston
SCL-BT   Records of the University Board of Trustees, 1873–75, University
                Archives, South Caroliniana Library, University of South Carolina,
                Columbia
SCL-EC   Edward Crosland Papers, South Caroliniana Library, University of
                South Carolina, Columbia
SCL-FB   Fisk Brewer Papers, South Caroliniana Library, University of South
                Carolina, Columbia
SCL-MM   Michael Mounter Research Files, South Caroliniana Library, Univer-
                sity of South Carolina, Columbia
SCL-NS   State Normal School Curriculum File, South Caroliniana Library,
                University of South Carolina, Columbia
SCL-RG   Richard Greener Research Collection, South Caroliniana Library,
                University of South Carolina, Columbia
SCL-RR   Reconstruction Records, University Archives, South Caroliniana
                Library, University of South Carolina, Columbia
UM-DB   W. E. B. Du Bois Papers, Special Collections and University Archives,
                University of Massachusetts Libraries, Amherst
WL-SHC   Southern Historical Collection, Wilson Library, University of North
                Carolina, Chapel Hill

Introduction

1. Janssen, Kim, "'It Gives Me Gooseflesh': Remarkable Find in South Side Attic,"
Chicago Sun-Times, Mar. 10, 2012. See, also, Tim Lacy, "'I Had to Get Their Attention':
Race, Class and Intellectual History on Chicago's South Side," Jan. 23, 2014, Society for
US Intellectual History blog, S-USih.org/2014/01/.

2. RTG, "Speech at the Harvard Club of New York, Feb. 21, 1881," quoted in *Philadelphia Christian Recorder*, Mar. 3, 1881.

3. Turner, "Sponsored and Contest Mobility and the School System," 857.

4. RTG, "The Intellectual Position of the Negro," 169; RTG, "The White Problem,"
355; Henry Louis Gates Jr., quoted in "First Black Alumnus's Papers Found," *Harvard
Magazine*, Mar. 21, 2012, harvardmagazine.com/2012/03/greener-papers-found.

5. RTG to W. E. B. Du Bois, Feb. 4, 1910, in Aptheker, *The Correspondence of W. E. B.
Du Bois*, 1:168.

6. Mounter, "Richard Theodore Greener: The Idealist," 4.

Chapter 1. Boyhood Interrupted

1. *Doylestown (PA) Democrat*, Sept. 16, 1847, quoted in Biddle and Dubin, *Tasting
Freedom*, 85.

2. Biddle and Dubin, *Tasting Freedom*, 85; Litwack, *North of Slavery*, 64; Du Bois, *Philadelphia Negro*, 36.

3. Robert Vaux to Samuel Emlen, May 31, 1831, quoted in Litwack, *North of Slavery*, 64; Du Bois, *Philadelphia Negro*, 32.

4. Mounter, "Richard Theodore Greener: The Idealist," 6–7.

5. RTG, "Richard T. Greener," unpublished handwritten biographical sketch, May 19, 1870, HUA.

6. William H. Crogman, "Negro Education—Its Helps and Hindrances," address to the National Educational Association, Madison, Wisconsin, 1884, quoted in Foner and Branham, *Lift Every Voice*, 632.

7. RTG, "Richard T. Greener."

8. RTG to Mishiyo Kawashima, Sept. 12, 1917, private collection of Evelyn Bausman. This letter states that Greener was ten years old when his father took him to Liverpool. Given the timing of his father's subsequent move to California, it is more likely Greener was seven years old at the time, as stated in Mounter, "Richard Theodore Greener: The Idealist," 10.

9. Du Bois, *Philadelphia Negro*, 86.

10. RTG, "Richard T. Greener;" Mounter, "Richard Theodore Greener: The Idealist," 12.

11. Litwack, *North of Slavery*, 143; Horton and Horton, *Black Bostonians*, 4, 7.

12. City of Boston, "Report of a Special Committee of the Grammar School Board, 1849," 33, quoted in Litwack, *North of Slavery*, 144, 145.

13. City of Cambridge, "Mayor's Address and Reports, 1852," 103; RTG, "Richard T. Greener."

14. A Bostonian, quoted in Woodward, *The Strange Career of Jim Crow*, 19; Douglass, quoted in Philip Foner, *Life and Writings of Frederick Douglass*, 2:250; Macon B. Allen to John Jay, Nov. 26, 1845, quoted in J. Clay Smith Jr., *Emancipation*, 95.

15. RTG, "Richard T. Greener."

16. Holmes, *The Autocrat of the Breakfast Table*, 74, 91.

17. RTG to Lewis H. Latimer, Jan. 5, 1915, QB-LL.

18. George W. Williams, *History of the Negro Race in America*, 2:40–41.

19. See Martin Duberman, "The Northern Response to Slavery," in Duberman, *The Antislavery Vanguard*, 395–413.

20. RTG, "Reminiscences of Frederick Douglass," 291.

21. Ibid., 294; Philip S. Foner, *Frederick Douglass*, 188. See, also, Levesque, *Black Boston*, 326.

22. Douglass, "The Boston Mob," 1.

23. Horton and Horton, *Black Bostonians*, 417–21; Mounter, "Richard Theodore Greener: The Idealist," 22–24; Douglass, "The Boston Mob," 1.

24. RTG, "Richard T. Greener."

25. "An Old Boston Firm Suspends," *New York Times*, May 3, 1884.

26. RTG, "Richard T. Greener."

27. Petrulionis, *To Set This World Right*, 125–53; "Antislavery in Concord," Concord Free Library, www.concordlibrary.org/scollect/antislavery/06_essay.html#70.

Chapter 2. Being Prepared

1. RTG, "Richard T. Greener"; Baumann, *Constructing Black Education*, 28.

2. Baumann, *Constructing Black Education*, 20; Litwack, *North of Slavery*, 140; Blodgett, *Oberlin History*, 15.

3. Lawson and Merrill, "The Antebellum 'Talented Thousandth,'" 151–52.

4. Coppin, *Reminiscences*, 12.

5. Butchart, "Mission Matters," 13–14; RTG, "Richard T. Greener."

6. RTG, "Richard T. Greener."

7. RTG, "First Lessons."

8. Coppin, *Reminiscences*, 19.

9. McPherson, *Battle Cry of Freedom*, 610; J. Brent Morrison, *Oberlin*, 413; RTG, "Richard T. Greener"; Baumann, *Constructing Black Education*, 52.

10. RTG, "Richard T. Greener"; *Boston Commonwealth*, May 27, 1864; Linda M. Perkins, *Fanny Jackson Coppin*, 38–39; Mounter, "Richard Theodore Greener: The Idealist," 36–37.

11. Perkins, *Fanny Jackson Coppin*, 39–40; *National Anti-Slavery Standard*, July 9, 1864.

12. RTG, "Richard T. Greener"; *Catalogue of Phillips Academy, Andover, Mass., July 1865* (Andover, MA: Warren F. Draper, 1867), quoted in Mounter, "Richard Theodore Greener: The Idealist," 39.

13. Allis, *Youth from Every Quarter*, 51–52.

14. Ibid., 180–217.

15. "Address of Colonel Richard Theodore Greener," 28.

16. Allis, *Youth from Every Quarter*, 287; RTG, "Richard T. Greener."

17. Allis, *Youth from Every Quarter*, 198–200.

18. Ibid., 198–99; "Address of Colonel Richard Theodore Greener," 29.

19. Frances Marchant, "Richard Theodore Greener: A Story of a Busy Man," unpublished handwritten manuscript, 1882, SCL-RG; Mounter, "Richard Theodore Greener: The Idealist," 43; RTG, "Richard T. Greener."

20. Allis, "Hurrah. Hurrah," 6.

21. Allis, *Youth from Every Quarter*, 215; RTG to Lewis Howard Latimer, June 2, 1915, QB-LL.

22. "Abraham Lincoln," 1–3.

23. Horace Deming Autograph Book, PAA, quoted in Mounter, "Richard Theodore Greener: The Idealist," 46.

24. RTG to Latimer, June 2, 1915.

Chapter 3. Experiment at Harvard

1. RTG, "Speech at the Harvard Club of New York, February 21, 1881."

2. Caldwell Titcomb, "The Black Presence at Harvard: An Overview," in Sollors et al., *Blacks at Harvard*, 2; RTG, "Richard T. Greener."

3. Thomas Hill to Augustus Batchelder, n.d., quoted in West, "Harvard's First Black

Graduates," 25; Samuel Eliot Morison, *Three Centuries*, 305, 301–19; Thomas Hill to Augustus Batchelder, July 17, 1866, HUA-TH.

4. Samuel Eliot Morison, *Three Centuries*, 303, 315–16.

5. *Nation*, December 17, 1878, 12; Samuel Eliot Morison, *Three Centuries*, 317, 306–8. See, also, Samuel Eliot Morison, introduction to *Development of Harvard University*, xxv–xxxix.

6. Samuel Eliot Morison, *Three Centuries*, 310, 313–17; "Harvard Presidential Report of 1863," quoted in Morison, *Three Centuries*, 313.

7. "Negro Equality," *Columbus Ohio Statesman*, October 3, 1865, reprinted from *Boston Herald*; *Catalogue of the Officers and Students*, 25; Samuel Eliot Morison, *Three Centuries*, 442; RTG, "Richard T. Greener."

8. John Langdon Sibley, "John Langdon Sibley's Diary," Oct. 14, 1865, 722, HUA.

9. *Catalogue of the Officers and Students*, 29. See, also, Mounter, "Richard Theodore Greener: The Idealist," 50–51.

10. RTG, "Richard T. Greener"; RTG, "Speech at the Harvard Club of New York, February 21, 1881"; Hill to Batchelder, Feb. 1, 1866, HUA-TH.

11. Harvard College Faculty minutes, Jan. 31, 1866, HUA.

12. Hill to Batchelder, Feb. 1, 1866, HUA-TH.

13. Batchelder to Hill, Feb. 2, 1866, HUA-TH.

14. Hill to Batchelder, Mar. 6, 1866, and Hill to Batchelder, July 17, 1866, HUA-TH; RTG, "Richard T. Greener."

15. Testimony of Richard T. Greener, Apr. 29, 1880, "Proceedings of the Court of Inquiry in the Case of Johnson C. Whittaker," Part 10, 2097, quoted in Mounter, "Richard Theodore Greener: The Idealist," 55; Samuel Eliot Morison, *Development of Harvard University*, xli–xlii.

16. *Collegian*, n.d., quoted in *The Harvard Advocate Catalogue, 1866–1886*, 3–7, *Collegian* files, HUA.

17. *Harvard Advocate*, June 25, 1869; Mounter, "Richard T. Greener: The Idealist," 59–60.

18. "Introduction," *Records of the Pi Eta Society, 1866–1953*, 4, HUA; RTG, "Richard T. Greener."

19. Thomas Hill, printed circular, August 11, 1865, Records of the Thayer Club, HUA. See, also, "The Thayer Club," *Harvard Crimson*, February 21, 1873, available at www.the crimson.com/article1823/2/21/the-thayer-club/.

20. RTG, "Richard T. Greener"; Frances A. Rollin, "Diary," quoted in Sterling, *We Are Your Sisters*, 455.

21. Du Bois, "A Negro Student at Harvard at the End of the Nineteenth Century," 441.

22. Marchant, "Richard Theodore Greener"; Mounter, "Richard Theodore Greener: The Idealist," 66.

23. "Harvard Boys," *Philadelphia Evening Bulletin*, August 12, 1869, reprinted in *Philadelphia Christian Recorder*, Aug. 21, 1869.

24. RTG, "Reminiscences of Frederick Douglass," 292–93.

25. "Class-Day at Harvard," *New York Times*, June 25, 1870; "The Colleges," *New York Times*, June 29, 1870.

26. Harvard University, *Harvard . . . Tenth Report.*

27. RTG, "Richard T. Greener."

28. Ibid.

Chapter 4. An Accidental Academic

1. Mounter, "Richard Theodore Greener: The Idealist," 49.

2. The will of Richard Humphreys, quoted in Biddle and Dubin, *Tasting Freedom*, 156.

3. US Census, 1870, quoted in Snyder, *120 Years of American Education*, 13. For ICY history, see Perkins and Taylor, "The Bible in the Educational Philosophies of Fanny Jackson Coppin and Nannie Helen Burroughs," and Linda Marie Perkins, "Quaker Beneficence and Black Control: The Institute for Colored Youth, 1852–1903," in Franklin and Anderson, *New Perspectives on Black Educational History*, 19–43.

4. Biddle and Dubin, *Tasting Freedom*, 402; Perkins, *Fanny Jackson Coppin*, 99.

5. Perkins, *Fanny Jackson Coppin*, 90; Henry C. Silcox, "Nineteenth Century Black Militant," 70; Biddle and Dubin, *Tasting Freedom*, 403; Alfred Cope to Octavius Catto, April 23, 1869, quoted in Perkins, "Quaker Beneficence," 26.

6. Coppin, *Reminiscences*, 22–23; Mounter, "Richard Theodore Greener: The Idealist," 34–36, 70–71.

7. Du Bois, *The Philadelphia Negro*, 50–51; Biddle and Dubin, *Tasting Freedom*, 323–54.

8. Isaiah Wears, speech at the National Convention of Colored Men, 1868, quoted in Biddle and Dubin, *Tasting Freedom*, 399; Coppin, *Reminiscences*, 14; Perkins, "Quaker Beneficence," 40.

9. Harris, "Historic Schools in Washington, D.C.," 9–13; Biddle and Dubin, *Tasting Freedom*, 413–14.

10. *Chicago Tribune*, Oct. 20, 1870, 2.

11. Biddle and Dubin, *Tasting Freedom*, 420–27.

12. Ibid., 429–31.

13. *Philadelphia Inquirer*, Oct. 16 and 17, 1871.

14. Du Bois, *The Philadelphia Negro*, 40, 42.

15. Isaiah Wears, "The Ku Klux of the North," in Foner and Branham, *Lift Every Voice*, 511.

16. Du Bois, *The Philadelphia Negro*, 42.

17. *New National Era*, Jan. 18, 1872.

18. *New National Era*, July 13, 1872.

19. RTG to Charles Sumner, Mar. 18, 1872, HL-CS.

20. "A Civil Rights Delegation," *New National Era*, January 18, 1872. See, also, Robert B. Elliott, "The Civil Rights Bill," in Foner and Branham, *Lift Every Voice*, 520–63.

21. "A Civil Rights Delegation."

22. Ibid.

23. *Congressional Globe*, 42nd Congress, 2nd Session, Jan. 31, 1872, 727, quoted in Mounter, "Richard Theodore Greener: The Idealist," 79; Henry McNeal Turner, speech to a convention of black newspapermen, quoted in Egerton, *The Wars of Reconstruction*, 311.

24. RTG to Sumner, Mar. 18, 1872.

25. Norman B. Wood, *The White Side of a Black Subject*, 355; Mary Gibson Hundley, *The Dunbar Story*, 15–24.

26. Mounter, "Richard Theodore Greener: The Idealist," 83–84.

27. "Prof. Richard T. Greener, Principal of the Male Department," *Philadelphia Christian Recorder*, Sept. 28, 1872.

28. Frazier, *Black Bourgeoisie*, 197–98.

29. Mounter, "Richard Theodore Greener: The Idealist," 87–88.

30. John E. Bruce, quoted in Gatewood, *Aristocrats of Color*, 160; RTG, "An Address," *New National Era*, Apr. 17, 1873; RTG, "Suffrage for Women," *New National Era*, Feb. 20, 1873; RTG, "Young Men to the Front," *New National Era*, Apr. 24, 1873.

31. Mounter, "Richard Theodore Greener: The Idealist," 91, 94–95.

32. "Negro Hate in the School Board," *New National Era*, June 5, 1873.

33. D. A. Straker, "Examination of the Preparatory High School," *New National Era*, June 19, 1873; *New National Era*, June 19, 1873.

34. *Philadelphia Christian Recorder*, Sept. 25, 1873; "The Colored Gang," *Washington Republican*, July 17, 1873; Mounter, "Richard Theodore Greener: The Idealist," 106; *New National Era*, July 3, 1873.

35. Carlton Fletcher, "Glover Park History: Historical Sketches of Glover Park, Upper Georgetown, and Georgetown Heights," Gloverparkhistory.com.

36. J. K. Jillson to RTG, Oct. 10, 1873, SCL-RR; Mounter, "Richard Theodore Greener: The Idealist," 112; J. K. Jillson to RTG, Oct. 28, 1873, SCL-RR.

Chapter 5. Professing in a Small and Angry Place

1. Taylor, *The Negro in South Carolina During Reconstruction*, 68.

2. Ibid., 153–70. See, also, Simkins and Woody, *South Carolina*, 186–99.

3. Taylor, *The Negro in South Carolina During Reconstruction*, 5. See, also, Sinclair, *The Aftermath of Slavery*, 154.

4. T. McCants Stewart, "Rumbles in the South," *New York Freeman*, Apr. 25, 1885. For definitions of carpetbaggers and scalawags, see Simkins and Woody, *South Carolina*, 73–74.

5. A South Carolinian [Belton Townsend O'Neall], "South Carolina Society," 676.

6. Edward Crosland to George Crosland, Feb. 27, 1869, SCL-EC; *Charleston Daily News*, Mar. 10, 1871, 2.

7. *Fairfield Herald* (Winnsboro, SC), Nov. 20, 1872, 1; *Georgetown Times*, quoted in *Anderson (SC) Intelligencer*, Nov. 27, 1873, 3.

8. *Charleston Daily News*, Jan. 22, 1872, 1; Pike, *Prostrate State*, 33–34.

9. "A History of Columbia, South Carolina," www.carolina.com/SC/Towns/Columbia_SC_2.html. See, also, Simkins and Woody, *South Carolina*, 278–79.

10. Speech by Woodrow Wilson, July 29, 1913, quoted in Baker, *Woodrow Wilson*, 222.

11. Green, *History of the University*, 44–55.

12. Matalene and Reynolds, *Carolina Voices*, 56–62. See, also, Hollis, *University of South Carolina*, 65–71.

13. Litwack, *North of Slavery*, 292.

14. Katherine Thompson Allen, *The University*, 5–6.

15. *New York Times*, Dec. 25, 1868, 2.

16. Hollis, *University of South Carolina*, 58; Resolution of the Board of Trustees, quoted in Simkins and Woody, *South Carolina*, 441.

17. Mounter, "Richard Theodore Greener: The Idealist," 117–18.

18. Green, *History of the University*, 279–81; Katherine Thompson Allen, *The University*, 5.

19. Minutes, Oct. 28, 1873, SCL-BT; "Biographical Notes," Erastus Everson Papers, 1861–1893, SCHS; Henry Fulmer, "Richard T. Greener."

20. Hollis, *University of South Carolina*, 69; Vaughn, "South Carolina University"; James Reynolds, quoted in LaBorde, *History of the South Carolina College*, xv.

21. Mounter, "Richard Theodore Greener and the African American Individual," 135; *Philadelphia Christian Recorder*, July 9, 1874, 1.

22. Photography Collection of Richard Greener, SCL-RR.

23. "Educational Meeting," *Columbia Daily Union Herald*, Dec. 12, 1873, 1.

24. *Columbia Daily Phoenix*, Dec. 30, 1873, 1; *Columbia Daily Union Herald*, undated clippings, quoted in Hollis, *University of South Carolina*, 71; Fisk Parsons Brewer Scrapbook, SCL-FB.

25. "Report of the Chairman of the Faculty of the University, 1875," quoted in Hollis, *University of South Carolina*, 74; RTG to Charles Sumner, Jan. 15, 1872, HL-CS; *South Carolina Reports and Resolutions, 1874–1875* (Columbia, SC), 329, quoted in Mounter, *At Freedom's Door*, 135; *Sixth Annual Report of the State Superintendent of Education, 1874–1875*, 2, quoted in Hollis, *University of South Carolina*, 73.

26. *South Carolina Reports and Resolutions, 1874–1875* (Columbia, SC), 55, quoted in Mounter, *At Freedom's Door*, 136.

27. *Sixth Annual Report of the State Superintendent of Education, 1874–1875*, 2, quoted in Hollis, *University of South Carolina*, 73; printed circular in Fisk P. Brewer Papers, SCL-FB; J. K. Jillson to RTG, June 17, 1875, SCL-RR.

28. Cornelius C. Scott, "When Negroes Attended the University," *Columbia State*, May 8, 1911, quoted in Matalene and Reynolds, *Carolina Voices*, 58.

29. RTG to Isaiah Wears, Feb. 12, 1886, MSR-JW.

30. Hollis, *University of South Carolina*, 73; Matalene and Reynolds, *Carolina Voices*, 63; RTG, "The Swallows," *Columbia Daily Union Herald*, Feb. 3, 1875.

31. Marchant, "Richard Theodore Greener." See, also, e.g., Gatewood, *Aristocrats of Color*, and Holt, *Black Over White*.

32. Holt, *Black Over White*, 59; *Charleston Daily News*, Mar. 10, 1871.

33. T. McCants Stewart, *Washington (DC) New National Era*, Apr. 16 and July 9, 1874.

34. *Columbia Daily Union Herald*, Feb. 10, 1875.

35. RTG, Benjamin Babbitt, and Anson Cummings, memo to Daniel Chamberlain, Mar. 26, 1876, SCL-RG; Mortimer Warren memo, June 27, 1875, SCL-RR; Minutes, May 9, 1874, SLC, Faculty Meeting Files.

36. RTG, "Civil Rights Again," *Columbia Union Herald*, Jan. 12, 1875.

37. "Greener, Richard Theodore," in Harvard University, *Harvard College Class of 1870, Sixth Report*, 25–26.

38. Erastus Everson Papers, SCHS, indicate that Everson went to New York and later to Massachusetts as a journalist. See, also, "Erastus Everson," http://genforum.geneal ogy.com/everson.

39. B. F. Whittemore, "Report of the Sub-Committee of the Board of Trustees of the University of South Carolina Relative to the Library of the University," handwritten report, Oct. 31, 1874, SCL-BT; RTG to University Board of Trustees, Oct. 30, 1875, SCL-BT.

40. Meeting minutes, University Board of Trustees, Nov. 1, 1875, SCL-BT.

41. *Charleston (SC) News and Courier*, Nov. 1, 1875, NewsBank, Inc.; Fulmer, "Richard T. Greener," 37.

42. RTG to University Board of Trustees, Oct. 30, 1875, SCL-BT.

43. Quoted in Foner, *A Short History*, 230; quoted in Du Bois, *The Gift of Black Folk*, 117.

44. Foner, *A Short History*, 230; A South Carolinian [Belton O'Neall Townsend], "The Political Condition of South Carolina," 182.

Chapter 6. The Brutal Retreat

1. Circular, photo copy in Everson Papers, SCHS.

2. Logan, *The Betrayal*, 9. See, also, Eric Foner, *A Short History*, 235–47, and Taylor, *The Negro in South Carolina*, 33–51.

3. *Evidence taken by the Committee of Investigation*, 26.

4. Eric Foner, *A Short History*, 202–3, 239; Brown, *The Year*, 73–110.

5. Thomas Holt, *Black over White*, 180–82. See, also, Taylor, *The Negro in South Carolina*, 214–30.

6. Simkins and Woody, *South Carolina*, 494–95.

7. Williamson, *After Slavery*, 259–73. See also Du Bois, *Black Reconstruction*, 673–76.

8. Wade Hampton, quoted in Randel, *Centennial*, 254.

9. Hampton, quoted in Williamson, *After Slavery*, 408.

10. Ibid., 268–73.

11. A South Carolinian [Belton O'Neall Townsend], "The Result in South Carolina," 6.

12. RTG to Francis J. Grimké, November 19, 1907, MSR-FG; Benjamin Tillman, speech, "The Struggles of 1876: How South Carolina Was Delivered from Carpetbag and Negro Rule," n.d., quoted in Simkins, *Pitchfork Ben Tillman*, 61; Benjamin Tillman, gubernatorial inaugural address, Dec. 4, 1890, quoted in Logan, *The Betrayal*, 74.

13. Mounter, "Richard Theodore Greener: The Idealist," 167.

14. "The Radical Meeting Friday," *Newberry (SC) Herald*, Nov. 1, 1876; "The Republican Meeting," *Pickens (SC) Sentinel*, Oct. 26, 1876.

15. "Editorial Notes," *Anderson (SC) Intelligencer*, Oct. 26, 1876; Mounter, "Richard Theodore Greener: The Idealist," 171; Williamson, *After Slavery*, 349.

16. RTG to Francis J. Grimké, Nov. 19, 1907, MSR-FG; Alfred Williams, "Redeeming the Prostrate State," *Charleston Evening Post*, Jan. 8, 1927.

17. Du Bois, *Black Reconstruction*, 687; A South Carolinian [Belton O'Neall Townsend], "The Political Condition in Carolina," 187.

18. Brown, *The Year*, 315–40; Simkins and Woody, *South Carolina*, 514–41; Holt, *Black Over White*, 195, 196.

19. W. Lewis Burke, "The Radical Law School," in Underwood and Burke, *At Freedom's Door*, 90–115; "Richard Theodore Greener," in Harvard University, *Harvard . . . Tenth Report*, 67.

20. Brown, *The Year*, 329, 343.

21. Hollis, *University of South Carolina*, 2:78–79; RTG to Rutherford B. Hayes, Mar. 9, 1877, Rutherford B. Hayes Papers, Rutherford B. Hayes Presidential Center, Fremont, Ohio, quoted in Mounter, "Richard Theodore Greener: The Idealist," 182.

22. "Gov. Chamberlain's Address," *New York Times*, Apr. 11, 1877; Daniel Chamberlain to William Lloyd Garrison, June 11, 1877, quoted in Walter Allen, *Governor Chamberlain's Administration*, 504.

23. "Minutes of the Richland Democratic Club," Aug. 24, 1876, quoted in Williamson, *After Slavery*, 408.

24. Fisk Brewer, "The University," unpublished sketch, 1877, Fisk Brewer Papers, Amistad Research Center, American Missionary Archives, Tulane University, quoted in Matalene and Reynolds, *Carolina Voices*, 65.

25. Mortimer A. Warren to the University Board of Trustees, 1877, SCL-NS; Hollis, *University of South Carolina*, 78; Du Bois, *Black Reconstruction*, 30.

26. Mounter, "Richard Theodore Greener: The Idealist," 4.

Chapter 7. Unsettled Advocate

1. Charles H. Simonton to William P. Miles, May 25, 1877, William Porcher Miles Papers, WL-SHC; *Edgefield (SC) Observer*, May 25, 1877; Cohen, *Reconstructing the Campus*, 127.

2. Lesko, Babb, and Gibbs, *Black Georgetown Remembered*, 39.

3. Ardizzone, *An Illuminated Life*, 32; Davison, *The Presidency*, 54. See, also, Mounter, "Richard Theodore Greener; The Idealist," 193.

4. Gatewood, *Aristocrats of Color*, 39.

5. Frazier, *Black Bourgeoisie*, 198; W. Calvin Chase, *Washington Bee*, Dec. 20, 1890; US Census, as described in Ardizzone, *An Illuminated Life*, 33, 493.

6. RTG to Charles Sumner, Jan. 15, 1872, HL-CS; Davison, *The Presidency*, 54.

7. Philip S. Foner, *Frederick Douglass*, 323; Wade Hampton, speech to the Washington Light Infantry, quoted in *Yorkville (SC) Inquirer*, Apr. 26, 1877.

8. Rutherford B. Hayes, diary entries for Oct. 24, 1878, Mar. 14, 1877, and Apr. 22, 1877, quoted in Harry Williams, *Hayes*, 164, 81, 86.

9. Davison, *The Presidency*, 138.

10. Quoted in Williams, *Hayes*, 101.

11. Rutherford B. Hayes to Frederick W. Seward, Rutherford B. Hayes Papers, Rutherford B. Hayes Presidential Center, Freemont, Ohio, quoted in Mounter, "Richard Theodore Greener: The Idealist," 190.

12. Davison, *The Presidency*, 55; RTG to Nathaniel B. Barnwell, Aug. 30, 1877, SCL-RR; RTG to Wade Hampton, May 11, 1877, SCDAH-WH; Greener to Nathaniel B. Barnwell, Aug. 20, 1877, SCL-RR.

13. RTG to Isaiah Wears, Apr. 25, 1878, MSR-JW.

14. RTG to Isaiah Wears, Apr. 6, 1878, MSR-JW.

15. Logan, *Howard University*, 86–87; Harvard University, *Harvard . . . Sixth Report*, 26.

16. RTG to Thomas Ticknor, May 2, 1878, SCL-MM; RTG to Isaiah Wears, n.d., MSR-JW.

17. Greener, "The Intellectual Position of the Negro," 165, 166, 189.

18. "Lecture Course in Washington City," *Philadelphia Christian Recorder*, July 4, 1878.

19. "Ireland's Wrongs," *Washington National Republican*, Oct. 29, 1881; "The Colored People," *Baltimore American*, Apr. 16, 1879.

20. RTG to James A. Garfield, Nov. 3, 1880, in SCL-MM.

21. Ackerman, *Dark Horse*, 173, 367.

22. Mounter, "Richard Theodore Greener: The Idealist," 191–94, 201–2.

23. Gulliver, "Minutes of the Meetings of the Negro American Society," 68; RTG, "Letter," *Philadelphia Christian Recorder*, Mar. 21, 1878.

24. Philip S. Foner, *Frederick Douglass*, 327–30.

25. RTG to Dear Sir, Apr. 12, 1879, copy of a mass mailing from the National Emigration Aid Society, in SCL-MM; Douglass, "The Negro Exodus from the Gulf States: A Paper Read on 12 September 1879," Blassingame and McKivigan, *Frederick Douglass Papers*, 4:523; RTG, "The Emigration of Colored Citizens from the Southern States," *Journal of Social Science* (May 1880): 22–34.

26. Frederick Douglass, quoted in "The Colored Exodus," *Washington Evening Star*, May 22, 1879.

27. RTG, quoted in "Professor Greener Ably Sustains the Flight of His Race from Southern Oppression," *Washington National Republican*, May 22, 1879.

28. *Washington National Republican*, May 22, 1879.

29. Douglass, "The Negro Exodus," 519, 524.

30. RTG, "The Emigration," 23.

31. Ibid., 30.

32. Blake, "The Great Exodus," 59–67.

33. Harvard University, *Harvard . . . Sixth Report*, 28.

34. "The Stone Wife Murder Case," *Washington Evening Star*, Sept. 23, 1879.

35. "A Persecuted Freedman," *New York Times*, Oct. 30, 1880.

36. Ibid.

37. "Perry, the Exodus Leader," *Washington Evening Star*, Nov. 10, 1880.

38. "A Persecuted Freedman," *New York Times*, Oct. 30, 1880.

39. Frederick Douglass to Charles Hall, Apr. 10, 1888, quoted in Philip S. Foner, *Frederick Douglass*, 331.

40. Greener, "The Future of the Negro," 90.

41. "News Brevity," *Maysville (KY) Evening Bulletin*, Sept. 21, 1882.

42. Harvard University, *Harvard . . . Tenth Report*, 67.

Chapter 8. A Violent Attack and Hopeless Case

1. Quoted in Flipper, *Colored Cadet*, 241–42.

2. Marszalek, *Court-Martial*, 18–22.

3. *Colored Cadet*, 120, 161, 167.

4. Mounter, "Richard Theodore Greener: The Idealist," 162–63.

5. *Philadelphia Christian Recorder*, June 10, 1877.

6. *New York World*, Aug. 29, 1877, quoted in Flipper, *Colored Cadet*, 280–81.

7. Johnson C. Whittaker, quoted in "Whittaker's Lecture," *Atlanta Constitution*, Aug. 2, 1882; Whittaker to Flipper, n.d., quoted in Flipper, *Colored Cadet*, 281–82.

8. Marszalek, *Court-Martial*, 40, 42; Davison, *The Presidency*, 168.

9. Marszalek, *Court-Martial*, 44–49; "Villainy at West Point," *New York Times*, Apr. 7, 1880.

10. Lieutenant Colonel Henry M. Lazelle to Adjutant, Apr. 7, 1880, in Court of Inquiry Records, Appendix, Part XI, 2825–29, quoted in Marszalek, *Court Martial*, 57.

11. "The Colored Cadet's Troubles," *New York Times*, Apr. 8, 1880.

12. "The West Point Mystery," *Charleston News and Courier*, Apr. 10, 1880, News-Bank, Inc.

13. Johnson C. Whittaker to "Dear Friend," Apr. 7, 1880, The Proceedings of the General Court Martial of Johnson C. Whittaker, US Military Academy, Records of the Judge Advocate General, Record Group 153 QQ 2774, National Archives, quoted in Marszalek, *Court-Martial*, 64; "Whittaker as a Witness," *New York Times*, May 19, 1880.

14. Justin D. Fulton to Alexander Ramsey, Apr. 10, 1880, copy in SLC-MM.

15. Marszalek, *Court-Martial*, 115.

16. *Lancaster (PA) Daily Intelligencer*, May 31, 1880.

17. *Charleston News and Courier*, May 31, 1880; Peter S. Michie, "Caste at West Point," *North American Review* 31, no. 283 (June 1880): 604–13; Marszalek, *Court-Martial*, 132.

18. Johnson Whittaker to RTG, May 27, 1880, quoted in Marszalek, *Court-Martial*, 131.

19. RTG, "Letter to *The Christian Recorder*," *Philadelphia Christian Recorder*, July 29, 1880.

20. Davison, *Presidency*, 168–69.

21. Marszalek, *Court-Martial*, 152–53; *Washington Post*, Dec. 30, 1880; *Memphis Daily Appeal*, Feb. 8, 1881; *Press and Daily Dakotaian* (Yankton, Dakota Territory), Jan. 4, 1881.

22. Harvard University, *The Sixth Report*, 26; Edgar A. Poe and Henry B. Hirst, "Poets and Poetry of Philadelphia," in Fisher, *Poe in His Own Time*, 23–40; Wert, *The Controversial Life of George Armstrong Custer*, 39–40; Davidson, "Court-Martialing Cadets," 657–58.

23. Current, *Those Terrible Carpetbaggers*, 398–99; Mounter, "Richard Theodore Greener: The Idealist," 254.

24. "To Try Cadet Whittaker," *New York Times*, Jan. 21, 1881; Mounter, "Richard Theodore Greener: The Idealist," 255–56.

25. Marszalek, *Court-Martial*, 165–77, 187.

26. Ibid., 177–83.

27. Ibid., 200–206, 214–15; Mounter, "Richard Theodore Greener: The Idealist," 260–62.

28. Marszalek, *Court-Martial*, 232.

29. "Cadet Whittaker's Case," *Washington Post*, June 18, 1881; *Charleston News and Courier*, Aug. 31, 1880; Mounter, "Richard Theodore Greener: The Idealist," 264; Daniel

Chamberlain to James Garfield, Dec. 28, 1880, James Garfield Papers, quoted in De Santis, *Republicans*, 137.

30. "Cadet Whittaker's Case."

31. Flipper, *Black Frontiersman*, 77–80; Mounter, "Richard Theodore Greener: The Idealist," 270–71.

32. Marszalek, *Court-Martial*, 241–44.

33. Mounter, "Richard Theodore Greener: The Idealist," 275–76.

34. "Whittaker's First Lecture," *Buffalo Commercial Advertiser*, June 2, 1882, quoted in *New York Times*, June 4, 1882; *Sumter (SC) Watchman*, Aug. 29, 1882.

35. Todd S. Purdum, "Black Cadet Gets a Posthumous Commission," *New York Times*, July 25, 1995.

36. Marchant, "Richard Theodore Greener."

37. D. Augustus Straker, "A Criticism on Prof. Greener's Views on the Chinese Bill," *Philadelphia Christian Recorder*, May 11, 1882.

38. Mounter, "Richard Theodore Greener: The Idealist," 278; *Washington People's Advocate*, Apr. 1, 1882; *Washington Bee*, May 12, 1883.

39. *New York Evening Post*, Oct. 16, 1883, quoted in Mounter, "Richard Theodore Greener: The Idealist," 306.

40. *Philadelphia Christian Recorder*, Apr. 13, 1882, May 15 and July 17, 1884; RTG, "The Future of the Negro," *North American Review* (July 1884), 89.

41. "Editorial," *Boston Daily Advertiser*, Jan. 26, 1885, clipping file, HUA; RTG, Feb. 21, 1881 (see chap. 3, n. 1).

42. "Colored Voters Rebelling," *Stark County Democrat*, July 8, 1885; Scheiner, *Negro Mecca*, 180; Nevins, *Hamilton Fish*, 2:898–99; RTG to John E. Bruce, Sept. 15, 1885, John E. Bruce Papers, Manuscript Division, Schomburg Center for Research in Black Culture, New York Public Library, quoted in Sharfstein, *The Invisible Line*, 204.

Chapter 9. Monumental Plans

1. James, *Merchant Adventurer*, 144–75, 196–202; Telegram, Mayor W. R. Grace to Colonel Frederick Grant, July 15, 1885, NPS-GF, Manhattan Historical Sites Archive.

2. General Philip Sheridan to Colonel Frederick Grant, July 23, 1885, NPS-GF; Frederick Grant, quoted in James, *Merchant Adventurer*, 202; "Where Will the Hero Be Buried?" *New York Sun*, July 24, 1885.

3. RTG to Isaiah Wears, Dec. 7, 1885, MSR-JW; RTG, *Grant Monument Association Minute Book*, *No. 1*, "First Meeting of the Committee of 100," July 28, 1885; "Act of the Majority of the Grant Association," Mar. 3, 1886, NPS-GMA, Manhattan Historical Sites Archive.

4. Stewart and Kahn, *Richard T. Greener*, 10; Brands, *The Man Who Saved the Union*, 634–35; "An Excellent Appointment," *Philadelphia Christian Recorder*, Dec. 24, 1885.

5. Mounter, "Richard Theodore Greener: The Idealist," 343–45; *Washington Bee*, Dec. 18, 1886; RTG to Isaiah Wears, Dec. 7, 1885, MSR-JW.

6. Du Bois, *The Black North in 1901*, 18; Gatewood, *Aristocrats*, 104–5; Dodson, Moore, and Yancy, *The Black New Yorkers*, 17; Scheiner, *Negro Mecca*, 177.

7. RTG to Isaiah Wears, Dec. 7, 1885, MSR-JW.

8. *South Bend (IN) Evening Register*, Sept. 5, 1885; *Brazil (IN) Clay County Enterprise*, Sept. 2, 1885.

9. *New York Times*, Aug. 14 and Sept. 1, 1885, June 11 and Dec. 11, 1886.

10. *New York Times*, Aug. 14, Oct. 14 and 20, 1885, Feb. 19 and Oct. 13, 1886; Leland Stanford to Horace Porter, May 10, 1892, NPS-GMA.

11. "The Grant Monument," *New York Times*, July 22, 1886.

12. Calvert Vaux to John Crimmins, Sept. 3, 1885; Charles Burns to Richard Greener, Oct. 10, 1885, NPS-GMA; *New York Times*, Dec. 3, 1886.

13. *Southwestern Christian Advocate*, June 17, 1886, quoted in Mounter, "Richard Theodore Greener," 353–54; *Philadelphia Christian Advocate*, July 14, 1887.

14. *Washington Bee*, May 26, 1883; *New York Times*, Feb. 21, 1886.

15. RTG to Isaiah Wears, Dec. 7, 1885, MSR-JW; "Richard Theodore Greener," Harvard University, *Harvard . . . Tenth Report*, 67; Mounter, "Richard Theodore Greener: The Idealist," 359.

16. Dodson, Moore, and Yancy, *Black New Yorkers*, 222–24; Mounter, "Richard Theodore Greener: The Idealist," 374.

17. RTG to Francis J. Grimké, Dec. 27, 1890, in Woodson, *The Works of Francis J. Grimké*, 4:25–26.

18. RTG to Isaiah Wears, Dec. 12, 1888, MSR-JW; Ardizzone, *An Illuminated Life*, 46; Mounter, "Richard Theodore Greener: The Idealist," 363.

19. RTG to Sir, Apr. 12, 1890, form letter to five architects; "Finding Aid to Grant Monument Association Records," 9, MPS-GMA; Stewart and Kahn, *Richard T. Greener*, 13–14.

20. *Congressional Record*, 51st US Congress, 2nd session, Dec. 10, 1890, 238, 240, 241.

21. "New York's Memorial to Grant," *New York Times*, Aug. 9, 1890; "Work Has Begun at Last," *New York Times*, Apr. 29, 1891; "Grant Monument Plans," *New York Times*, May 5, 1891.

22. "President Grace Resigns," *New York Times*, Nov. 27, 1891; Stewart and Kahn, *Richard T. Greener*, 14; "Secretary Greener Out," *New York Age*, Feb. 22, 1892.

23. *New York Times*, Mar. 23, 1892; "President Horace Porter's Speech," n.d., 1892, NPS-GMA; *New York Times*, Apr. 7, 1892.

24. "Laid by the President: The Cornerstone," *New York Times*, Apr. 28, 1892; "Grant Monument," *New York Times*, June 1, 1892; "The Negro Left in the Cold," *Charleston (SC) Sunday News*, May 16, 1897.

Chapter 10. Off White

1. RTG to Booker T. Washington, May 26, 1894, in Harlan, *The Booker T. Washington Papers*, 3:448; Ellen Collins to Booker T. Washington, Aug. 23, 1892, in Harlan, *The Booker T. Washington Papers*, 3:258.

2. Thomas Junius Calloway to Booker T. Washington, May 2, 1894, in Harlan, *The Booker T. Washington Papers*, 3:415.

3. Sinkler, *Racial Attitudes*, 334; Benjamin Harrison, quoted in Calhoun, *Benjamin Harrison*, 89–90.

4. Ford, *The Cleveland Era.*

5. Booker T. Washington, "Atlanta Exposition Address," Sept. 18, 1895, in Foner and Branham, *Lift Every Voice*, 802–5; Philip S. Foner and Robert J. Branham, introduction to Washington, "Atlanta Exposition Address," 802; Woodward, *Strange Career*, 82.

6. Woodward, *Strange Career*, 7, 82.

7. T. Thomas Fortune, *New York Age*, Feb. 27, 1892; Logan, *Betrayal of the Negro*, 327.

8. Fortune, *New York Age*, Feb. 27, 1892; RTG, "T. M'Cants Stewart Flayed," *Indianapolis Freeman*, Jan. 25, 1896.

9. RTG to George A. Myers, Sept. 2, 1896, George Myers Papers, Ohio Historical Society. Copy in Michael Mounter Research Files, SCL-MM.

10. Harvard University, *Harvard . . . Sixth Report*, 26–27. See, also, Mounter, "Richard Theodore Greener: The Idealist," 403–7.

11. RTG to Isaiah Wears, Apr. 27, 1894, MSR-JW.

12. Nussbaum, *Cultivating Humanity*, 156–57.

13. RTG, "The White Problem," 356, 358.

14. Ibid., 359, 367.

15. "The White Problem: Professor Greener's Splendid Effort Attracting Much Attention," *Cleveland Gazette*, Sept. 22, 1894; RTG to Washington, May 26, 1894, in Harlan, *The Booker T. Washington Papers*, 3:447, 449.

16. Mounter, "Richard Theodore Greener: The Idealist," 417, 428; Richard T. Greener to William M. K. Olcott, Feb. 15, 1895, Records of U.S. Attorneys, New York District, National Archives. Copy in Mounter Research Files, SCL-MM.

17. Mounter, "Richard Theodore Greener: The Idealist," 408; RTG, "Address to the Congress of the United States," quoted in Aptheker, *A Documentary History*, 765–67; *Philadelphia Press*, Feb. 8, 1896.

18. RTG to Archibald Grimké, Jan. 27, 1896, MSR-JW; RTG to Booker T. Washington, Mar. 26, 1897, Harlan, *Booker T. Washington Papers*, 4:266.

19. *Washington Bee*, Aug. 29, 1896; RTG to Whitefield McKinlay, Sept. 16, 1896, LOC-WM.

20. Mounter, "Richard Theodore Greener: The Idealist," 428; RTG to Isaiah Wears, Sept. 27, 1896, MSR-JW.

21. "William McKinley," in Graff, *The Presidents*, 306–22.

22. RTG to Lewis Howard Latimer, Apr. 7, 1897, QB-LL, copy in SCL-MM.

23. Sinkler, *Racial Attitudes*, 372; RTG to Latimer, Apr. 7, 1897, QB-LL, copy in SCL-MM; RTG to Washington, Mar. 26, 1897, and RTG to Washington, Apr. 5, 1897, Harlan, *Booker T. Washington Papers*, 4:266, 4:269.

24. Ardizzone, *An Illuminated Life*, 49–50; Mounter, "Richard Theodore Greener: The Idealist," 432; RTG to Isaiah Wears, Apr. 24, 1898, MSR-JW.

25. Alexander Crummell to John E. Bruce, Jan. 21, 1898, NYPL-JB, copy in SCL-MM.

26. "Bethel Literary," *Washington Bee*, Nov. 21, 1896; "The Color Line," *Washington Bee*, Apr. 11, 1896; "Greener a Leader," *Washington Bee*, Apr. 11, 1896; "Not Satisfied," *Washington Bee*, June 18, 1896.

27. "Mr. Greener Appointed," *Washington Bee*, Jan. 29, 1898.

28. "Address of Colonel Richard Theodore Greener," 29; RTG to Isaiah Wears, Apr. 18 and 24, 1898, MSR-JW.

Chapter 11. Our Man in Vladivostok

1. RTG to Whitefield McKinlay, Aug. 27, 1898, LOC-WM.

2. Ibid.

3. Ibid.

4. RTG to Mishiyo Kawashima [his daughter], Dec. 12, 1916, private collection of Evelyn Bausman.

5. RTG to Thomas Cridler, Sept. 20, 1898, quoted in Mounter, "Richard Theodore Greener: The Idealist," 441.

6. RTG to Whitefield McKinlay, Oct. 25, 1898, MSR-JW; Blakely, "Richard Greener," 311, 309.

7. RTG to Thomas Cridler, Sept. 30, 1898, NA-DV.

8. "Development of Siberia," 304.

9. Birgitta Ingemanson, "Vladivostok Scenes," in Pray, *Letters*, 47; Ingemanson, introduction to Pray, *Letters*, xxxii.

10. RTG to Thomas Cridler, Sept. 30, 1898, NA-DV.

11. RTG to Isaiah Wears, Jan. 7, 1899, MSR-JW.

12. Blakely, "Richard Greener," 312.

13. William McKinley, speech to the Cincinnati (Ohio) Commercial Club, 1897, quoted in "William McKinley," in Graff, *The Presidents*, 313–14.

14. Rhodes, *The McKinley and Roosevelt Administrations*, 125–26; Blakely, *Russia and the Negro*, 44–46.

15. RTG to Whitefield McKinlay, Oct. 25, 1898, MSR-JW.

16. RTG to Isaiah Wears, Jan. 7, 1899, MSR-JW.

17. RTG to Thomas Cridler, Nov. 7, 1898, NA-DV.

18. Blakely, "Richard Greener," 311.

19. RTG to Isaiah Wears, Jan. 7, 1899, MSR-JW.

20. Harvard University, *Harvard . . . Sixth Report*, 28; Ardizzone, *An Illuminated Life*, 51–52.

21. RTG to Isaiah Wears, Jan. 7, 1899, MSR-JW.

22. Ardizzone, *An Illuminated Life*, 53–57; US Census Bureau, "Twelfth Census of the United States," Manhattan, New York City, 1900.

23. Williamson, *New People*, 101.

24. RTG, "Educational Progress in Eastern Siberia," 1427–30; Greener, "Educational Progress in Siberia," 868.

25. RTG, "Reports of Commercial Agent R.T. Greener," 60:437–45.

26. Allison Blakely, *Russia and the Negro*, 46.

27. RTG, "Reports of Commercial Agent R. T. Greener," 65: 232–33; 67:401; 72:140.

28. Eleanor Lord Pray to Clara Lord McCue, Oct. 11, 1898, and Pray to Home, Oct. 21, 1898, in Pray, *Letters*, 81, 82.

29. Ibid., 82–83.

30. Eleanor Pray to Sarah, Oct. 23, 1899; Pray to Home, Sept. 20, 1901; Pray to Home, Apr. 14, 1904, in Pray, *Letters*, 82, 83.

31. Evelyn Bausman to Michael Mounter, Apr. 24, 2002, SCL-MM.

32. Evelyn Bausman, interview by author, June 30, 2015; RTG to Third Assistant Secretary of State, Apr. 1, 1901, NA-DV.

33. Bausman, interview; Roger S. Greene, "Report Regarding Mr. R. T. Greener," Dec. 6, 1906, NA-DS, copy in SCL-MM; Evelyn Bausman to the author, Jan. 9, 2016.

34. RTG to Alvey A. Adee, Jan. 2, 1900, with attached letters, NA-DV, quoted in Mounter, "Richard Theodore Greener: The Idealist," 446–48.

35. Mounter, "Richard Theodore Greener: The Idealist," 448.

36. Preston, *The Boxer Rebellion*, 105–210.

37. Mounter, "Richard Theodore Greener: The Idealist," 449–50.

38. RTG to Whitefield McKinlay, Feb. 18, 1902, LOC-WM; Greener to H. H. D. Peirce, Jan. 25, 1902, NA-DV. See, also, Mounter, "Richard Theodore Greener: The Idealist," 455–56.

39. RTG to Isaiah Wears, n.d., MSR-JW.

40. RTG to Whitefield McKinlay, Feb. 18, 1902, LOC-WM.

41. Blakely, "Richard Greener," 315; Laurits S. Swenson to Jacob Riis, Jan. 3, 1905, LOC-TR.

42. White, *The Diplomacy of the Russo-Japanese War*, 11.

43. Ibid., 33. See, also, Dennett, *Roosevelt*.

44. Harvard University, *Harvard . . . Tenth Report*, 67.

45. Takahira (Secretary of the Japanese Legation in the United States) to US Secretary of State John Hay, May 9, 1904; Takahira to Alvey A. Adee, Aug. 5, 1904. Notes from the Japanese Legation in the United States to the Department of State, vol. 8, 1858–1906, National Archives, copy in SCL-MM.

46. Baron Komura (Japanese Foreign Minister) to John Hay, Feb. 16, 1904. Notes from the Japanese Legation, copy in SCL-MM.

47. Blakely, *Russia and the Negro*, 47.

48. Mounter, "Richard Theodore Greener: The Idealist," 459–60.

49. "Vladivostok Expects Siege," *New York Times*, May 19, 1905; Blakely, *Russia and the Negro*, 48.

50. Theodore Roosevelt to George Meyer, Aug. 25, 1905, in Elting Morison, *Letters of Theodore Roosevelt*, 6–8.

51. "Greener's Action Was Undiplomatic," *Washington Times*, Apr. 13, 1905; Haynes, *Biographical Sketch*.

52. Joseph Choate to Theodore Roosevelt, Dec. 12, 1904, LOC-TR.

53. Blakely, "Richard Greener," 316.

54. Theodore Roosevelt to Secretary of State, Jan. 16, 1905, LOC-TR.

55. Herbert Peirce to William Loeb, Dec. 21, 1904, LOC-TR.

56. Quoted by Huntington Wilson to Roger S. Greene, Nov. 3, 1906, NA-DS, copy SCL-MM.

57. "Greener's Action Was Undiplomatic."

58. Harlan, *Booker T. Washington*, x, 7.

59. Booker T. Washington to Theodore Roosevelt, Dec. 27, 1904, LOC-TR; Booker T. Washington to Samuel Laing Williams, Feb. 15, 1905, in Harlan and Smock, *Booker T. Washington Papers*, 8:193–94.

60. Booker T. Washington to Elihu Root, Feb. 23, 1906, LOC-TR.

61. Mounter, "Richard Theodore Greener: The Idealist," 462–64.

62. Roger Greene to Assistant Secretary of State, June 26, 1906, NA-DV.

63. Theodore Roosevelt to George Kennan, Mar. 30, 1905, quoted in Dennett, *Roosevelt*, 160.

64. Takahira to Elihu Root, Oct. 27, 1905, "Notes from the Japanese Legation," copy in SCL-MM.

65. "A More Representative Foreign Service: African Americans," usdiplomacy.org.

66. Harlan, *Booker T. Washington*, 7.

67. Bausman, interview.

Chapter 12. Closure in Black and White

1. Mounter, "Richard Theodore Greener: The Idealist," 463; RTG to Mishiyo Kawashima, Dec. 12, 1916, private collection of Evelyn Bausman.

2. Woodward, *The Strange Career of Jim Crow*, 91, 97; C. Vann Woodward, "Tom Watson and the Negro in Agrarian Politics," in Wynes, *The Negro in the South Since 1865*, 39–61. See, also, Sinclair, *Aftermath*, 157. Tillman quoted in Francis Butler Simkins, *Pitchfork Ben Tillman*, 396.

3. RTG to Francis Grimké, Nov. 18, 1907, MSR-FG.

4. Ibid.; RTG to Arthur Grimké, Jan. 1, 1908, MSR-AG.

5. *Charleston News and Courier*, June 21, 1906, 10; June 22, 1906, 10; July 03, 1906, 3, Newsbank, Inc.

6. RTG to Francis Grimké, Nov. 18, 1907, in Woodson, *The Works of Francis Grimké*, 4:104–9; *Charleston News and Courier*, Nov. 26, 1907, 3.

7. RTG to Kawashima, Sept. 5, 1916, private collection of Evelyn Bausman; RTG to Booker T. Washington, May 17, 1906; Washington to RTG, May 18, 1906; and Washington to John S. Durham, Apr. 10, 1905, Booker T. Washington Papers, Library of Congress, quoted in Harlan and Smock, *Washington Papers*, 9:10, 8:254.

8. RTG to Elihu Root, Oct. 17, 1906, copy in SCL-MM.

9. Roger S. Greene, "Report Regarding Mr. R. T. Greener," Dec. 6, 1906, Case No. 2079/9/1, RG 59, NA-DS.

10. Ibid.

11. Thomas Platt to Elihu Root, Feb. 12, 1907, and Elihu Root to Thomas Platt, Feb. 14, 1907, Case No. 2079/1, RG 59, NA-DS.

12. RTG to Henry Cabot Lodge, Feb. 1907, and Elihu Root to Henry Cabot Lodge, Mar. 2, 1907, Case No. 2079/1, RG 59, NA-DS. See, also, Mounter, "Richard Theodore Greener: The Idealist," 476–78.

13. Mounter, "Richard Theodore Greener: Idealist," 477; RTG to Kawashima, Dec. 12, 1916, private collection of Evelyn Bausman.

14. RTG to Kawashima, Sept. 5, 1916, private collection of Evelyn Bausman.

15. RTG to Booker T. Washington, July 31, 1906, Harlan and Smock, *Washington Papers*, 9:48; Harlan, *Booker T. Washington*, 85.

16. Harlan, *Booker T. Washington*, 85.

17. Emmett Scott, docketing note, Aug. 2, 1906; Booker T. Washington to RTG, Aug. 7, 1906; RTG to Washington, Aug. 11, 1906; Washington to RTG, Aug. 11, 1906, Harlan and Smock, *Washington Papers*, 9:48, 51, 55, 56.

18. Harlan, *Booker T. Washington*, 89; Mounter, "Richard Theodore Greener: The Idealist," 467–68.

19. Logan, *The Betrayal of the Negro*, 348; Woodward, *Origins of the New South*, 337–38; RTG to Whitefield McKinlay, Nov. 23, 1908, LOC-WM.

20. RTG to Whitefield McKinlay, Nov. 23, 1908, LOC-WM; RTG to Archibald Grimké, Apr. 28, 1913, MSR-AG.

21. RTG to Whitefield McKinlay, Nov. 23, 1908, LOC-WM.

22. Ibid.; Sinclair quoted in Shawn Alexander, "New Introduction," in Sinclair, *Aftermath*, xii.

23. RTG to W. E. B. Du Bois, Feb. 4, 1910, Aptheker, *The Correspondence of W. E. B. Du Bois*, 1:168, 169. See, also, Mounter, "Richard Theodore Greener: The Idealist," 500.

24. RTG to Kawashima, Dec. 12, 1917, private collection of Evelyn Bausman.

25. James B. Bradwell, "Women Lawyers of Illinois," *Chicago Legal News* 32 (June 2, 1900); RTG to Kawashima, Sept. 12, 1917, private collection of Evelyn Bausman.

26. See, e.g., Greener's articles, "The First Congress of Colored Women," 23–30; "The Birth of a World Power," 308–09; "Russia's Financial Position During the Russo-Japanese War," 93–98; "A Britisher in the South," 250–52.

27. RTG to Jerry C. Calloway, Dec. 23, 1910, MSR-JW; RTG to Kawashima, Dec. 12, 1916, private collection of Evelyn Bausman; "For Good Government and Urban Politics," 268.

28. RTG to Kawashima, Sept. 12, 1917, and Sept. 5, 1916, private collection of Evelyn Bausman.

29. RTG to Jerry C. Calloway, Oct. 11, 1912; Greener to McKinlay, Aug. 1, 1910, MSR-JW; Mounter, "Richard Theodore Greener: The Idealist," 509–11; RTG to McKinlay, Sept. 5, 1916, MSR-JW.

30. Sherman, *Republican Party*, 71–76.

31. Woodward, *Origins of the New South*, 479; Sherman, *Republican Party*, 101, 113; RTG to Francis Grimké, in Woodson, *The Works of Francis Grimké*, 4:236.

32. "Anniversary of Charles Sumner," *Chicago Defender*, Jan. 14, 1911; "Many Races Enjoy Lincoln Day Banquet," *Chicago Defender*, Feb. 17, 1912; "Richard T. Greener Addresses St. Mark's Lyceum," *Chicago Defender*, July 20, 1918; "Judge Olson Lauds Name of Frederick Douglass," *Chicago Defender*, Feb. 27, 1915; RTG to Jerry C. Calloway, Dec. 18, 1914, MSR-JW; RTG to Kawashima, May 3, 1917; "Prof. Greener Off to Graduation Exercises," *Chicago Defender*, June 23, 1917, 7.

33. RTG to Howard L. Latimer, June 2, 1915, QB-LL.

34. RTG to Roy Nash, July 20, 1916, MSR-JS, quoted in Mounter, "Richard Theodore

Greener: The Idealist," 518; W. E. B. Du Bois, "Notes on Amenia Conference, 1916" and Joel Spingarn, "Amenia Conference Album," UM-DB.

35. RTG to Kawashima, Sept. 5, 1916, and Dec. 12, 1916, private collection of Evelyn Bausman.

36. RTG to Kawashima, Sept. 12, May 3, and July 20, 1917, Apr. 28, 1919, private collection of Evelyn Bausman; Evelyn Bausman, personal communication to the author, Apr. 3, 2016.

37. RTG to Carter Woodson, Oct. 24, 1917, LOC-WM; Ardizzone, *An Illuminated Life*, 54.

38. Ardizzone, *An Illuminated Life*, 78–80; "Annual Commencement Program," Columbia University, June 13, 1906, 11; Commencement Programs, University Archives, University of Tennessee.

39. Mounter, "Richard Theodore Greener: The Idealist," 512–17.

40. Ardizzone, *An Illuminated Life*, 313; Belle da Costa Greene to Bernard Berenson, Jan. 4 and 7, 1914, quoted in Ardizzone, *An Illuminated Life*, 311; cover of the *Crisis* 14, no. 4 (Feb. 1917).

41. "Sudden Death of Prof. Greener at His Home in This City," *Chicago Broad Ax*, May 13, 1922; "Richard Greener," *Chicago Defender*, May 13, 1922; State of Illinois Death Certificate.

Epilogue

1. Eric Foner, "Why Reconstruction Matters," *New York Times*, Mar. 28, 2015.

2. Blakely, "Richard T. Greener," 305, 311, 318.

3. Richard Greener, "Reply to T. McCants Stewart," *Indianapolis Freeman*, Jan. 25, 1896.

4. Du Bois, *The Souls of Black Folk*, 3.

5. Harry C. Silcox, "The Black 'Better Class' Political Dilemma," 65.

6. Sharfstein, *Invisible Line*, 258, 9.

7. Williamson, *New People*, 101.

8. Aridizzone, *An Illuminated Life*, 315, 363, 433, 458.

9. Lawrence S. Mayo to Mrs. Knierim, December 7, 1938, private collection of Evelyn Bausman.

10. Evelyn Bausman, interview by author, June 30, 2015.

11. Ibid.

12. "Ida Platt," scholarship.kentlaw.itt.edu.

13. Du Bois, "The Talented Tenth," 31–76, 42.

BIBLIOGRAPHY

"Abraham Lincoln." *Mirror of the Philomathean Society* 11, no. 3 (July 1865): 1–3.

Ackerman, Kenneth C. *Dark Horse: The Surprise Election and Political Murder of President James A. Garfield*. New York: Carroll and Graf, 2003.

"Address of Colonel Richard Theodore Greener." *Phillips Bulletin* 10, no. 5 (1915): 28.

Allen, Katherine Thompson. *The University of South Carolina Horseshoe: Heart of Campus*. Columbia: University of South Carolina Libraries, 2014.

Allen, Walter. *Governor Chamberlain's Administration in South Carolina: A Chapter of Reconstruction in the Southern States*. New York: Putnam, 1888.

Allis, Frederick S., Jr. "Hurrah. Hurrah. Write. Write." *Andover Bulletin* 59, no. 1 (April 1965): 5–7.

———. *Youth from Every Quarter: A Bicentennial History of Phillips Academy, Andover*. Hanover, NH: University Press of New England, 1979.

Aptheker, Herbert, ed. *The Correspondence of W. E. B. Du Bois*. Vol. 1, *1877–1934*. Amherst: University of Massachusetts Press, 1973.

———. *A Documentary History of the Negro People in the United States*. New York: Citadel Press, 1951.

Ardizzone, Heidi. *An Illuminated Life: Belle da Costa Greene's Journey from Prejudice to Privilege*. New York: W. W. Norton, 2007.

Baker, Ray S., ed. *Woodrow Wilson, Life and Letters*. Vol. 4, *1913–1914*. New York: Doubleday, Doran, 1931.

Baumann, Roland M. *Constructing Black Education at Oberlin College: A Documentary History*. Athens: Ohio University Press, 2010.

Biddle, Daniel R., and Murray Dubin. *Tasting Freedom: Octavius Catto and the Battle for Equality in Civil War America*. Philadelphia: Temple University Press, 2010.

Blake, Lee Ella. "The Great Exodus of 1879 and 1880 to Kansas." MA thesis, Kansas State College, 1942.

Blakely, Allison. "Richard Greener and the 'Talented Tenth's' Dilemma." *Journal of Negro History* 59 (October 1974): 305–17.

———. *Russia and the Negro: Blacks in Russian History and Thought*. Washington, DC: Howard University Press, 1986.

Blassingame, J. W., and J. R. McKivigan, eds. *The Frederick Douglass Papers*. Series 1, Vol. 4. New Haven, CT: Yale University Press, 1991.

Blodgett, Geoffrey. *Oberlin History: Essays and Impressions*. Kent, OH: Kent State University Press, 2006.

Brands, H. W. *The Man Who Saved the Union: Ulysses Grant in War and Peace*. New York: Doubleday, 2012.

Brown, Dee. *The Year of the Century: 1876*. New York: Charles Scribner's Sons, 1966.

Butchart, Ronald. "Mission Matters: Mt. Holyoke, Oberlin and the Schooling of Southern Blacks." *History of Education Quarterly* 42, no. 1 (Spring 2002): 1–17.

Calhoun, Charles William. *Benjamin Harrison*. New York: Macmillan, 2005.

The Catalogue of the Officers and Students of Harvard University for the Academical Year 1865–66. Cambridge, MA: Harvard University, 1865.

City of Cambridge. "Mayor's Address and Reports, 1852." Cambridge, MA: Chronicle, 1852.

Cohen, Michael David. *Reconstructing the Campus: Higher Education and the American Civil War*. Charlottesville: University of Virginia Press, 2012.

Coppin, Fanny Jackson. *Reminiscences of School Life, and Hints on Teaching*. New York: G. K. Hall, 1995.

Current, Richard Nelson. *Those Terrible Carpetbaggers: A Reinterpretation*. New York: Oxford University Press, 1988.

Davidson, Michael J. "Court-Martialing Cadets." *Capital University Law Review* 36, no. 3 (2008): 636–73.

Davison, Kenneth E. *The Presidency of Rutherford B. Hayes*. Westport, CT: Greenwood, 1972.

Dennett, Tyler. *Roosevelt and the Russo-Japanese War*. New York: Doubleday, Page, 1925.

De Santis, Vincent P. *Republicans Face the Southern Question: The New Departure Years, 1877–1897*. Baltimore: Johns Hopkins University Press, 1959.

"Development of Siberia." *Journal of the American Asiatic Association* 8 (November 1908): 289–320.

Dodson, Howard, Christopher Moore, and Roberta Yancy. *The Black New Yorkers*. New York: John Wiley and Sons, 2000.

Douglass, Frederick. "The Boston Mob of December, 1860." *Douglass' Monthly*, January 1861.

Du Bois, W. E. B. *The Black North in 1901: A Social Study*. New York: Arno, 1969.

———. *Black Reconstruction in America (1860–1880)*. New York: Russell and Russell, 1935.

———. *The Gift of Black Folk: The Negroes in the Making of America*. New York: Washington Square, 1970.

———. "A Negro Student at Harvard at the End of the Nineteenth Century." *Massachusetts Review* 1 (May 1960): 439–58.

———. *The Philadelphia Negro: A Social Study*. New York: Benjamin Bloom, 1899.

———. *The Souls of Black Folk*. New York: Modern Library Edition, 2003.

———. "The Talented Tenth." In *The Negro Problem: A Series of Articles by Representative American Negroes of Today*, edited by Booker T. Washington, 31–76. New York: James Pott, 1903.

Duberman, Martin, ed. *The Antislavery Vanguard: New Essays on the Abolitionists*. Princeton, NJ: Princeton University Press, 1965.

Egerton, Douglas R. *The Wars of Reconstruction: The Brief, Violent History of America's Most Progressive Era*. New York: Bloomsbury, 2014.

Eppinga, Jane. *Henry Ossian Flipper: West Point's First Black Graduate.* Plano: Republic of Texas Press, 1996.

Evidence taken by the Committee of Investigation of the Third Congressional District, General Assembly of the State of South Carolina. Columbia, SC: John W. Denny, Printer to the State, 1870.

Fisher, Benjamin F., ed. *Poe in His Own Time.* Iowa City: University of Iowa Press, 2010.

Flipper, Henry Ossian. *Black Frontiersman: The Memoirs of Henry O. Flipper, the First Black Cadet.* Edited by Theodore D. Harris. Fort Worth: Texas Christian University Press, 1997.

———. *The Colored Cadet at West Point.* New York: Homer Lee, 1878.

Foner, Eric. *A Short History of Reconstruction, 1863–1877.* New York: Harper and Row, 1990.

Foner, Philip S. *Frederick Douglass.* New York: Citadel Press, 1964.

———, ed. *The Life and Writings of Frederick Douglass.* 5 vols. New York: International, 1950.

Foner, Philip, and Robert Branham, eds. *Lift Every Voice: African-American Oratory, 1787–1900.* Tuscaloosa: University of Alabama Press, 1998.

"For Good Government and Urban Politics: The Career of Richard T. Greener, '70." *Harvard Alumni Bulletin* 67 (Dec. 12, 1964): 266–68.

Ford, Henry Jones. *The Cleveland Era: A Chronicle of the New Order in Politics.* New Haven, CT: Yale University Press, 1919.

Franklin, Vincent P., and James D. Anderson, eds. *New Perspectives on Black Educational History.* Boston: G. K. Hall, 1978.

Frazier, E. Franklin. *Black Bourgeoisie: The Rise of a New Middle Class.* New York: Free Press, 1957.

Fulmer, Henry. "Richard T. Greener and the Radical University Library." *Ex-Libris* (1995): 34–37. Annual publication of University of South Carolina, University Libraries.

Gatewood, Willard B. *Aristocrats of Color: The Black Elite, 1880–1920.* Bloomington: Indiana University Press, 1990.

Graff, Henry F., ed. *The Presidents: A Reference History.* 3rd ed. New York: Charles Scribner's Sons, 2002.

Green, Edwin L. *The History of the University of South Carolina.* Columbia, SC: The State Company, 1916.

Greener, Richard T. "The Birth of a World Power." *A.M.E. Review* 30 (April 1914): 308–9.

———. "A Britisher in the South." *A.M.E. Review* 32 (April 1916): 250–52.

———. *Charles Sumner: The Idealist, Statesman, and Scholar.* Columbia, SC: Republic, 1874.

———. "Educational Progress in Eastern Siberia." In *Annual Report of the Department of the Interior for the Fiscal Year Ended June 30, 1900,* 1427–30. Washington, DC: Government Printing Office, 1901.

———. "Educational Progress in Eastern Siberia." In *Annual Report of the Department of the Interior for the Fiscal Year Ended June 30, 1902,* 868–84. Washington, DC, Government Printing Office, 1903.

———. "The Emigration of Colored Citizens from the Southern States." *Journal of Social Science* (May 1880): 22–34.

———. "The First Congress of Colored Women." *A.M.E. Review* 30 (July 1913): 23–30.

———. "First Lessons in Greek—Prof. W. S. Scarborough." *Christian Recorder*, September 29, 1881.

———. "The Future of the Negro." *North American Review* 149, no. 332 (July 1884): 88–93.

———. "The Intellectual Position of the Negro." *National Quarterly Review* 127 (July 1880): 168–89.

———. *An Oration at the Celebration of the Festival of Saint John the Baptist, June 24, 1876.* Savannah, GA: D. G. Patton, Stern, 1876.

———. "The Progress of the Negro Race." *Colored American Magazine* 12 (February 1907): 115–17.

———. "Reminiscences of Frederick Douglass." *Champion* (February 1917): 291–95.

———. "Reports of Commercial Agent R. T. Greener." In *Consular Reports: July 1900: Commerce, Manufactures, Etc.* Vols. 60, 65, 67, and 72.Washington, DC: Government Printing Office, 1901 and 1903.

———. "Richard T. Greener." Unpublished handwritten biographical sketch, May 19, 1870. HUA.

———. "Russia's Financial Position during the Russo-Japanese War." *A.M.E. Review* 32 (October 1915): 93–98.

———. "Speech at the Harvard Club of New York, February 21, 1881." Reprinted in *Harvard Register* 3 (March 1881): 154–55.

———. "The Tenure of Land in Ireland." Senior diss., Harvard College, 1870. HUA.

———. "The White Problem." *Lend a Hand: A Record of Progress* 12 (January–June 1894): 354–67.

Gulliver, Adelaide Cromwell. "Minutes of the Meetings of the Negro Americans Society." *Journal of Negro History* 64 (Winter 1979): 58–69.

Harlan, Louis R. *Booker T. Washington: The Wizard of Tuskegee, 1901–1915.* New York: Oxford University Press, 1983.

———, ed. *The Booker T. Washington Papers.* Vol. 3, *1889–95.* Urbana: University of Illinois Press, 1974.

Harlan, Louis R., and Raymond W. Smock, eds. *The Booker T. Washington Papers.* Vol. 8, *1904–6.* Urbana: University of Illinois Press, 1979.

Harris, Gabriela. "Historic Schools in Washington, D.C.: Preserving a Rich Heritage." MA thesis, University of Maryland, 2008.

Harvard University. *Harvard College Class of 1870, Sixth Report.* Cambridge, MA: Riverside, 1895.

———. *Harvard College Class of 1870, Tenth Report.* Cambridge, MA: Riverside, 1920.

Haynes, Thornwell. *Biographical Sketch of Governor B. R. Tillman of South Carolina.* Columbia, SC: B. C. DuPre, 1894.

Hollis, Daniel Walker. *University of South Carolina.* Vol. 2, *College to University.* Columbia: University of South Carolina Press, 1956.

Holmes, Oliver Wendell. *The Autocrat of the Breakfast Table.* Boston: Phillips, Sampson, 1859.

Holt, Thomas. *Black over White: Negro Political Leadership in South Carolina during Reconstruction.* Urbana: University of Illinois Press, 1977.

Horton, James O. "Black Education at Oberlin College: A Controversial Commitment." *Journal of Negro Education* 54, no. 4 (Autumn 1985): 477–99.

Horton, James O., and Lois E. Horton. *Black Bostonians: Family Life and Community Struggle in the Antebellum North.* New York: Holmes and Meier, 1979.

Hundley, Mary Gibson. *The Dunbar Story (1870–1955).* New York: Vantage, 1965.

James, Marquis. *Merchant Adventurer: The Story of W. R. Grace.* Wilmington, DE: Scholarly Resources Books, 1993.

LaBorde, Maximilian. *History of the South Carolina College from Its Incorporation, December 19, 1801 to December 19, 1865.* Charleston, SC: Walker, Evans and Cogswell, 1874.

Lawson, Ellen N., and Marlene Merrill. "The Antebellum 'Talented Thousandth': Black College Students at Oberlin Before the Civil War." *Journal of Negro Education* 52, no. 2 (1983): 142–55.

Lesko, Kathleen M., Valerie Babb, and Carroll R. Gibbs. *Black Georgetown Remembered: A History of Its Black Community from the Founding of "Town of George" in 1751 to the Present Day.* Washington, DC: Georgetown University Press, 1991.

Levesque, George A. *Black Boston: African American Life and Culture in Urban America, 1750–1860.* New York: Garland, 1994.

Litwack, Leon F. *North of Slavery: The Negro in the Free States, 1790–1860.* Chicago: University of Chicago Press, 1961.

Logan, Rayford W. *The Betrayal of the Negro: From Rutherford Hayes to Woodrow Wilson.* 3rd ed. New York: Da Capo Press, 1997.

———. *Howard University: The First Hundred Years, 1867–1967.* New York: New York University Press, 1969.

Marchant, Frances. "Richard Theodore Greener: A Story of a Busy Man." Unpublished handwritten manuscript, 1882. SCL-RG.

Marszalek, John F., Jr. *Court-Martial: A Black Man at West Point.* New York: Scribner's, 1972.

Matalene, Carolyn B., and Katherine C. Reynolds. *Carolina Voices: Two Hundred Years of Student Experiences.* Columbia: University of South Carolina Press, 2001.

McPherson, James. *Battle Cry of Freedom: The Civil War Era.* New York: Oxford University Press, 1988.

Michie, Peter S. "Caste at West Point." *North American Review* 130, no. 283 (June 1880): 604–13.

Morison, Elting E., ed. *The Letters of Theodore Roosevelt.* Cambridge, MA: Harvard University Press, 1952.

Morison, Samuel Eliot. *Three Centuries of Harvard: 1636–1936.* Cambridge, MA: Harvard University Press, 1936.

——, ed. *The Development of Harvard University Since the Inauguration of President Eliot, 1869–1929*. Cambridge, MA: Harvard University Press, 1930.

Morrison, J. Brent. *Oberlin, Hotbed of Abolitionism: College, Community, and the Fight for Freedom and Equality*. Chapel Hill: University of North Carolina Press, 2014.

Mounter, Michael Robert. "Richard Theodore Greener: The Idealist, Statesman, Scholar, and South Carolinian." PhD diss., University of South Carolina, 2002.

——. "Richard Theodore Greener and the African American Individual in a Black and White World." In J. L. Underwood and W. L. Burke, eds. *At Freedom's Door: African American Founding Fathers and Lawyers in Reconstruction South Carolina*, 130–65. Columbia: University of South Carolina Press, 2000.

Nevins, Allan. *Hamilton Fish: The Inner History of the Grant Administration*. Vol. 2. New York: Frederick Ungar, 1957.

Nussbaum, Martha C. *Cultivating Humanity: A Classical Defense of Reform in Liberal Education*. Cambridge, MA: Harvard University Press, 1997.

Perkins, Linda M. *Fanny Jackson Coppin and the Institute for Colored Youth, 1865–1902*. New York: Garland, 1987.

Perkins, Linda M., and Traki Taylor. "The Bible in the Educational Philosophies of Fanny Jackson Coppin and Nannie Helen Burroughs." In Wimbush, *African Americans and the Bible*, 403–17.

Petrulionis, Sandra Harbert. *To Set This World Right: The Antislavery Movement in Thoreau's Concord*. Ithaca, NY: Cornell University Press, 2006.

Pike, James S. *The Prostrate State: South Carolina under Negro Government*. New York: D. Appleton, 1874.

Pray, Eleanor L. *Letters from Vladivostok, 1894–1930*. Edited by Birgitta Ingemanson. Seattle: University of Washington Press, 2013.

Preston, Diana. *The Boxer Rebellion: The Dramatic Story of China's War on Foreigners That Shook the World in the Summer of 1900*. New York: Berkley, 2001.

Randel, William P. *Centennial: American Life in 1876*. Philadelphia: Chilton, 1969.

Rhodes, James F. *The McKinley and Roosevelt Administrations, 1897–1909*. Port Washington, NY: Kennikat, 1965.

Saville, Julie. *The Work of Reconstruction: From Slave to Wage Laborer in South Carolina, 1860–1870*. London: Cambridge University Press, 1994.

Scheiner, Seth M. *Negro Mecca: A History of the Negro in New York City, 1865–1920*. New York: New York University Press, 1965.

Sharfstein, Daniel. *The Invisible Line: Three American Families and Their Secret Journey from Black to White*. New York: Penguin, 2011.

Sherman, Richard B. *The Republican Party and Black America: From McKinley to Hoover, 1896–1933*. Charlottesville: University Press of Virginia, 1973.

Silcox, Henry C. "The Black 'Better Class' Political Dilemma: Philadelphia Prototype Isaiah C. Wears." *Pennsylvania Magazine of History and Biography* 63, no. 1 (January 1989): 45–66.

——. "Nineteenth Century Black Militant: Octavius V. Catto (1839–1871)." *Pennsylvania Magazine of History and Biography* 44 (January 1977): 53–76.

Simkins, Francis B. *Pitchfork Ben Tillman: South Carolinian*. Baton Rouge: Louisiana State University Press, 1944.

Simkins, Francis B., and Robert H. Woody. *South Carolina during Reconstruction*. Chapel Hill: University of North Carolina Press, 1932. Reprint, Gloucester, MA: Peter Smith, 1966.

Simmons, William J. *Men of Mark: Eminent, Progressive and Rising*. Cleveland, OH: George M. Rewell.

Sinclair, William A. *The Aftermath of Slavery: A Study of the Condition and Environment of the American Negro*. Columbia: University of South Carolina Press, 2012. First published in 1905 by Small, Maynard.

Sinkler, George. *The Racial Attitudes of American Presidents: From Abraham Lincoln to Theodore Roosevelt*. Garden City, NY: Anchor, 1972.

Smith, J. Clay, Jr. *Emancipation: The Making of the Black Lawyer, 1844–1944*. Philadelphia: University of Pennsylvania Press, 1993.

Smith, John David. *Black Judas: William Hannibal Thomas and the American Negro*. Athens: University of Georgia, 2000.

Snyder, Tom, ed. *120 Years of American Education: A Statistical Portrait*. Washington, DC: National Center for Educational Statistics, 1993.

Sollors, Werner, Caldwell Titcomb, Thomas Underwood, and Randall Kennedy, eds. *Blacks at Harvard: A Documentary History of African-American Experience at Harvard and Radcliffe*. New York: New York University Press, 1993.

A South Carolinian [Belton O'Neall Townsend]. "The Political Condition of South Carolina." *Atlantic Monthly* 39 (February 1877): 177–94.

———. "The Result in South Carolina." *Atlantic Monthly* 41 (January 1878): 1–12.

———. "South Carolina Society." *Atlantic Monthly* 39 (June 1877): 670–84.

Sterling, Dorothy, ed. *We Are Your Sisters: Black Women in the Nineteenth Century*. New York: W. W. Norton, 1984.

Stewart, Ruth Ann, and David M. Kahn. *Richard T. Greener, His Life and Work: An Exhibit and Tribute Sponsored by the National Park Service and the National Park Foundation*. Exhibit catalog. New York: National Park Service, 1980.

Taylor, Alrutheus Ambush. *The Negro in South Carolina during Reconstruction*. New York: Russell and Russell, 1969. First published in 1924 by the Association for the Study of Negro Life and History.

Turner, Ralph H. "Sponsored and Contest Mobility and the School System." *American Sociological Review* 25, no. 6 (1960): 855–62.

Vaughn, William P. "South Carolina University and Fisk Parsons Brewer." *South Carolina Historical Magazine* 76, no. 4 (October 1975): 225–31.

Washington, Booker T., ed. *The Negro Problem: A Series of Articles by Representative American Negroes of Today*. New York: James Pott, 1903.

Wert, Jeffrey D. *The Controversial Life of George Armstrong Custer*. New York: Simon and Schuster, 1996.

West, Emery. "Harvard's First Black Graduates: 1865–1890." *Harvard Bulletin* (May 1972): 24–28.

White, John A. *The Diplomacy of the Russo-Japanese War*. Princeton, NJ: Princeton University Press, 1964.

Williams, George W. *History of the Negro Race in America, 1619–1880*. Vol. 2. New York: G. P. Putnam's Sons, 1883.

Williams, Harry, ed. *Hayes: The Diary of a President, 1875–1881*. New York: David McKay, 1964.

Williamson, Joel. *After Slavery: The Negro in South Carolina during Reconstruction, 1861–1877*. Chapel Hill: University of North Carolina Press, 1965.

———. *New People: Miscegenation and Mulattoes in the United States*. New York: Free Press, 1980.

Wimbush, Vincent L., ed. *African Americans and the Bible: Sacred Texts and Social Structures*. New York: Continuum, 2000.

Wood, Norman B. *The White Side of a Black Subject: Enlarged and Brought Down to Date*. Chicago: American Publishing House, 1897.

Woodson, Carter G., ed. *The Works of Francis J. Grimké*. Vol. 4, *Letters*. Washington, DC: Associated Publishers, 1942.

Woodward, C. Vann. *Origins of the New South, 1877–1913*. Baton Rogue: Lousiana State University Press, 1951.

———. *The Strange Career of Jim Crow*. 3rd ed. New York: Oxford University Press, 2002.

Wynes, Charles E., ed. *The Negro in the South since 1865*. New York: Harper and Row, 1968.

INDEX

abolitionist activities, 2, 7, 11–13, 14
African Methodist Episcopal Church, 91
Agassiz, Louis, 26
Alexander, Charles T., 92
Allen, Macon B., 10
Allis, Frederick S., Jr., 20
A.M.E. Review, 154
American Negro Academy, 126
American Philological Association, 60
American Social Science Association (ASSA), 84
Antioch College, 25
Ardizzone, Heidi, 126, 160, 165
Arthur, Chester A., 100, 101, 107
Assault at West Point, 167
Associated Press, 105, 165
Astor, John Jacob, 107
Atlanta Compromise Address, 119
Avery Normal Institute, 101, 146

Bagby, George K., 87
Baltimore American, 80
Banneker, Benjamin, 102, 122, 159
Barnwell, Robert W., 51
Bassett, Ebenezer D., 36
Batchelder, Augustus, 13–15, 19, 24, 27–29, 35
Bausman, Evelyn K., 136, 165
Bausman, John, 165
Beecher, Henry Ward, 2, 13
Bird, James
   and Lombard Street School (Bird school), 8
Blakely, Allison, 130, 140, 162
Blaney, Charles, 11
Blodgett, Geoffrey, 15
Bombay consulate, 127–28, 133
Boston, MA, 2, 26
   employment, 10
   public schools, 9
   race relations, 9–10, 11–13
Boston Daily Advertiser, 105
Boston Massacre, 82, 122

Bowley, James Alfred, 46
Boxer Rebellion, 4, 137, 154
Brewer, Fisk P., 53–54, 72
Broadway Grammar School, 9–10
Brooklyn Daily Times, 127
Brown, John, 11–12, 14, 150, 152
Bruce, John Edward, 124
Bryan, William Jennings, 124–25
Buffalo Commercial Advertiser, 101
Bureau of Colored Troops, 18
Burnett, George R., 92
Butchart, Ronald, 17

Calhoun, John C., 17, 61
Calloway, Thomas J., 117
Cambridge, MA, 2, 9, 10–11, 113, 167
Cambridge African American Heritage Trail, 167
Cardozo, Francis L., 57–58, 62
Carnegie, Andrew, 116
carpetbaggers, 48–49, 53, 58, 65, 89
Catto, Octavius, 36–40
Chamberlain, Daniel
   defense counsel for Johnson C. Whittaker, 97–99
   governor of South Carolina, 59, 62–63, 65–67, 71–72, 74, 76, 78
Charleston Daily News, 49, 53
Charleston News and Courier, 61, 93–94, 95, 146
Chase, W. Calvin, 127
Chesnut, Mary Boykin, 90
Chesterfield Democrat, 49
Chicago, 1, 144, 151, 153
   RTG work and activities in, 5, 124, 154, 156
Chicago Broad Ax, 154, 160
Chicago College of Law, 154
Chicago Daily Tribune, 160
Chicago Defender, 154, 160
China, 130, 131, 138–39, 142. *See also* Boxer Rebellion
Chinese Exclusion Act, 101